ENEMIES KNOWN AND UNKNOWN

T0386723

JACK MCDONALD

Enemies Known and Unknown

Targeted Killings in America's Transnational War

HURST & COMPANY, LONDON

First published in the United Kingdom in 2017 by
C. Hurst & Co. (Publishers) Ltd.,
41 Great Russell Street, London, WC1B 3PL
© Jack McDonald, 2017
All rights reserved.
Printed in the United Kingdom by Bell & Bain Ltd, Glasgow

The right of Jack McDonald to be identified as the author of
this publication is asserted by him in accordance with the
Copyright, Designs and Patents Act, 1988.

A Cataloguing-in-Publication data record for this book
is available from the British Library.

ISBN: 9781849046442 *paperback*

This book is printed using paper from registered sustainable
and managed sources.

www.hurstpublishers.com

CONTENTS

For Heather

PREFACE

The origin of this book lies in one of the overriding questions of the 'drone debate':[1] Do targeted killings work?[2] In particular, it lay in the available data, which was being used to support two competing arguments at the same time: that targeted killings were excessive, useless and illegal; and that targeted killings were precise, useful and legal. The data supports both arguments, depending upon your definition of terms, and therein lies the problem: Who gets to judge? More to the point: Who is making these judgements, defining these terms and why does it matter?

This book was written during Barack Obama's second term as president of the United States. During his first term, Obama and a number of senior government figures provided a defence of the continued use of targeted killings, one of a number of his predecessor George W. Bush's controversial policies in the 'War on Terror'. Obama oversaw a drastic rise in the quantity of targeted killings, while also seeking to normalise America's ongoing conflict with al-Qaeda. Obama used his first major speech on the topic of national security to announce his intention to close the Guantanamo Bay military detention facility, reiterate the prohibition on torture and articulate a vision of the War on Terror as a clean war.

Obama played the hand dealt to him by the Bush administration. Whether or not he played it well is for others to argue. The three most significant foreign policy decisions of the Bush administration were to go to war with al-Qaeda over the 9/11 attacks, to go to war with the Taliban for sheltering al-Qaeda and to go to war with Iraq in 2003 ostensibly due to Saddam Hussein's refusal to abandon his (non-existent) weapons of mass destruction programmes. By the time I started on this book, Osama Bin Laden, the enemy face of America's war, had been killed by US Special Forces in 2011. The United States had withdrawn its troops from Iraq, Obama had announced the future withdrawal of troops from Afghanistan, and the use of targeted killings in Pakistan, Yemen and Somalia had slumped. Yet America's war continued. As I write this in 2016, the United States is waging an aerial war in Iraq and Syria, it still has Special Forces in Afghanistan and it is still at war with al-Qaeda.

This book is about that 'third war', as Micah Zenko calls it,[3] whether it can even be called a war, and how America wages it. It is about the role that law plays in the constitution of war and the way it is waged. The great policy debate of the last fifteen years—how the United States could, or should, defeat al-Qaeda—is in part defined by law and legal questions. My focus here runs in parallel to that debate, as I am interested, like a growing number of scholars, in the relationship between law, technology, violence and war.[4] My caveat for this work is that it is a book about how American interpretations of law operate at this intersection—I am not seeking to advance a particular legal standard, and the policy-relevant elements consist of observations and warnings. Instead, my focus is the construction of categories of permissible violence, the role of knowledge and truth in these categories, and how they can inform our study of US strategy and warfare. Lest I sound too high-minded, I am mostly interested in what happens after the real world gives the ideal world a bloody nose.

There are a great many people who have helped me develop the ideas for this book and supported me during the writing process. All faults or flaws contained herein are entirely my own. James Gow gave me the idea to break from my previous research on American justifications for targeted killings and zoom out to the big picture. Michael Dwyer, my publisher, has been exceedingly patient and I am thankful for him giving me the time to write this book a couple of times to get it right. Thanks are also due to Jon de Peyer, Alison Alexanian and the rest of the team at Hurst for helping the book cross the finish line. This book would be quite different, and worse, without the comments and constructive feedback from the anonymous reviewers. The research time for this book was supported by the Economic and Social Research Council under an RCUK Global Uncertainties Science and Security Programme Grant: 'SNT Really Makes Reality: Technological Innovation, Non-Obvious Warfare and the Challenges to International Law' (ESRC Ref: ES/K011413/1) and engaging with these topics with Guglielmo Verdirame and Rachel Kerr helped me sketch out the framework of this book. While writing this up, I was lucky enough to find a home within a home at the Centre for Science and Security Studies, part of the Department of War Studies where I currently work. I share an office with a mathematician, a US foreign policy specialist and a Middle East non-proliferation expert, so I can blame some of the delay for this book on the fascinating discussions on international politics and security that arose from this mix. Robert Downes, Heather Williams and Dina Esfandiary have also been polite enough not to complain when my desk overflowed with drafts and corrections for weeks at a time. I would also like to thank the rest of my colleagues at the Centre for Science and Security Studies for their support, so thanks go to Wyn Bowen, Chris Hobbs, Susan Martin, Matt Moran, Jessica Marcos, Hassan Elbahtimy, Daniel Salisbury and Luca Lentini, who was there to celebrate with a cold beer when I submitted the first draft of this manuscript while in Indonesia. John Gearson and Michael Rainsborough guided me through the process of a PhD, from which many of these ideas originated. Conversations with Thomas Rid, David Betz and Neville Bolt shaped some of the ideas contained within. Thanks are also due to Adam Elkus and Ana Flamind who read early drafts of this work. Students on the courses that I've taught at King's over the last four years are likely to recognise many of the arguments made within this book. Although the views and mistakes contained herein are mine and mine alone, having my ideas and arguments tested in seminars improved the ones presented here. Last, and due strong compliments, help and tremendous support from friends and family made this book possible. Without the love and support of Heather Swain I would likely have missed even more deadlines, and this book is dedicated to her.

INTRODUCTION

THE BALKAN CRUCIBLE

What is the origin of American targeted killings? We could start with the National Security Act of 1947 that created the Central Intelligence Agency.[1] Or we could fast forward to the 1975 report by a Congressional Committee led by Frank Church that examined the CIA's involvement in political assassinations.[2] This led to the series of presidential declarations that outlawed 'political assassination' by US government agents.[3] But skipping past the Vietnam War would miss important details like the US use of remote reconnaissance vehicles such as the Firebee,[4] or the development of targeting bombing runs based on remote sensors alone.[5] We could move to the tail end of the Cold War, and the CIA's role in bolstering Afghan resistance to a Soviet-backed regime, and thence to the American abandonment of the regime as geopolitical priorities changed. This is a common stop, since this is the war that is key to understanding the formation of al-Qaeda, America's current *bête noire*.[6]

These narratives have been told elsewhere in far greater depth. The argument that I hope to convince you of in this book is that America's current war, and way of waging it, has neither a single cause nor origin. Both the kind of war and means of warfare are, however, inextricable from one another. What is interesting is the degree to which the various threads that I will cover in this book are all present, for better or for worse, in the Yugoslav Wars of the 1990s.

Years before Predator drones were deployed to track down Osama Bin Laden in the border regions of Afghanistan and Pakistan, they were flying over Bosnia.[7] Before the CIA and US Special Forces units were hunting al-Qaeda across the world, they were tracking and capturing 'Persons Indicted For War Crimes' (PIFWCS, in slang 'pifwicks') across the former Yugoslavia.[8] If America's war with al-Qaeda is indeed 'a new kind of war against a new kind of enemy',[9] we should consider that Mary Kaldor's *New Wars* was written about violence committed by 'hybrid networks' for public and private ends in the Yugoslav Wars and beyond.[10] To understand the present conflicts over international law, sovereignty and the resort to war, we need to consider the creation and judgements of the International Criminal Tribunal for the Former Yugoslavia (ICTY, or the Hague Tribunal) and NATO's intervention in the Kosovo War. We also need to consider the movement to reject the underpinning norms of 'business as usual' in the international system. The unwillingness of powerful states to intervene in the Balkans horrified many observers. The atrocities of the former Yugoslavia loomed large in later debates regarding the responsibility to protect, human security and global governance. While it would be impossible to claim that the Balkan Wars were a single causal factor in this movement, the apparent failure of the state system to prevent mass atrocity gave many of the emerging critical accounts of state sovereignty both urgency and moral force. At the root of these movements and ideas was a re-imagination of war, security and law in cosmopolitan ideals, ethics and politics. Cosmopolitanism, the idea that humans belong to a single political community with shared universal values, stands in opposition to a world order centred on sovereign states. Cosmopolitan approaches to war and security reflect this—they are primarily concerned with protecting individuals from the depredations of states and non-state actors, rather than the security of the state. While these ideas did not transform the world—we still live in a world of states—the increased focus on the obligations that states owe to individuals regardless of state borders forced states to defend long-standing practices and claimed rights to use violence.

The Balkan Wars do not explain America's current situation. The interplay of factors that link the two are better described as accident, coincidence and irony, rather than driven by a single overarching narrative or force. After all, who could have predicted that the CIA and US Special Forces' use of 'habeas grab-ass'[11]—capturing indicted war criminals and rendering them to the custody of the Hague Tribunal— would also serve as practice for the capture and rendition of al-Qaeda suspects in the early War on Terror? Who could have known that the first jury-rigged communications link that allowed generals in the Pentagon to witness battlefields in real time would one day enable a complex legal bureaucracy to track and kill America's enemies as a matter of routine?[12]

The Yugoslav Wars demonstrated the limits of US power in terms of both capability and will.[13] In particular, armed forces designed for confronting (and perhaps fighting) the Soviet Union and state threats were not necessarily suited to confronting genocidal warlords and the carnage of overlapping wars of independence and expansion. Conversely, the wars were also demonstrations of key military technologies and concepts that the United States would rely upon to wage war on al-Qaeda. Fundamentally, however, the Balkans are most important for the changes that they demonstrate in the international system.

Take, for example, the ICTY. The post-Cold War era saw rapid advances in the development of international criminal law, which had stalled since the war crimes tribunals at the end of the Second World War. If we are thinking about the distance between Yamamoto and al-Harithi,[14] then we need to consider both the reshaping of international order and international law. The ICTY was established by the United Nations Security Council (UNSC), the organ of the United Nations charged with 'the maintenance of international peace and security'.[15] At the time Yamamoto was killed, the UN did not exist. Not only were international criminal law prosecutions non-existent,[16] but key classes of criminal behaviour that the ICTY later sought to prosecute—crimes against humanity—did not exist in international law. Between the killings of Yamamoto and al-Harithi, the character and structure of international politics and law changed to the point that individuals were now held responsible for some violations of international law.[17] One fundamental consequence of the ICTY was the addition of influential voices in international jurisprudence regarding the definition of war and armed conflict. As we will see in the next chapter, who 'gets to speak' on the definition of armed conflict in international law is a central question in America's transnational war.

The Balkan Wars also raised important questions regarding state sovereignty and the resort to the use of force in international politics. Many important groups involved in the breakup of Yugoslavia had no formal international status. Some fragments sought (and achieved) statehood through recognition by states, regional actors like the European Economic Community (EEC, predecessor of the European Union) and integration into the international system.[18] In places, however, there was so much overlap and cooperation between formal political entities, paramilitaries and criminal groups that such formal distinctions and definitions could not describe many of the belligerents. If 'in the land of the blind, the one-eyed man is king', then in a land lacking formal sovereigns, the possession of guns, money and a loyal fighting force created them. Many of these local warlords committed genocide and war crimes in the pursuit of sectarian political goals.[19]

If we take a moment to reflect here, many of the debates regarding how al-Qaeda should be treated—as a terrorist group, or something akin to a belligerent in a war—bear similarities to debates about the recognition and treatment of these new 'hybrid' forms of non-state actors. A central conundrum that the Yugoslav Wars posed for the international community was the recognition and treatment of non-state actors in international affairs. What the Yugoslav Wars demonstrated was that these were no longer solely political questions, that international politics and sovereignty was now framed in legal questions, while at the same time international politics fundamentally affected the reach and application of international law.[20] The legal dimension to political hostility, something that I will cover in Chapter 3, is integral to understanding contemporary war and warfare.

As America's experience of the Balkans demonstrates, these developments in international law and international politics shape strategy and the use of force. Four months before the start of Slovenia's ten-day war of independence in June 1991, the United States had decisively defeated Iraq's military at the head of a coalition force of over 900,000 service personnel. The seeming decisiveness of this military coalition (mindful that Saddam Hussein remained in power, a situation that America would later change by forming a coalition to overthrow him in 2003) could be compared to America's unhappy experience working with the UN and NATO in support of UNPROFOR—the UN's protection force in Bosnia.[21] Airpower, the key to coalition victory in Desert Storm, proved both contentious and indecisive when faced with Bosnian Serbs who were willing to take UN personnel hostage, playing upon the multiple political fault lines that existed in the UN and NATO. It took the open defiance of the Srebrenica massacre for the international community to agree to the use of levels of force that helped bring the warring parties to the negotiation table. Towards the end of the decade, the same problems of negotiating the use of force between coalition partners, and the political utility of force itself, would reappear in NATO's 1999 bombing of the Federal Republic of Yugoslavia and Kosovo to eject Serb and Yugoslav forces from Kosovo.[22] Whereas NATO used force in Bosnia at the behest of the UN, its actions in Kosovo lacked such a mandate.[23] Who or what has the proper authority to go to war, or use force, without the positive authorisation of the UNSC, and on what basis, are key questions that hang over America's current transnational war. What the Balkan Wars and the post-Cold War era in general demonstrated is that international law shapes and constitutes these questions of international politics.

If the first Gulf War was a demonstration of America's conventional capabilities, the Balkans proved to be a testing ground for innovations that would later become central to its war with al-Qaeda. Both of these wars were ultimately shaped and informed by the 'revolution in military affairs'—the technological capability to wage precision warfare, and the subsequent adaptation of military practice to these emerging capabilities. This revolution (in practice, more of an evolution of existing capabilities) was itself informed by American culture, its concepts of war-fighting and its 'strong bias towards techno-centric warfare'.[24] The pressure to develop precision capabilities arose not only from the perceived need to destroy Soviet tanks but from cultural understandings of warfare that militate towards reducing the harms of war to the minimum necessary.[25] Military culture and professional identity also plays a significant role in the development of technologies for military purposes.[26] Law played an increasing role in military affairs in the 1980s and 1990s: the concept of operational law—the combination of national and international law relevant to the conduct of operations—matured into its own field,[27] and legal issues shaped the success of military operations.[28]

The key technology that symbolises American targeted killings are drones, the remotely piloted aerial vehicles now loaded with surveillance pods and precision-guided weapons.

The Balkans saw the first operational deployment of General Atomics' RQ-1 Predator drone. The deployment and use of the Predator demonstrates some of the issues inherent in drawing straight trajectories from history to the present. After all, as Richard Whittle's history of the Predator drone highlights, many of what we now consider to be its most vital aspects were not present when they were used in the Balkans. Predators were first deployed to Bosnia in 1995, but it was not until February 2001 that the United States first tested firing a missile from one.[29] The Predator's capability to produce full motion video is what we now see as a key element of its utility, but in its original deployment, American military intelligence analysts were not able to process the full motion video feeds that the Predator provided in the 1990s because they were used to working with still imagery.[30] US engagement in the Balkans also featured the first tentative steps towards the use of drones to conduct lethal operations. While drones over Bosnia could pass intelligence to aid military operations, NATO's 1999 war in Kosovo also saw the first field test of using laser designators to guide strikes by other traditional platforms.[31] These tentative steps towards the arming of drones highlight something that I think is in some ways more important than armed drones: the instant and near-seamless communication of information and intelligence.

The Balkans also featured the CIA and the US military in the opening phases of a turf war over which organisation should control America's drone fleet.[32] The military origins of the CIA and its overlap with the US Special Forces community are integral to understanding its role in present-day targeted killings.[33] Just as interesting is the relationship between the two communities in the hunt for Balkan War criminals after the Dayton Accords. The role of law and legal authority to conduct detention operations is a key issue in American targeted killings. Again, law, or cultural attitudes about law, shape military practice as well as the adoption of technology, but organisations matter since they have different cultural norms, and different legal constraints. The CIA's employment of 'contractors' to abduct ICTY-indictee Stevan Todorović and present him to NATO forces is an example of the exercise of power where the law is unclear or uncertain.[34]

INTRODUCTION: THE BALKAN CRUCIBLE

Todorović was a Bosnian-Serb police chief, responsible for the torture and persecution of civilians. Although he was able to cut a plea deal with the ICTY due to the circumstances of his appearance before the court, I doubt many people were too fussed that a degree of force had to be used to bring him to justice.[35] The same cannot be said for America's actions after 9/11. If the Balkan Wars highlighted the uncertainties inherent in the international system, American conduct after 9/11 demonstrates the limits of this system in constraining the action of powerful states. Yet the Balkan example also demonstrates the powerful link between law, politics and legitimacy in the contemporary world. Moreover, it provides a perspective on an international system facing challenges from below, where traditional categories of violence seem ill-equipped to describe the world. In this context, the idea of a war between a state and a terrorist group does not seem completely unworldly. Nonetheless, it is highly controversial, and this controversy has been with us since 9/11 due to America's claim that it is 'at war' with al-Qaeda.

This is a book about the world after 9/11. Specifically, it is about the concept of transnational war and the concept of targeted killings. The idea that underpins this book is that American targeted killings are somewhat unique, and for that reason, they provide a way of thinking about the war that America currently claims to be waging against al-Qaeda, and, most importantly, the way that social rules and values constitute both war and methods of warfare, and the relationship between the two. The central theme of this book is the relationship between law, legal concepts and the physical acts of violence that we colloquially refer to as warfare. I will try to explain myself in as intelligible terms as possible. A good window into this way of thinking is to question why American presidents might say that America is at war with al-Qaeda, but the government lawyers working away behind closed doors writing memos that define the legal constraints for the use of violence talk about an 'armed conflict' with al-Qaeda. There is more to this than a mere semantic difference. If you think that these details are unimportant to the people on the receiving end of a Hellfire missile, then the point of this book is to convince you that you are wrong: you do not get Hellfire missile attacks without legal authorisation, and, for lawyers signing off on acts of violence, such details matter. No memo: no missile. No missile: no deaths of people that the US thinks are lawful targets, no deaths of nearby civilians that the United States does not think are lawful targets.

The problem with transnational war, or, to frame it in the language of the law of armed conflict, a transnational non-international armed conflict, is that if such a war or armed conflict exists, it would give the American government the right to use military force against its opponents anywhere they are found. When we think about war, in layman's terms, our understanding of the concept is usually tied to territory and states. The existence of a state of war between France and Prussia in 1870, for example, did not give either state the right to kill people in faraway countries. The custom of neutrality limits the spread of armed conflict. More to the point, the limits of technology in the nineteenth century meant that if either state wanted to kill people in, say, America, it would be very difficult and expensive to project force at such a distance. Nowadays, some states possess the means to kill at distances and speeds that would shock their nineteenth-century forebears. More importantly, however, is that the people with whom they consider themselves to be at war (in colloquial terms) are not states, and are not tied to geographical locations in the way that states are. In this sense, transnational armed conflict is really encapsulating the idea of being in an armed conflict with a transnational opponent.

We cannot get to grips with targeted killings unless we also consider the kind of war that America is waging, and we cannot understand that war without specific reference to American culture and its relationship with al-Qaeda. In other words, the choices that the United States makes and the boundaries to those choices are important. If we are going to ask 'why use targeted killings?', then the first question should really be: 'why bother to use targeted killings?' Consider this: in the discussions that led up to the Special Forces' raid that killed Osama Bin Laden in Pakistan in 2011, one mooted alternative was to use a B-2 Spirit bomber to drop a 500-pound bomb on Bin Laden's Abbottabad complex. This was apparently rejected as the US government could not be sure that it would work, and because they wanted proof that Bin Laden was dead. The B-2 bomber can carry 40,000 pounds of ordnance, and up to eighty guided bombs. If the US government wanted to be sure that it killed Bin Laden, then a single B-2 could drop enough explosives for it to be certain of this outcome. The reasons why this option was not picked tells us a lot about the current American approach to war and warfare, which is defined by the American interpretation of the law of armed conflict, and US social values.

Targeted killings, then, are a product of law, politics and social values, as much as they are enabled by technology. While elements of 'high value targeting' can be found in many contemporary American military campaigns, the idea of a war that can only be waged by targeted killings is something new. You do not get targeted killings unless a state is willing to go to war with a network that obfuscates itself. Even then, you do not get the kind of precision we see with American targeted killings without the kind of restraint that America demonstrates. If the use of the word precision offends you in this context, please consider the example of the B-2 above. Precision in this context does not mean 'no civilian casualties'; it means tailoring methods of warfare to reduce them to the minimum possible. Above all, however, targeted killings represent a turn to war at the individual level. What differentiates targeted killings from other forms of warfare is the need to pick out and identify individuals from the societies they live in. This would not be too strange to someone who fought against guerrillas or insurgents; however, some argue that the distance at which this identification is performed differentiates the two. Distance is important, but in my mind, the true differentiator is the process of targeted killing that the US government has created. Drones are an important surveillance platform, and they are tailor-made to carry out precision strikes, but their true importance lies in the fact that they are useful for a form of bureaucratic warfare that is the product of a legalistic society. Legal and moral discussion of drone strikes tends to focus upon the act of killing, yet many of the more troubling questions and issues lie in the process of decoding who can be killed.

Book map

This book is divided into two parts, the first focused upon the concept of transnational war, and the second focused upon targeted killings and their consequences. In some chapters, I focus upon individuals or incidents. These are intended to highlight particular aspects and problems inherent in America's use of targeted killings. Naturally, this means that my focus in each case is weighted towards the chapter's theme, rather than providing an exhaustive account in each case. For example, the life and crimes of Duško Tadić get a rather short shrift, since the main reason he features in this book is the substantive elements of ICTY jurisprudence related to his case.

In the next chapter, I cover the connection between war, warfare and law. My argument is based on the idea that all three are social constructions rooted in culture. This highlights two roles that law plays in war and warfare: as a frame of observation or judgements, and as a constitutive aspect of war itself. In Chapter 2, I examine the connection and disconnection between the political concept of war and the law of armed conflict. This chapter highlights many of the problems that America's claim that it is engaged in an armed conflict presents to the legal framework that regulates state violence. Here I argue that the idea of war as a social construction conflicts with the idea that the existence of an armed conflict can be measured using objective criteria.

Law, and interpretations of law, are integral to the constitution of war and armed conflict in the contemporary world. In Chapter 3, I draw attention to the role of law, and legal arguments, in the politics and policy decisions that constitute war and armed conflict. This continues in Chapter 4, where I explore the role of law 'all the way down' as legal concepts inform both the strategy and conduct of war. I argue that legal concepts permit a war of attrition against al-Qaeda, as well as bounding the means to do so, hence targeted killings. This draws attention to the normative values reflected in the legal interpretations that constitute America's war. In Chapter 5, I examine the relationship between two ideas associated with liberalism—cosmopolitanism and pluralism—and argue that America's war is only reconcilable with a pluralist approach to liberal values. This is strongly related to America's interpretation of its human rights obligations, and is at odds with many of its close allies.

Targeted killings highlight numerous problems in contemporary warfare. In Chapter 6, I look at the role of law as a constitutive element of American targeted killings. Here I focus on the problems that al-Qaeda (and irregular opponents in general) pose states such as America. I argue that, by thinking about targeted killings as a process of individuating terrorist or militant networks from their milieu, we arrive at a better understanding of this activity. This, I argue, is inherent in many forms of military practice, and draws attention to the fundamental role that information-processing and intelligence plays in contemporary American targeted killings. Rethinking warfare on an individual or case-by-case basis draws attention to the difference between identity and the processes of identification designed to satisfy the criteria of permissible targets in the law of armed conflict. I tackle this subject in Chapter 7, and use this frame to address the distinction between so-called 'personality strikes' aimed at 'known' individuals and 'signature strikes' that are used to kill otherwise unknown individuals based upon multiple fragments of information associated with them that indicate their 'pattern of life'. At heart, I argue that the distance between the two is perhaps overstated, given that both are attempts to reconcile the imperfect information present in the world with the theoretically perfect categories of person in the law of armed conflict.

Transnational war and targeted killings highlight the problem of civilian harm and new forms of harm that are not specified in the law of armed conflict. In Chapter 8, I focus upon the role of civilian agency as an inherent element of the way that civilians attempt to protect themselves from the effects of warfare. I argue that by reducing the information available to civilian populations, wars waged by targeted killings and remote means also substantially reduce the ability of civilian populations to save themselves. Given the nondescript limits to America's war, I identify this as a significant problem with America's conduct that is independent of American attempts to reduce the physical impact of its war on affected civilian populations. In Chapter 9, I consider the implications of my analysis for the current coalition war against Islamic State. Here I argue that many of the problems associated with America's transnational war against al-Qaeda apply against this new enemy. The coalition efforts also demonstrate that America's allies are faced with many of the same problems identified in this book. By drawing attention to the close relationships between Britain and the United States, I argue that each faces different problems accounting for their actions against Islamic State, which are perhaps exacerbated by their close coupling in coalition operations.

1

THE CLEANEST WAR

'Rules and responsibilities: these are the ties that bind us. We do what we do because of who we are. If we did otherwise, we would not be ourselves.'

Morpheus, *Sandman: The Kindly Ones*

Introduction

At the heart of this book is a seemingly simple question: What happens when a state goes to war with a transnational opponent? The immediate answer is that people die, and many of those people have little, if any, connection to the aforementioned conflict. However, unpacking this question is somewhat difficult, not least because many of the terms that it contains appear not to fit together. Can states 'go to war' with a transnational terrorist network like al-Qaeda? Can al-Qaeda even constitute an 'opponent' in a military sense, the type of framing that people commonly associate with war? And what does 'transnational' mean in this context, and why does it matter?

The salience of these questions lies in the fact that the US government defends its transnational targeted killing campaign to 'disrupt, dismantle and defeat'[1] al-Qaeda and 'associated forces'[2] as lawful and moral acts of war. In other words: whether or not you or I agree with the possibility of such a war, the US government is currently killing people on the basis that one exists. However, the way in which the

13

United States wages war on al-Qaeda does not appear to be very similar to the industrial wars of years past. Once one looks beyond the boundaries of America's recent large-scale conflicts in Afghanistan and Iraq, targeted killings appear to be the de facto method the US government now uses to attack al-Qaeda. In this sense, targeted killings are integral to America's transnational war: they are the primary means by which it is waged. The problem is that the term 'targeted killing' can cover a lot of different activities: drone strikes, special forces raids, even the use of cruise missiles can be folded into the same category. What links these myriad methods of killing is a mode of killing, one that is again driven by the underlying principles of the rules of war: distinction and proportionality. Despite substantial numbers of civilian casualties—The Bureau of Investigative Journalism identifies between 488 and 1,073 civilians killed from 2002 to 2015[3]—targeted killings represent a way of waging war on a terrorist network that is driven by rule-abidance and a mind-set that reduces war and warfare to a bureaucratic process of identification and killing.

The US government believes that the existing law governing the conduct of war also applies to its armed conflict with al-Qaeda, and that its use of targeted killings is legitimate and lawful in the context of this framework. This body of law, as will be explained in this book, permits states to kill people lawfully to a far greater degree than they can in peace, or, rather, than they can without the existence of an armed conflict of some form. At the same time, war is not entirely the same as armed conflict, and the distinction between these two terms defines where and when the law of armed conflict applies, and therefore where the use of lethal force is legitimate. Before we move on to make sense of America's claim that it is at war with al-Qaeda, it is first necessary to examine the relationship between war, armed conflict and warfare. In particular, it is necessary to look at the social construction of political violence—in this case war—and its connection to changing forms of warfare. It is clear that both law and technology play a vital role in the social construction of war, as well as the forms of warfare that arise from a war waged against transnational opponents. These theoretical points are necessary to make because, as we will encounter in later chapters, different sides to the debate on targeted killings have quite different understandings of what war is, what armed conflict is, and therefore whether or not targeted killings are at all lawful. Before explaining that, I first need to explain why I consider contemporary American targeted killings to be a new class of violent activity.

Distinguishing targeted killings

How best to define targeted killings? In his book on the ethics of war, Christopher Coker uses the notion of a 'turn' used by philosopher Richard Rorty to describe that 'a significant shift in cultural and intellectual *attitudes* has taken place' without being able to point to a precise inflection point or direction of change.[4] Coker argues that a 'security turn' occurred after 9/11, but for present purposes, I think American targeted killings constitute a similar sort of turn in the conduct of warfare. In recent years, there has been much written about the 'changing character of war', and particularly what brings about the changing patterns of organised violence between human beings.[5] The problem is that targeted killings tend to be analysed as a class of military activity independent of a particular war. A drone strike that kills an individual in Afghanistan, Iraq, Yemen or Palestine is, to some, one and the same thing. In their recent book *Drone Warfare*, John Kaag and Sarah Kreps argued that 'Targeted killings and signature strikes have always been in the repertoire of military planners, but never, in the history of warfare, have they cost so very little to use.'[6] This statement is far from their central concern—the moral hazard that drones might engender—but I use it here because it encapsulates a prevalent idea that, in my view, is incorrect: targeted killings are nothing new.

At an extreme level of abstraction, Kaag and Kreps are right: assassination plays an important role in irregular warfare, and irregular warfare is hardly a novelty. However, the degree of abstraction required to define American targeted killings as nothing more than killing individuals also erases almost everything that is important about them. In particular, this isolation of targeted killings as individually targeted violence creates a second erasure: it ignores the nature of the state using force. As we will see in this book, particular American attitudes to war, law and violence are central to American targeted killings, but other states approach the same issue in their own specific ways. We should question whether one state's targeted killings are the same as another's. American targeted killings, in the sense of large-scale killing by remote platforms operated halfway around the world from the point of weapons release, are intimately tied to the war that America wages against al-Qaeda.[7]

Many states have used similar methods, notably Israel, but the American campaign is of a different scale and scope.[8] Whereas Israel has used targeted killings abroad in a limited sense, America has, over the past thirteen years, conducted hundreds of targeted killings in countries such as Pakistan and Yemen.[9] This can be described in terms of cultural or legal differences, such as Israeli attitudes towards the human rights of those it uses targeted killings against, or in terms of constitutional difference, such as the right of the British Prime Minister David Cameron to define a British citizen as a lawful target of attack, or a functional one: no state can currently replicate the technological apparatus that enables America to wage war on al-Qaeda wherever it can find its members.

It is this ability for the American state to 'reach out' across the globe and do violence to its enemies that worries many. Still, there are numerous other reasons to pay specific attention to American targeted killings. One is that they appear to be an 'easier' form of killing. A better reason, I think, is that we should be cautious about casting today's understandings into the past in order to justify present-day actions. A good example of this is John Yoo's use of history to defend current American targeted killings. Yoo points out that America killed the Japanese Admiral Isoroku Yamamoto in the Second World War in a manner that looks very much like a targeted killing.[10] Indeed, that is the reason why Yoo uses this example: If targeted killing was lawful in the Second World War, then why would it be a problem in the present day?

Admiral Isoroku Yamamoto was killed on 18 April 1943 by American pilots in P38G Lightning aircraft who shot down his plane over the Solomon Islands. Yamamoto was the commander-in-chief of Japan's Combined Fleet in the Second World War, but America did not have a strategy or operational concept built around killing men like him. The selection and intentional killing of Yamamoto was an exception to the direction of military activity at the time, and required political authorisation from Frank Knox, the secretary of the navy, as well as the president, Franklin D. Roosevelt. Historian E.B. Potter noted that Admiral Nimitz, the commander in chief of the US Pacific Fleet, checked with Washington about killing Yamamoto, since 'assassination of so eminent a personage might have political repercussions'.[11] The moral unease in this instance emphasises the role of ethical constraints regarding killing on an individual basis which are evidently different to today. Notably, and contrary to Potter's account of Secretary Knox's decision-making, John Costello states that Knox took 'the advice of leading churchmen on the morality of killing enemy leaders' before agreeing to the operation to kill Yamamoto.[12] American officers understood that targeting Yamamoto would have an effect on morale,[13] but military concerns were foremost in Nimitz's mind: whether Yamamoto could be replaced by a better officer.[14]

Compare the case of Yamamoto to that of Qaed Salim Sinan al-Harithi, the first person targeted and killed 'beyond the battlefield' in America's war with al-Qaeda. The use of an MQ-1 Predator drone to kill al-Harithi in Yemen in November 2002 was the start of over a decade's worth of ongoing targeted killings outside of identifiable conflict zones such as Afghanistan and Iraq. Like Yamamoto, al-Harithi, too, was a leader, being al-Qaeda's leader in Yemen, tied to the 2000 bombing of the USS *Cole* and ongoing al-Qaeda operations in Yemen. But while armed MQ-1 Predator drones had been developed before 9/11, and first used for lethal action in Afghanistan,[15] the Hellfire missiles that killed al-Harithi and five other men in his vehicle were far removed from America's operations in Afghanistan. Unlike Yamamoto, al-Harithi was not a one-off—his name was on the CIA's 'kill or capture' list of al-Qaeda operatives.[16] The Second World War was a war between industrialised nation states that involved the clash of armies, navies and air forces. The technology that enabled the United States to wage war across the globe against Japan and Nazi Germany also enabled the US military to kill Yamamoto. In contrast, America's war with al-Qaeda was, to a large extent, directed at al-Qaeda themselves, severing any ties to state support. In 2001, America toppled the Taliban regime in Afghanistan in order to remove al-Qaeda's safe haven there, and once that had occurred, America's war with al-Qaeda was reduced to hunting down the members of the network itself. Consider this when we think about the Yamamoto strike: American operations in the Pacific theatre were built around fleet engagements and 'island hopping' towards Japan. Yamamoto might have been a legitimate target of attack, but American military planners were more concerned with winning naval engagements like the Battle of Midway, or defeating Japanese forces entrenched on islands like Saipan than they were with hunting Japan's top-tier military leadership. The killing of Yamamoto was incidental to the main effort; the killing of al-Harithi and capturing or killing others like him, on the other hand, is America's main objective in its war with al-Qaeda.

There are, however, some similarities between the two cases. In both, the president of the United States authorised the lethal action. Also notable is the role of signals intelligence in each killing. Signals intelligence, which intelligence professionals often refer to as SIGINT, is intelligence derived from communications media. The production of signals intelligence requires the collection, processing and analysis of information gleaned from communications networks, be they letters in the mail, or the packets of information that make up their digital equivalent. Despite the contemporary focus on the internet-snooping activities of America's National Security Agency (NSA) and the UK's Government Communications Headquarters (GCHQ), the signals intelligence agencies of both countries, this activity is one of the oldest and widespread forms of espionage.

US naval intelligence managed to identify and verify Yamamoto's probable location using signals intelligence because they had broken the cryptographic codes the Japanese used to protect their communications. By intercepting details of Yamamoto's itinerary, the intelligence analysis capabilities that the United States developed to wage war across the Pacific also allowed them to identify a time and a place where US aircraft would be able to intercept Japan's most famous admiral. The intercepted transmission's value was also helped by Yamamoto's punctuality, a feature of his personality that, according to David Kahn, meant that 'The cryptanalyzed intercept amounted to a death warrant for the highest enemy commander.'[17] The American operation that killed al-Harithi, however, did not need to rely upon his punctuality: by tracking the signal from his mobile phone, they were able to identify the vehicle he was travelling in.[18] Moreover, Lt. General Michael DeLong, the US CENTCOM (Central Command, a military command structure) deputy commander, was able to watch the video feed of al-Harithi's vehicle while authorising the strike to kill him.[19]

This does, however, point to key differences between the two strikes. Kahn's analysis of Yamamoto's killing is predicated on the fact that Yamamoto would be targeted, but this connection between identification and action was not a foregone conclusion at the time. The strike that killed al-Harithi, although authorised by DeLong, was also checked over by military lawyers, judge advocates-general (JAGS), and conducted by an MQ-1 Reaper under the CIA's control. The processes of defining whether lethal action was lawful fundamentally differed between the two strikes, even though both ultimately took their authorisation from a decision by the president of the United States.

Yamamoto was killed at a point in time when it was becoming possible to single out men such as himself, but the routine killing of people such as al-Harithi comes at a point when it is possible to make such routine identifications from communications technology. It would have been physically impossible to identify and kill Yamamoto without technology developed to wage industrial war, whereas tracking mobile phones like the one al-Harithi used is integral to a functioning cellular phone network. If anything, the al-Harithi strike demonstrates how reliant America's war is upon the widespread use of civilian communications technology. At the same time, the ultimate purpose and orientation of the US military at the time did not allow this kind of fine-grained targeting as a general purpose method of waging war. Eventual victory in the Second World War came not from winning a battle, but from winning a steady stream of battles in multiple theatres over the space of years. In the process, over fifty million people died: Yamamoto's death was a drop in the ocean of human suffering. The war could not have been won by a military that thought about its opponents as individuals, and expended substantial resources to kill a single person. As daring as the raid that killed Admiral Yamamoto was, it remained an exception, not the rule. Compare this to al-Harithi: once we move beyond the battlefields of Afghanistan and Iraq, America's war has killed thousands, but not tens of thousands. Despite its global scope, it is, in terms of blunt statistics, a very small war. That is not to say that there aren't consequential effects—America operates in extremely unstable states, some of which, like Pakistan, Somalia and Yemen, tip between uneasy peace and civil war. Nonetheless, America is not waging an industrial war against al-Qaeda but is waging a war that reduces warfare to singling out men like al-Harithi. It is the consequences of seeing the rights and wrongs of war in this way that the latter third of this book will address.

At the time, Yamamoto's death did not prove controversial in the way that targeted killings are in the present day. Although Secretary Knox consulted clergy, the death of Yamamoto did not inspire a large degree of public controversy. Unlike President Obama's walk down to the East Room of the White House to announce the death of Osama Bin Laden at the hands of US forces less than eight hours after the event, the United States waited until Japan announced Yamamoto's death just over a month later. There was good reason for caution, particularly since American forces did not want to tip off their opponents that they had in fact cracked Japan's naval codes.

Ultimately, Yamamoto was a military commander in one of the most brutal wars in human history. Whether or not it was right to kill Yamamoto, the greatest controversy over his death came from the competing claims of naval aviators regarding who had in fact shot down his plane. This leads to the use of Yamamoto's death in defence of targeted killings in the present day: If a targeted killing was not a problem then, why all the talk of legal and moral problems now? Contemporary targeted killings are certainly controversial. More to the point, they occur in a half-light of recognition, somewhere between an honest accounting and the repetition of rote-learned lines regarding state secrecy in the face of media reporting. Again, al-Harithi is a hallmark here. When pressed by the media about America's role in the strike, Donald Rumsfeld, then secretary of state for defence, noted that al-Harithi was in that car and that 'It would be a very good thing if he were out of business.'[20]

A defence of targeted killings that rests on the premise that 'it was okay when we did it in the Second World War' obfuscates much of what is most important or worrying about targeted killings of individuals like al-Harithi in the present day. Yes, Yamamoto was indeed targeted by the United States and killed, but if that is all we mean by targeted killing, then this combination of actions covers far more military killing than Yamamoto. The difference—between the US navy turning its attention to kill a single man in the context of a global industrial war and the United States developing the capability to identify, track and kill individuals across the globe—is important. Moreover, if we only examine targeted killings in order to figure out if they are lawful, or under what circumstances they are morally permissible, or whether they 'work' or not, then we will be missing an opportunity to explore what targeted killings can tell us about war and warfare itself. In short, targeted killings are not only an interesting subject of analysis but a window into a way of thinking about the rights, wrongs and role of political violence in the present day.

For this reason, Coker's use of Rorty's concept of a turn is a good method for analysing the practice of targeted killings. Rorty, according to Coker, 'insists that we should all tell stories to make sense of the world around us'.[21] By understanding the American justification for targeted killings, it is possible to see that very different stories can be told about targeted killings using the lingua franca of war—the rules of war, both legal and moral. Even though targeted killings are described and justified in a common language, it is clear that they differ from earlier forms of warfare. The role of law and legal concepts in the constitution of targeted killings, and America's wider war, provides a way of understanding the role of law in America's war. So what is it about this war that is new?

The social construction of war

America's war has gone by many names since 9/11. Some of these are formal aspirations—the 'War on Terror', and latterly the 'Global War on Terror' and the 'Long War'. Others are official definitions, such as 'Operation Enduring Freedom'—the US government's formal name for the war in Afghanistan which change to mark different deploy-ments (the United States has been engaged in 'Operation Freedom's Sentinel' to support the Afghan government since 2014).[22] In parallel, formal legal definitions are used to describe war as armed conflict. It is the connection between war in a political, social and strategic sense of the term and the legal definitions of war and armed conflict that is important to understand here.

Part of the problem is that we are discussing a social concept and an idea. The link between war as an idea and war in our world is a key feature of one of the primary texts for those who seek to understand war and warfare: Carl von Clausewitz's *On War*.[23] Clausewitz identified the difference between war as a concept and war as a phenomenon and differentiated between an ideal form of war, absolute war and war as it existed in the world. Peter Paret explains that Clausewitz sees real war as an antithesis: 'that war, even in theory, is always influenced by forces external to it'.[24] Warfare in part defines the phenomenon—how war is fought dictates how humans experience it. Targeted killings are the form of warfare tied to America's war, and it is this form of warfare that we can directly experience.

Changes in the methods that humans use to do violence to one another change the way we can perceive wars. War, as experienced by humans, 'is a social phenomenon involving specific, dedicated social organisations (armed forces) in the management of restrained coercive violence for political purpose, governed by rules and conventions'.[25] As the difference between the killing of Yamamoto and al-Harithi demonstrates, America's contemporary use of targeted killings shows significant changes in every category of this definition.

The 'specific, dedicated social organisations' that currently do violence on behalf of the United States now include the CIA and US special forces from its Joint Special Operations Command (JSOC), neither of which existed in the Second World War (though it should be noted that the CIA's predecessor, the Office of Strategic Services, was a product of the Second World War). The 'restrained coercive violence' in America's transnational war is directed at a terrorist network, not a state. Furthermore, the precision warfare capabilities integral to American targeted killings enable far greater restraint, even as they expand the possible use of violence.

The political purpose of American targeted killings is to preserve America's national security, a concept that grew to dominate American society during the Cold War. National security also demonstrates a mode of thinking closely tied to the concept of risk and the practice of risk management. As Coker argues: 'Ours is an age of risk, and insecurity is its definitive feature.'[26] But one of the most important shifts lies in the rules that govern war.

While the rules of war are often talked about as timeless, the law of armed conflict in the contemporary world reflects important evolutions and events that occurred after Yamamoto's death. The lawyers responsible for determining whether the killing of al-Harithi was lawful were basing their analysis upon subsequent treaties, such as the 1949 Geneva Conventions and the disputes arising from the 1977 Additional Protocols to these conventions. The changing processes of adherence to the law of armed conflict, in the form of these military lawyers integrated at the operational level, shapes American military operations and has transformed military practice at a fundamental level.[27] Yet this also leads to the issue that has dominated international politics since the 9/11 attacks: Is the United States actually at war? While the legal team that judged al-Harithi's killing would likely answer yes, the way in which they would likely phrase this answer reflects a profound change in the law of armed conflict since Yamamoto's death: they would likely define it as an 'armed conflict', not a war.

The definitions of war that I have used so far are derived from philosophy and strategic studies, but given its importance, numerous academic disciplines contain and examine the concept of war. Even though these disciplines often share the same words, they frequently refer to the underlying concepts in quite different ways. In this regard, international law is no different, yet the difference between legal and conceptual terms matters because democratic states mostly define themselves by the rule of law. This is the idea that the law applies evenly, without exceptions.

So what is the problem? Well, if you happen to confuse the terms 'armed conflict' and 'war' when talking to someone versed in international law it is likely that you will receive a friendly rebuke: war and armed conflict are not the same thing, at least in international law. More importantly, while states do find themselves engaged in a variety of armed conflicts, they no longer wage wars, at least not in the legal sense of the term. Take, for example, the classical definition of war drawn from *On War*: 'War is thus an act of force to compel our enemy to do our will.'[28] Clausewitz's definition treats war in a wider sense than the classic legal definition of the concept of war offered by Lassa Oppenheim: 'War is a contention between two or more States, through their armed forces, for the purpose of overpowering each other and imposing such conditions of peace as the victor pleases.'[29]

The two definitions seem very close but contain important distinctions. While both Clausewitz and Oppenheim wrote with states in mind, Oppenheim's definition is fundamentally restricted to states: the law of war in Oppenheim's day was the law relating to conflict between states, defined by states. For all the development and permutation of international law since Oppenheim's day (his work contains readable definitions, but much has changed since the early twentieth century), war remains an inter-state concept. Non-state actors or groups do not count as participants in war, although (and this is important) they can engage in armed conflicts with states. Clausewitz's definition of war, however, could also relate to non-state groups even if during his day (and in Europe in particular) war was seen as an inter-state affair and mode of political relationship.

The difference between informal, conceptual and legal definitions of war can cause much confusion. Successive presidents—George W. Bush and Barack Obama—have used the language of war to refer to America's conflict with al Qaeda, which is why this book also uses the term 'trans-national war' to reflect this idea of a war. All the same, the government lawyers serving these presidents, and the US Supreme Court, have defined this political conflict with al-Qaeda as an armed conflict.[30] In theoretical and legal terms, this difference is very important. In international law, war is restricted to defining political violence between states, whereas armed conflict can occur between non-state armed groups as well as between states. To a certain extent, war and armed conflict refer to the same conceptual subject matter—organised armed violence—but the peculiarities of international law mean that the two diverge significantly in details. For lawyers, whether something is a war or an armed conflict are two distinct questions, since a state of war can be constituted by a declaration alone, whereas an armed conflict cannot. Where either exists, '[s]o far as the operation of the laws of war is concerned it makes little, if any, difference whether or not a conflict is characterised as war'.[31] This sentiment is true with regard to wars, armed conflicts and hostilities between states, but the existence of an armed conflict between states (an international armed conflict) and one that involves non-state armed groups (a non-international armed conflict) are two distinct issues, and although the principles of the law of armed conflict remain constant, the particular type of armed conflict alters specific legal rules on the conduct of war. As Gary Solis emphasises: 'In a non-international armed conflict, common Article 3 [which gives basic protections to civilians and detainees] and, perhaps, Additional Protocol II [that develops and extends common Article 3 protections in non-international armed conflicts], apply. No other portion of the Geneva Conventions applies.'[32] In other words, the legal classification of armed conflict not only determines the overarching authority to use violence but also the rules by which violence must be employed.

For those not versed in international law, it is easy to see this difference as a matter of splitting hairs. After all, one could quite easily look at any recent instance of armed conflict between states that a lawyer would claim is not a war and apply the 'I know it when I see it' test: the violence of armed conflicts resembles the violence found in wars, political leaders often refer to them as wars, and the people asked to wage them often consider them to be wars. If you go to your local bookshop, you are quite likely to find shelves of books that happen to make the apparent mistake of using the word 'war' when 'armed conflict' is the correct term, at least in terms of law. However, the difference between the two is not academic, nor a matter of mere semantics. Rather, it points to the important issue of how political violence is shaped by social concepts and ideas.

International law structures and frames the language of violence conducted by states, even in silence. A state wishing to break all the established laws and norms of the international community will be called upon by other states to abide by international law. Arguing against the constraints imposed by international law usually requires engaging with the very body of law that is being dismissed. Scholars disagree over the force of international law, notably the realist school of international relations, and legal scholars sometimes use rational choice theory to argue that states only comply with international law out of their own self-interest.[33] Yet whether states care for its restrictions or not, the fact remains that even states that challenge or disrupt the system speak the language of law when doing so. For this reason, the disappearance of war in law (and subsequent analysis of political violence in terms of armed conflict) is important, since states have retained the political (and perhaps customary) understanding of war, whereas the legal framework has shifted to armed conflict.

Transnational war is a product of the era in which we live. In the broadest sense, war refers to the public and restrained use of violence by two or more political entities in service of conflicting political aims—again, 'an act of force to compel our enemy to do our will', in Clausewitz's classical formulation.[34] Yet the realm of international politics has changed considerably since Clausewitz's day. Much of our world is now transnational, '[e]xtending or having interests extending beyond national bounds or frontiers'.[35] Transnational relations, 'contacts, coalitions, and interactions across state boundaries that are not controlled by the central foreign policy organs of governments', arguably constitute the majority of world politics, given the rise of the internet and globalisation.[36] This definition dates to 1971, predating the explosion of internet use and transnational communications networks, but the importance is not the novelty of transnational relations, but rather that the present day enables transnational social movements, and terrorist networks, to organise and persist. The two types of transnational phenomena that I am primarily concerned with are transnational jihad as an identity or idea,[37] and transnational networks[38] (made up of people adhering to a particular interpretation of broader ideals) that can enact acts of transnational terrorism (as defined in terrorism studies literature as acts that traverse state borders)[39] or inspire domestic terrorism. The reason for using transnational in this manner is that it references the character of a political entity (al-Qaeda) that has neither territorial, nor national, affiliation. The constitutive role that communications technology plays in such groups permits us to think of them as actors, or cohesive groups. From the perspective of states such as America, it also means they can be considered as possible opponents. Therein lies the novelty of America's war—one that is fought against a new type of group, but waged, justified and defined primarily according to rules devised for inter-state politics and war.

America's war requires social legitimation, and the definition of violence as war by states is an important component of this legitimation. Whereas Israel's covert killing of European and Iranian scientists or Palestinian militants sometimes blurs the boundaries of peace and war, occurring as they do in the context of the Palestinian conflict and confrontation with Iran, the United States defines its actions as legal and moral acts of war, yet one that is not directed at any state or territorial group. This transnational dimension is key. Al-Qaeda may have declared war on the United States in 1996 and 1998, but it was not until the United States declared war (and in the legal sense, determined that the United States was in an armed conflict with al-Qaeda) that a war could be said to exist between the two. The transnational aspect of this conflict arises because al-Qaeda is neither a state, nor is the conflict restricted to the territory of a state (or contiguous states).

The question of whether such a war could exist is often confused with the question of whether such a war does exist. I will address these issues in the next chapter, but for now, we need to look at the shifting legal boundaries of America's war, and why targeted killings are favoured by the Obama administration.

The rule of law, and the role of law

The wars that we see in the present day differ in many ways from those of the past. Former British General Sir Rupert Smith goes so far as to say that 'War no longer exists.'[40] If war is the violent settlement of disputes between states by means of battle, then Smith offers sufficient support for this statement. He notes, for example, that the last 'real tank battle' occurred in the 1973 Arab-Israeli War.[41] Smith's writing eloquently exposes the gap between the common social imagination of what war is, and the actual use of coercive force and violence in the twenty-first century.

Advances in technology mean that states and non-state actors can both use force in novel ways. Another difference is that the changing political landscape changes the nature of the actors involved, as well as their political aims. War in the contemporary world differs in character from the wars of the past, and this is partly due to the role that international law—and the legal arguments related to it—now play in defining war and the existence of wars. This suggests a closer relationship between the rules of war and war itself than that suggested in Clausewitz's opening statement that international law and custom are 'certain self-imposed, imperceptible limitations hardly worth mentioning' that 'attach' to physical force.[42]

Seeing the role of law as something independent of states, to be adhered to (or not) according to self-interest, misses the underlying role that legal concepts play in culture. In an influential critical account of the role of international law, Jack Goldsmith and Eric Posner argue that 'states provide legal or moral justifications for their actions, no matter how transparently self-interested their actions are'.[43] This claim that '[t]heir legal or moral justifications cleave to their interests, and so when interests change, so do rationalizations' is a powerful critique of the traditional view of international law as a code that states follow out of a sense of obligation. In Posner and Goldsmith's account, rational interest and self-interest trump any obligations arising from international law:

> a kind of empty happy talk is common in the international arena just as it is in other areas of life; it is largely a ceremonial usage designed to enable the speaker to assert policies and goals without overtly admitting that he or she is acting for a purpose to which others might object.[44]

Goldsmith and Posner's account clearly hews close to Clausewitz's idea of law. Yet the idea that states follow international law out of self-interest is more about the relationship between self-interest, obligation and the concept of law.[45] In his book criticising Goldsmith and Posner's 'New Realist' school of international law, Jens Ohlin points out that 'self-interest and the essential normativity of international law are not mutually exclusive' since international law reflects states' self-interest in the form of long-term cooperation.[46] Moreover, our structures and concepts of law reflect a tradition and cultural approach to that which they are supposed to regulate. Whether or not they exert a measurable effect at a given point in time misses the fact that they structure the way in which certain issues are approached. Here, international law plays the important role of ordering the very concept of war.

If we see war as a social practice and custom, albeit one that involves a violent adversarial relationship between actors, then the ideas that states have that permit and constitute the use of force also constitute war. If the anarchy of the international system is 'what states make of it', to quote Alexander Wendt, then war, too, is what states make of it.[47] What states 'make of it', and why, is dependent upon cultural factors and identity.[48] International law therefore has the force and influence that states consider it to hold. The importance of identity as a frame is that shared values inherent in a given identity give rise to orders based around a shared set of rules. As Ohlin observes: 'When it comes to law, ideas really matter ... academic arguments questioning the validity and scope of international law affect how the U.S. Government conducts its business ... arguments about international law implicate every corner of our foreign relations.'[49] This is in part why law permeates what contemporary states consider to be war, as James Gow writes:

> lawfulness is essential to the military. It is also vital to strategy and the conduct of operations. It is in the interest of the armed forces to ensure that war crimes allegations are dealt with, and seen to be dealt with, both internally and externally, for the sake of professional ethos and also to ensure wider legitimacy and public support for the armed forces, generally.[50]

Do states rationally choose to obey or disobey international law? Social constructivism offers an alternative perspective that stands aside from this question but can inform it. In the words of Janina Dill, international law 'is a compromise between pre-existing motivational forces and normative codes'.[51] These codes not only contain a common understanding of behaviour but they also contain ontological assumptions—what exists, or how the world is categorised and ordered—implicit within the way that they describe the world. The importance of the law of armed conflict is that it consists of a shared way of thinking about what war is, a grammar of war. This grammar, we must note, informs the 'grammar of killing'—'how we perceive [killing], how we reflect on why others do what they do and how we tend to experience it once done'.[52]

What most people, including lawyers, would agree is that war in the present is fought in a very different context from the wars of the past. America's war occurs in the context of larger shifts in international politics and international order, something that Philip Bobbitt frames as a shift from the society of nation states to the society of market states.[53] The changes in international society, with its differing states, social movements and armed groups, all with varied political goals, have resulted in many different types of wars. Even though the international law of states is intended to cover all such conflicts, there is still considerable difference in its scope of application, interpretation and, pointedly, willingness to adhere to its strictures. Notably, terrorist networks like al-Qaeda not only fail to abide by international law but they also do not see themselves as bound by this body of law. This, however, is only one side of the coin, so to speak, with how states see themselves as bound by international law found upon the other. This is an important factor in how international law constitutes wars. To understand this, we need to consider the changing character of America's war with al-Qaeda.

The idea that law constitutes war might seem strange given that the symbols of the early War on Terror were the orange-jumpsuited detainees at Guantanamo Bay, and, later, the issue of torture. The early stages involved known or suspected al-Qaeda members being transferred (in a process of 'extraordinary rendition') to third-party authoritarian states where they were tortured or mistreated for information that they were thought to possess.[54] Others were transferred to CIA-operated detention facilities, the so-called 'black sites', where some were tortured by CIA operatives.[55] The point I wish to make here is that this does not demonstrate the weakness of law, but instead its centrality. The early conduct of the War on Terror was defined as lawful by the US Department of Justice's Office of Legal Counsel and was sanctioned by the American Psychological Association.[56] Actions that constitute torture were defined as legal until the Office of Legal Counsel opinion that supported these practices was withdrawn by Jack Goldsmith in December 2003.[57] The same could be said of many of the contentious practices of both the Bush and Obama administrations. US conduct in the War on Terror cannot be understood without reference to the work of government lawyers, interpreting the limits of executive authority, the American courts deciding on the limits of this authority, the US Congress reshaping the legal landscape, and innumerable legal advocates challenging the government in court throughout. Regardless of your stance on which actions were or were not legal, the law mattered.

Of course, politics drives policy choices, but law and politics are near-inseparable in contemporary America. As a political act, President Obama sought to define his national security policy as a break from that of the Bush administration in his important 2009 National Archives speech: 'the decisions that were made over the last eight years established an ad hoc legal approach for fighting terrorism that was neither effective nor sustainable—a framework that failed to rely on our legal traditions and time-tested institutions, and that failed to use our values as a compass'.[58]

It made political sense for the Obama administration to distance itself from the actions authorised by the Bush administration, including torture, since they were widely reviled by Democrats and international

society. The Bush administration was perceived to have tried to legitimise torture as a necessary action in order to fight al-Qaeda, and in this
speech, Obama sought to emphasise that this was not the case. In the
grand tradition of 'good war/bad war' binaries, some would like to
recast America's war with al-Qaeda under Obama as somehow better
or cleaner than its conduct under the Bush administration, something
that critics like Jeremy Scahill deride as a 'fantasy'.[59] Obama promised
to wage war on al-Qaeda 'with an abiding confidence in the rule of law
and due process; in checks and balances and accountability', but
Obama's war still aimed to 'defeat' al-Qaeda.[60] As important as these
policy distinctions are, we should bear in mind two things: first, the
near-primacy of law as a source of authority; and second, that even
though the Obama administration set about 'cleaning up' the war that
it inherited, it still argued that it existed, and, more importantly, it
escalated the use of targeted killings to wage it. In short, Obama promised to continue his predecessor's war against al-Qaeda, but to do so
without resort to torture.

The Obama administration's explicit rejection of torture meant
that, unlike the Bush administration, it sought to veer away from the
zone of ambiguity inherent in the law regulating torture and interrogation. Yet for all the differences between the two administrations, there
is considerable overlap and continuity in the methods employed to
wage war against al-Qaeda. Critics note that Obama's use of drones
exceeded that of the Bush administration, and some even argue that
Obama is 'worse than Bush' on this and other related foreign policy
decisions.[61] The grey area of overlap between the CIA, the military and
America's intelligence community appears to be a core feature of this
conflict, and not an aberration.

America's hostile political relationship with al-Qaeda and the Obama
administration's rejection of 'dirty' means of waging war set the stage for
the considerable increase in targeted killings under Obama. For liberals
who thought that Obama would represent a clean break from the Bush-
era, this came as a disappointment. As David Rohde wrote in 2013: 'The
candidate that liberals thought would return the rule of law to the
struggle against terror continues to embrace many of President George
W. Bush's practices.'[62] As such, the multiple constraints levied on the
presidency, from the legal retrenchment spearheaded by Jack Goldsmith,

to the pioneering Supreme Court decisions on military detention at Guantanamo Bay, and acts of Congress, have resulted in the notion of a clean war waged largely by remote weapons systems against al-Qaeda and its affiliated organisations.[63]

The difference between the Bush and Obama administrations is about the role of law in America. Liberal states, according to Stephen Holmes, are defined by their pluralistic nature and governance by popular consent; they protect the rights of individuals, the state is subject to the rule of law and all citizens are considered politically equal.[64] Obama's revisions of the War on Terror are therefore an attempt to reconcile this war with liberal political norms, most notably by normalising this war with processes that ensure adherence to the rule of law.[65]

In the early stages of America's war, then Vice-President Dick Cheney referred to this conflict as 'a struggle of years, a new kind of war against a new kind of enemy'.[66] However, the conduct of America's war under Obama appears to be the application of old law to this 'new kind of enemy' rather than an attempt to transform the law of armed conflict. Despite the ongoing use of targeted killings, the character of America's war has changed since 9/11. Through a mixture of political change, public revulsion and court rulings, Obama's war is now explicitly defined in traditional military terms, and as a lawful activity. This leads us to the issue of strategy: Why are targeted killings the preferred means of warfare? The answer is not 'drones'—it is the relationship between the legal, political and strategic requirement for a form of warfare that can identify and attack America's opponents at a distance. The missing ingredient is technology, but it is technology in a wider sense than a class of remote platforms.

Technology should never be confused for tools, even though the two are related. Instead, as Martin Bridgstock defines it, technology is a 'body of skills and knowledge by which we control and modify the world'.[67] Technology is the way that humans think about and relate to the world, and the tools that they devise in order to interact with and shape their environment. For this reason, technology is both social and political by definition. Technology shapes society, but different cultures often adopt and use technology for quite different purposes. Technology constitutes transnational politics. Without transnational communications networks, cohesive transnational social networks that could pose a threat to states would be almost impossible to sustain. In shorter form: no technology, no problem. At the same time, without the key technologies that permit the US government to identify, track and kill individuals at such distance, there would be no way for America to wage such a war. Technology is fundamentally social in character—while humans use technology to manipulate the world that we inhabit, until we create some form of self-sustaining artificial intelligence, technology will always be human-centric by definition.

American targeted killings are therefore situated in a given technological moment, but that should not be mistaken for deriving them from the platform. On its own, a Reaper is an inert lump of matter. Technology shapes the way in which societies wage war, as technology, culture and warfare are interrelated. Martin van Creveld explains that 'War is permeated by technology to the point that *every* single element is either governed by or at least linked to it.'[68] Debates over the legality and illegality of targeted killings tend to miss the constitutive role that law plays in the design and operation of targeted killings themselves. There are notable interesting exceptions to this. Gregory McNeal recounts how the battle damage assessments performed before and after missile strikes mean that the military's interpretations of its legal responsibilities create significant control mechanisms and in many respects reduce the autonomy of the drone pilots.[69] Adherence to the law of armed conflict is an integral component of the US military's self-image and culture—it perceives itself as a law-abiding entity. Law regulates targeted killings in its truest sense in that perceptions of law are a constitutive aspect of the practice itself.

The use of technology, even military technology, is governed to a large extent by cultural attitudes and assumptions. As John Ellis notes, cultural perceptions of war can dominate the use of a technology, as happened with the early development of the machine gun.[70] In Ellis's understanding, culture governs the use and adoption of technology. However, the conduct of war places constraints on pure cultural relativism, due to the fact that combat and other forms of military violence are typically lethal by design. John Lynn identifies this as a kind of feedback loop between cultural influences and reality—the plain facts of combat eventually alter or change the discourse of war.[71] This can be seen in the changing role of the machine gun by militaries in the nineteenth and early twentieth centuries, and the manner in which its use eventually altered the discourse on war, despite strong resistance from military cultures that sought to preserve it.[72] Targeted killings are a product of this kind of interaction, and I will explore this further in Chapter 6.

Conclusion

The central problem with America's war on al-Qaeda is that there is substantial disagreement regarding its very existence. The names used to describe targeted killings not only indicate whether a person considers them legitimate or not, but also whether they consider that the United States is actually at war with al-Qaeda. Targeted killings are also referred to as high-value targeting, drone warfare, extrajudicial killing, assassinations and murder. All of these names impart a specific focus on the same set of material activity, namely the targeting and killing of individuals by the American military and its intelligence services, notably the Central Intelligence Agency.

The American claim that the United States is at war with a transnational terrorist network is the primary focus of this book. How this war is constituted, why it gives rise to targeted killings and what this tells us about war itself are the central questions that concern us. The American belief that a war exists is central to understanding its use of targeted killings. At the same time, this is a subjective interpretation of the world. How can claims that a war does not exist be weighed or reconciled against America's claims? Moreover, a war waged by targeted killings against a transnational network in conditions of quasi-secrecy is at the very fringes of activity that could be considered war. The central problems are what can be counted as war, what evidence proves (or disproves) the existence of war, how the existence of war can be judged and whose judgement is important. Fundamentally: How is war constituted in the world in which we live? I will explore all these questions in the next two chapters, but before examining the role of law in the constitution of war, it is prudent to outline the connection between war and armed conflict in international law.

2

THE LENS OF LAW

Baldrick:

... the way I see it, these days there's a war on, right? And ages ago, there wasn't a war on, right? So there must have been a moment when there not being a war went away, right, and there being a war came along, right?[1]

Introduction

The distinctions between war, peace and armed conflict matter because they are essential to understanding the constitution and interpretation of political violence. If a state kills a person for no reason, in times of peace, then this is generally held to be a misdeed, and in addition, a violation of that person's right to life.[2] Conversely, killing (and the threat of killing) is essential to war and armed conflict. In this sense, the existence of an armed conflict or war is a key factor in assessing the rights and wrongs of violence.

The problem that America's transnational war poses is that it is an open question as to whether it even exists. It lies in a grey zone of interpretability between a state of peace, and an armed conflict that is recognised and acknowledged as such. Also, given that armed conflict is different from war, this makes the comparison between the mission that killed Admiral Yamamoto and Abu Ali al-Harithi less useful. After all, the Second World War is almost universally recognised as having been a war, whereas the existence of the transnational armed conflict that America insists it is engaged in is very much up for debate. For present purposes, it is better to compare the al-Harithi strike to the killing of Abu Musab al-Zarqawi in 2006. Zarqawi was killed by US forces at the end of an exhaustive hunt when an American F-16 dropped two bombs on his safe house in Iraq.[3] One reason that the strike that killed al-Harithi caused controversy was that it occurred 'beyond the battlefield', and the same could be said of the strike that flattened the house Zarqawi was staying in. Yet Zarqawi's death did not cause nearly the same level of controversy or introspection. The reason for this is important.

The difference between the two killings is that there was a recognised armed conflict in Iraq at the time of Zarqawi's death, but no recognised armed conflict in Yemen at the time of al-Harithi's. Unlike Admiral Yamamoto, neither al-Harithi nor Zarqawi were members of a state's armed forces. However, Zarqawi's connection to the armed conflict in Iraq was clear. Although a Jordanian, Zarqawi formed and led the group that would later become al-Qaeda in Iraq. In the aftermath of the American decision to invade Iraq in 2003, Zarqawi emerged as a brutal and effective jihadi leader, pursuing a two-pronged strategy of driving out foreign forces and targeting Iraq's Shia population in order to enflame civil war.[4] By any standard, the violence in Iraq was, at the time of Zarqawi's death, an armed conflict.

The difference between al-Harithi and Zarqawi lies in the framing of the violence that killed them. If a transnational armed conflict existed, then the Harithi strike could be considered as part of that armed conflict. The problem is that numerous figures in the group of practitioners and academics that constitute the international law community disagree. To them, there is little evidence that such an armed conflict exists, or that the violence being done in this frame rises to the level of armed conflict.[5] In the government's defence, the US Supreme Court has held that America is engaged in an armed conflict with al-Qaeda, its lawyers draw the same conclusion, and the political leadership act upon this advice. But is this enough?[6] After all, if all it takes for an armed conflict to exist is for a state to say that one does, then this would enable states to cover any kind of violence as armed conflict.

How, then, does armed conflict come to exist, and how should its existence be judged?

Many of the arguments about America's use of targeted killings hinge on the existence and classification of armed conflict. Is America at war with al-Qaeda, or is it engaged in an armed conflict with this group? These questions are designed to probe the existence of something: a state of war, or an armed conflict of some sort. These questions are, however, united by the fact that they are examining intangible objects. Unlike, say, a rock, a state of war is not something that can be perceived in and of itself. Similarly, an armed conflict is not something that can be prodded with a stick. This property is not unique to either war or armed conflict—many of our social concepts exist in the mind and are impossible to verify through the kind of empirical inquiry that allows humans to make sense of the physical world.

The mode of inquiry matters, and for that reason law and legal concepts are important: they give us the categories of investigation as well as the standards of assessment. However, there are two competing ideas about the role of law in the existence of armed conflict. One is that law acts as an impartial frame of observation and judgement. In this sense, the role of law is to provide a way of making sense of the world we collectively observe, such that judgements of legality can be made one way or the other. A second, sometimes competing, way of thinking about the role of law in this context is that it is a constitutive aspect of armed conflict. In this chapter, I want to examine this first idea, that the role of international law is to render impartial judgement on the actions of states.

Categories of armed conflict

Part of the confusion as to whether America is at war with al-Qaeda stems from the early arguments of the Bush administration after 9/11, as well as the wars in Afghanistan and Iraq. Although the status of American actions in both Afghanistan and Iraq were (and to some, remain) important legal issues, the subject of this book is the idea of a war between America and al-Qaeda, without restriction to a single country.[7] Here, the principal problem is that, at various stages,

President George W. Bush declared that the United States was at war with 'Terror', 'Terrorism' and 'Terrorists', as well as al-Qaeda. As Bush himself elaborated to a joint session of Congress soon after the 9/11 attacks: 'Our enemy is a radical network of terrorists, and every government that supports them. Our war on terror begins with al Qaeda, but it does not end there. It will not end until every terrorist group of global reach has been found, stopped and defeated.'[8]

Whether or not America had the right to use force in self-defence as a response to the 9/11 attacks lies beyond the scope of this book. In the early years of the war on terror, some senior legal figures vehemently protested the idea that the violence that terrorists could inflict would be serious enough to permit a state to respond with military measures.[9] States, we should note, retain the inherent right to self-defence under the UN Charter.[10] This is triggered—in international law—by an 'armed attack'. Some argue, like Sean Murphy, that 'our appreciation of these non-traditional means of engaging in an armed attack must also comprehend the pernicious methods of terrorist organizations'.[11] Article 51 of the UN Charter—the article explaining the right of self-defence—is worded 'broadly enough to allow for the use of self-defense against acts emanating from non-state actors'.[12] Nonetheless, successive US administrations have claimed to have the right to act in self-defence against terrorists should they pose a threat, building upon previous instances where it responded with force, such as the 1998 strikes in Sudan and Afghanistan.[13] But the scope for using force in self-defence is relatively indeterminate versus the authority to use force in the context of an armed conflict. International law experts do not necessarily agree on the limits of self-defence, particularly anticipatory or pre-emptive action.[14] Actions taken in self-defence are intended to be responses to imminent threats that have to be responded to with force, and some have difficulty reconciling this concept with a long-term transcontinental military campaign. A targeted killing could be justified as an act of self-defence, or as an act of violence in the context of an armed conflict. The important point here is that these are two concurrent justifications—the existence of an armed conflict doesn't preclude states from acting in self-defence and vice versa—and they place different explicit and implicit limitations upon the use of force. The difference between these two concepts is therefore important, since they place different limits upon state activity.

The lawyers for the US government argue that the United States and al-Qaeda are engaged in armed conflict rather than being at war with each other. However, the implied transnational nature of this armed conflict has led some senior legal figures to conclude that the conflict does not exist.[15] This disagreement is essential to understanding the problem that transnational war poses to the existing legal framework that regulates the resort to force by states, as well as their conduct in armed conflicts and wars.

The notion of a 'war on terror' was, to some, as absurd as a 'war on drugs' or a 'war on poverty'. Michael Howard, a leading historian of war and warfare, referred to this as 'a natural but terrible and irrevocable error' in part because '[t]o declare war on terrorists, or, even more illiterately, on terrorism is at once to accord terrorists a status and dignity that they seek and that they do not deserve'.[16] Although Howard was understanding of America's reaction and resort to war, he considered it unwise because '[t]errorists can be successfully destroyed only if public opinion, both at home and abroad, supports the authorities in regarding them as criminals rather than heroes'.[17] In response, Philip Bobbitt argued that 'the phrase "a war on terror" is not an inapt metaphor, but rather a recognition of the way war is changing'.[18]

Semantic disagreements regarding the nature of the conflict are common, but they inevitably reduce to the question of whether states could or should wage war on terrorists or terrorism. Michael Howard's argument is that states such as America could choose to wage war on terrorists, but that they should not do so, because this is both counterproductive and, in his judgement, futile. Bobbitt's argument is more expansive—states are not only at war with terrorists, but are at war to preserve 'states of consent' from 'states of terror' that new, globalised 'market state terrorists' seek to impose. Rather than war upon a tactic, Bobbitt proposes war against such groups to be necessary in order to preserve liberty and consent-based government and 'that it is precisely against terror—and not simply against terrorism or the arming of terrorists—that war must be waged if the war aim of market states of consent is to be achieved'.[19]

It is at this point that we must recognise the difference, and perhaps separation, of 'war' in the political and semantic sense, and the legal classification of war and armed conflict. Consider the words of Antonio Cassese, a leading Italian jurist, writing shortly after the 9/11 attacks: 'I shall not dwell on the use of the term "war" by the American President and the whole US administration. It is obvious that in this case "war" is a misnomer. War is an armed conflict between two or more states.'[20]

The idea that war can only occur between states is a reflection of the global order of states—since war confers legitimacy on political violence, states would only countenance referring to inter-state political violence as war. The international treaties that defined war and armed conflict in the nineteenth and twentieth centuries reinforced this, as Christopher Greenwood points out: 'only States had the legal capacity to wage war; for example, the laws of war are built around the assumption that the belligerents are States and have the apparatus of States (such as a criminal justice system) to draw upon'.[21]

The difference between war and armed conflict matters because they are distinct concepts in international law.[22] This may strike lay observers as a case of splitting hairs, but this difference reflects distinctions made in the treaties that have codified the law of armed conflict.[23] Whereas, in international law, although 'war' is a term reserved for the interactions of states, it takes almost no effort to find examples of wars in human history that concerned political entities that are barely comparable to the nation states that initially agreed upon this body of law. Armed conflict, however, can occur between states and non-state groups. It is now the dominant legal frame for assessing the use of violence in what we colloquially term wars. Even states that end up fighting one another, for example, the United States and Iraq in 2003, find themselves engaged in armed conflicts, despite the fact that their political leadership use the language of war. Some argue that it is even illegal for war to exist in its technical legal sense, although Yoram Dinstein points out that 'a negation of the existence of a state of war appears to be no more than a hollow semantic gesture' given that the law regulating the conduct of international armed conflicts would still apply.[24]

In this sense, what this book terms 'transnational war' translates, in law, to an armed conflict that is transnational. This is the essence of the claim articulated in some considerable detail by the Obama administration.[25] America's war with al-Qaeda involves two parallel processes: the conceptual articulation that the United States is at war, and the translation of this into legal terminology. Hence the president can use the language of war, while his legal advisors in the US Department of Justice's Office of Legal Counsel work with the language and constraints of national and international law to frame and bound this political discourse with legal opinions. What, then, should we make of the blunt American claim that 'As a matter of international law, the United States is in an armed conflict with al-Qaida, the Taliban, and associated forces'?[26]

One thing we should bear in mind is that the transition from war to armed conflict involved more than swapping one name for another. In international law, armed conflict requires violence. This differentiates armed conflict from war since 'war was a technical legal condition, distinct from actual hostilities; one could have fighting without war and war without fighting'.[27] Like war, the violence that is required for an armed conflict to exist needs to be conducted by an organised armed group, either a professional state military or the armed forces of a non-state actor.[28] How armed conflict exists, or could be judged to exist, remains a problem. In fact, it is the different ideas of how war and armed conflict are judged or deemed to exist that are crucial for understanding the disagreement regarding the existence of a transnational armed conflict. States used to be able to declare war without any actual violence taking place between states, but they cannot 'declare' armed conflict in the same way since its existence depends upon violence and violent acts. So who gets to judge, and how?

One problem is that there are different understandings of what does, and does not, constitute armed conflict. The International Law Association's Use of Force Committee reported in 2010 that:

> the existence of armed conflict is a significant fact in the international legal system, and, yet, the Committee found no widely accepted definition of armed conflict in any treaty. It did, however, discover significant evidence in the sources of international law that the international community embraces a common understanding of armed conflict.[29]

Here, the gap between widely accepted definitions of armed conflict and common understandings of the same concept is important. This seems illogical until we consider the nature of international law, both formal and customary. States often shy away from precise definitions of important concepts, while agreeing on a common legal language with which to discuss international affairs. For example, while aggression is a significant breach of international law, there is no universal agreement between states regarding its definition. The 1974 UN General Assembly Resolution 3314 offered both a general definition as well as a non-exhaustive list of specific acts, but also recognised that the UN Security Council was free to determine what constituted aggression under the UN Charter. In the modern day, the ICC's actionable definition of aggression, over which it is yet to exercise jurisdiction, is effectively limited to the states parties to the Rome Statute.[30] This tension between precise definitions and common agreement exists alongside the methods and purposes of international law. Here, armed conflict is a judgement and classification of reality. In order to make these classifications in a fair and impartial manner, it is necessary to have standards for judgement, hence the ever-present drive towards formal and technical definitions of legal concepts. The tension between the need to judge 'commonly understood' concepts in a fair manner produces arguments that seem illogical on face value, but entirely understandable once these wider tensions are brought into view. A good example of this relevant in this regard is the committee's recognition that armed conflict is 'a core concept in international law, but it is also a socially constructed concept and, as such, it is not amenable to any scientific litmus test', yet '[n]evertheless, whether or not armed conflict exists depends on the satisfaction of objective criteria'.[31]

Such tensions can be understood in the purpose of international law, as a wide variety of lawyers and NGOs see it, in reducing violence and harm. The existence of armed conflict means that the more specialised body of law, the law of armed conflict, governs state actions.[32] If the specialised law, *lex specialis*, permits greater or wider uses of force than the general rules that govern state conduct, *lex generalis*, then applying this law expands the lawful range of options to a state. There is therefore an inherent tension between legal positions that expand the applicable scope of the law of armed conflict, and jurists who seek to restrict the ability of states to define where it applies.[33] It is for this reason that a range of actors wish to restrict the ability of states to determine the application of the law of armed conflict, and one of the principal ways of doing so is to form objective criteria for assessing the existence of armed conflicts. This, we should note, is very far from the world of states declaring war, even if the actual underlying violence does not change. To understand the problem that leaving such definitions to states can cause, we need to consider the killing of Baitullah Mehsud.

The many conflicts problem

One of the key issues in the contemporary world is the degree to which armed conflicts can overlap. After all, states armed with ballistic or cruise missiles can project violence thousands of miles from their own forces. There are many problems associated with this, but the one I want to focus on here is the problem that arises when conflicts overlap. Although comprehensive datasets of individual strikes have now been compiled by organisations such as the Bureau of Investigative Journalism in London, these only provide a snapshot of the damage a strike causes. It is possible to try and guess the intended effect by the presence (or lack thereof) of persons identifiable as people that the United States might want to kill, but even then, it is difficult or impossible to know the precise reason for individual acts of violence from the public record.[34] We tend to think of war and armed conflict in a singular sense—a state 'goes to war'—but the reality of the modern world is that states sometimes have multiple overlapping legal rationales to use violence, and it is not readily apparent from their actions which is in play. In short, we lack the means to assess the legal justification of public violence from the available evidence.

On 5 August 2009, a CIA-operated drone attacked a compound where Baitullah Mehsud was staying, fatally wounding him, and killing a number of others. Baitullah Mehsud had founded the non-state militant group Tehrik-E-Taliban Pakistan (TTP) in December 2007, but, unlike al-Zarqawi, Mehsud's militants were not directly embroiled in a violent conflict with the United States. Rather, the TTP 'is an umbrella group for what were once locally-oriented tribal militias involved in varying, individualized conflicts with the state of Pakistan'.[35] Taliban elements fighting NATO forces in Afghanistan did, however, use Pakistan as a staging area for that conflict. Mehsud's death therefore provides a window into the overlapping conflicts that America finds itself engaged in.

Baitullah Mehsud was responsible for a significant amount of violence in Pakistan. To observers in the West, his most visible act of violence was his purported involvement in the 2007 assassination of Benazir Bhutto. The CIA, at the time led by Michael Hayden, reportedly came to the same conclusion as Pakistan's then-President Pervez Musharraf, placing the blame for Bhutto's murder at Mehsud's door.[36] The government of Pakistan declared war upon the group in 2008 and America placed a bounty of $5 million on Mehsud's head.[37]

Mehsud is an important case for a number of reasons. The first is that he did not die alone. As the Bureau of Investigative Journalism noted, 'As many as ten others also may have died, including his uncle, father-in-law Maulvi Ikramuddin and mother-in-law, and seven bodyguards. Four children were also injured.'[38] The strike that killed Mehsud therefore killed many people who were not, by any definition, military targets, including his wife and children. Georgetown Law Professor Mary Ellen O'Connell highlights this strike in her general criticism of American targeted killings in part because 'the strike killed twelve for one intended target'.[39] Nor were these apparently the first people to die due to America's pursuit of Mehsud. The human rights charity Reprieve published a report that accuses the US government of killing up to 164 people in its pursuit of Mehsud as part of a wider pattern of indiscriminate killing that killed up to 1,147 people while pursuing just forty-one named targets.[40]

Mehsud's death is also controversial because it is not immediately apparent why he was killed, or who is ultimately responsible. The thinking that applied to previous targeted killings of al-Qaeda operatives and Taliban elements did not necessarily apply to Mehsud. This is what I refer to as the 'many conflicts problem': the way that 'traditional' armed conflicts overlap with America's transnational one. This is a wider problem, but here I focus upon the American perspective.

Regardless of the controversy over America's claim of being engaged in a transnational armed conflict, by 2009 it was engaged in a number of armed conflicts that were less controversial. Afghanistan was (and remains) a good case study of non-international armed conflict in the contemporary world.[41] The same could be said about Iraq. The point is that the violence in Afghanistan and Iraq at this time was plain for the world to see, and intelligible as armed conflict. Both of these armed conflicts had a trans-border dimension. Militant networks in Iraq spilled across into both Syria and Iran, while Pakistan's border regions served as a staging area for Taliban groups in Afghanistan. A drone strike or targeted killing in Pakistan could therefore be performed in support of US forces in Afghanistan—attacking Taliban safe areas and staging locations to disrupt attacks.[42]

At the same time, Pakistan was having problems of its own. I do not have space to consider the full extent of Pakistan's involvement in conflicts in Afghanistan, nor with its neighbour, India, but it also faced significant internal opposition.[43] In 2009, President Obama expanded the CIA's operations in Pakistan to include targets that threatened the Pakistani state, not just the Taliban elements that used Pakistan's territory to rest and train for the war in Afghanistan.[44] Although Mehsud communicated with al-Qaeda's core group, located in Pakistan since their escape from Afghanistan in 2001, he was not a member of the organisation.[45] So on what basis did the Americans kill him?

Without clarification from the US government, it is impossible to identify the basis on which agents of the American state killed Mehsud. Yes, senior figures in the Obama administration, including the president himself, have made lengthy speeches providing a legal and moral justification for these killings, but the specific details needed to understand the actual rationale for killing men like Mehsud remain a closely guarded secret.[46] The perceived lack of transparency and accountability for the use of targeted killings is exacerbated by the unclear chains of responsibility for each strike: Are they the doing of the CIA or the US military? For lawyers, these distinctions matter. How, Philip Alston asks, can the CIA be held accountable for their actions in the same way that the US military can?[47] Moreover, how can the American public hold its government to account, if it does not even know the legal basis of violent acts committed in their name?

This is where the idea of conflict status becomes an issue. Until the end of combat operations in Afghanistan, a theoretical American strike in Pakistan could occur in the context of three separate conflicts: America's war with al-Qaeda, in support of NATO or American operations in Afghanistan, or in support of Pakistan's government. This leads to the interesting issue: If the United States is engaged in two declared conflicts, is it necessary to define the context of each act of violence when and where these conflicts overlap? It would be easy if the situation in Pakistan was an isolated case, but America has also committed targeted killings in Pakistan, Yemen and Somalia. In each country, the government of the state is threatened by armed groups in situations that hover between fragile peace and open civil war. To better understand this issue, we need to examine how, and why, armed conflict is judged to exist in law.

Law as observation

In domestic court cases, facts are determined from evidence, either by a jury or by a judge. The role of the trier of fact is in essence to decide upon what was true, or what occurred. This works well in domestic courts since in a political system governed by the rule of law there will exist some form of determining legal truth one way or the other for acts committed by all persons subject to the jurisdiction of the courts. However, the international system is defined by de facto anarchy, albeit a somewhat cooperative 'anarchical society' of states, as Hedley Bull phrased it.[48] How, then, does law operate in this system? How is the fact of an armed conflict's existence derived from available evidence? More importantly, who or what gets to make these kinds of determinations?

Before answering these questions, we need to consider the purpose of international law in this context. The law of armed conflict as a codified body of law is itself a relative novelty. Humans have organised to kill and coerce one another for thousands of years, yet written international law (as is understood to exist now) is less than 200 years old. Law matters, since, as Gary Solis writes:

> Rules of war are not the same as laws of war. A law is a form of rule that, within a particular sphere or jurisdiction, must be obeyed, subject to sanctions or legal consequences. A rule does not necessarily involve either sanctions or legal consequences. There have been *rules* for the battlefield

for thousands of years, but, with significant exceptions, there have been *laws* for the battlefield—LOAC [the law of armed conflict]—only in the past hundred years or so. LOAC is a relatively recent phenomenon.[49]

Yet the law of armed conflict is not neutral—it is biased towards states and reflects its European origins.[50] Moreover, every treaty reflects the differences of opinion that exist between states on the nature, purpose and content of international law. Despite such differences, significant rule-abidance characterises the relationship between states and international law. Louis Henkin's point that 'Almost all nations observe almost all principles of international law and almost all of their obligations almost all of the time' is still as valid as ever.[51]

Treaty law thus reflects the considerable convergence of state opinion in certain areas, including the conduct of wars. The law of armed conflict consists of both treaty and custom, and is rooted in the international system of states. The treaties that constitute the 'black letter' non-controversial aspects of this body of law were agreed by states, and originally applied between states. Importantly, this created a body of written law shared by states in a stable and accretive system, laying the foundations for fixed universal rules of conduct.[52]

The idea was that states would limit the suffering and hardships of war between themselves, and also agree to standards of conduct in these same wars. The primary sanction was that breaking these rules would render persons liable to the loss of protections inherent in the law, and possible sanctions. Of course, this implies limits. If the existence of war triggers obligations, then this gives states wishing to exceed said limits an incentive to wage war without declarations. No war, no obligations; no obligations, no limits on the means available to the state. This is particularly an issue in civil wars.

The modern law of armed conflict was in part an attempt to construct a more rigorous regime to regulate the use of violence by states. By taking armed conflict as the focus, the rules of the 1949 Geneva Conventions ostensibly attempted to circumvent the problem of undeclared war. In theory, states could still wage undeclared wars on one another, but their actions would still be an armed conflict, and therefore their obligations would apply. The four Geneva Conventions of 1949 shared specific language in the second article of each, namely that the treaties applied 'to all cases of declared war or of any other armed conflict which may arise between two or more of the High Contracting Parties, even if the state of war is not recognized by one of them'.[53] This also covered armed occupations of territory that were not resisted by a state's citizens. In short, regardless of how a state characterised its relations with another state, if this involved military force or occupation, then the new treaty obligations applied.

The increased regulation of the conduct of war worked in tandem with increased legal restrictions on the resort to war. The international system arranged around the United Nations, and its restriction on the use of force in international affairs, meant that going to war was prohibited,[54] unless, of course, a state is acting in self-defence, since the UN Charter recognised 'the inherent right of individual or collective self-defence' against an 'armed attack'.[55] The terms involved, aggression, self-defence, armed attack and so on, are all legal terms of art that are book-worthy of themselves.[56] But in theory, at least, states could no longer declare war, and they could only use force either in self-defence or with the authorisation of the UN Security Council. The problem of states using force against one another, or escaping their treaty obligations, was minimised. That was the theory, at least. In practice, '[t]he contemporary injunction against war has not yet eliminated its incidence'.[57]

One element of the 1949 Geneva Conventions was the creation of minimal standards of conduct in any type of armed conflict beyond inter-state ones. The shorthand for this is 'Common Article 3'—named because each of the four Geneva Conventions in 1949 shared the same Article 3. These standards are intended to apply a set of minimal standards to the conduct of non-international armed conflicts. Of course, what the drafters of the Geneva Conventions had in mind were civil wars, rebellions and so on. What we now encounter is the argument made by the United States that these rules also apply to its violence against al-Qaeda.

The law of armed conflict is not uniform. At any given point in time states have disagreed over both major and minor points of treaty and custom, and relatively extreme state opinions (and practices) are unlikely to disappear. This was exacerbated in 1977, when some states agreed to additional protocols to the Geneva Conventions of 1949, while others did not. Some states—including the United States—did not sign or ratify one or more of the additional protocols, notably

Additional Protocol I (API). This was because the language of API elevated 'national liberation wars' to the status of international armed conflicts, which some states found to be unacceptable, and President Reagan refused to submit it to the Senate for ratification as he claimed it would benefit terrorists.[58] However, many aspects of these treaties that regulate the conduct of hostilities are now recognised as customary international law.

From these overarching legal trends, we get a system that is dedicated to the application of basic principles of the rules of war—distinction, proportionality, necessity and humanity—to all wars and armed conflicts, including those between states and non-state groups. The idea that states would have to treat rebels with minimum standards of care, at least in theory, would enforce the general standards of war in situations of civil war that are usually bloody and unregulated.[59] Secondly, limiting the ability of states to declare war on sections of their own population in a legitimate fashion would prevent states from using war as a cover for massive human rights violations.[60] If these cover how the law of armed conflict is meant to apply and why the system is designed in this way, we need to consider the most vital element: who makes these legal determinations.

The ability to define violence as armed conflict, and to distinguish between international armed conflicts and non-international armed conflicts, is both a legal and political issue. The United Nations underpins global order, and the UN Security Council has 'primary responsibility for the maintenance of international peace and security'.[61] As the permanent members of the UN Security Council can veto any UNSC resolution, this means that the UNSC is often silent on major issues, or at least very vague on details.[62] The UN General Assembly can also pass resolutions, but these are non-binding, which means that even though they do represent a judgement or advance a common normative position, they cannot compel states to do something.[63] Given this, when international organisations like the UN don't provide legal determinations, what else can?

Many states look to international courts or accept their jurisdiction. Where courts have jurisdiction, they can render binding decisions. The International Court of Justice is one of the major courts with global jurisdiction, but the United States considers itself to be subject to this jurisdiction on a case-by-case basis.[64] The United States is traditionally hostile to subjecting itself to the jurisdiction of international courts, and this is something I will return to in Chapter 5.

The acceptance, or non-acceptance, of the jurisdiction of international courts displays the role of power in the international system. In 1984, Nicaragua filed proceedings against the United States at the ICJ, claiming that the American support for rebels (the Contras) and the mining of Nicaragua's harbours constituted a violation of international law.[65] The United States declared that the court had no jurisdiction, and ignored the resulting decision in Nicaragua's favour in 1986. Compare this to the situation in the former Yugoslavia, where the UNSC created an ad-hoc tribunal to try war crimes committed during the breakup of the country.[66] In that event, individuals were brought before a court that had no firm treaty basis, but that the Security Council had determined was necessary to pass judgement upon them. I will return to the ICTY later in this chapter, as some of its decisions were very important, particularly with regard to non-international armed conflict. For now, I wish only to draw attention to the power-disparity at work: the United States can avoid the judgement of international courts while simultaneously participating in processes that enforce judgements of the international system upon others.

The last class of international law actor is what academics refer to as 'norm entrepreneurs'—people and organisations that seek to advance a particular normative value, idea or understanding.[67] Norms are an important element of international law since both the norm of adherence to the law, as well as normative interpretations of the legal obligations that it creates, are important elements in understanding the evolution of international law over time. The law of armed conflict is no different. Henry Dunant, the founder of the organisation that became the International Committee of the Red Cross (ICRC), was what we would now term a norm entrepreneur. A private citizen, Dunant witnessed the aftermath of the Battle of Solferino in 1859. Horrified by the carnage of the battle and the sight of soldiers having been left to die on the field, Dunant organised locals to care for those left behind, and his subsequent activism helped lead to the creation of the first Geneva Convention in 1864.[68]

Norm entrepreneurs matter, but their activism finds its most effective expression when the norms that they advance change the formal inter-state system. Norm entrepreneurs are critical to understanding our current regimes of international human rights law,[69] as well as specific regulations, like the ban on anti-personnel landmines in the Ottawa Treaty of 1997.[70] The problem that norm entrepreneurs face is when powerful states politely (or rudely) say 'no'—and this is an issue that recurs throughout this book. There have been considerable amounts of critical legal analysis and writing upon the subject of targeted killing and the idea of a transnational armed conflict, yet this has not necessarily changed the legal opinion of the US government. I will return to this interaction at the end of this chapter.

The distributed character of the international system means that it is very rare for a single entity to have an opinion on a given question of international law, as well as the means to form a recognisable judgement and to enforce that judgement. Respected NGOs such as the ICRC have the respect of states in part because their neutrality declaims any enforcement capability. In the absence of a world government and world court mirroring the practice and functions of domestic courts, questions of international law are either resolved politically, through the UNSC or inter-state politics, or judicially, where states submit themselves to the jurisdiction of international courts. I need to be careful here to highlight that the questions considered in this book are perhaps the most sensitive questions in public international law. International commercial law is far better developed and abided by.[71] However, the point is that even if states disagree, they disagree with reference to the same body of law. While this book concerns itself with edge cases (that is, highly contentious political and legal disagreements), these disagreements are situated inside far wider zones of agreement. Returning to Henkin's earlier quote: as most states agree most of the time, this means that over seven billion human beings are guided by the same set of principles. With that in mind, let us consider the generally accepted elements of armed conflicts, and how they exist.

Classifying armed conflict

The concept of war in political theory and history is markedly more flexible than its counterpart in international law. Nonetheless, the legal classification of political violence is inseparable from the violence itself in the contemporary world. So what are the generally accepted categories of armed conflict, and why is the concept of a transnational armed conflict seen as transgressive?

As an intellectual discipline, international law has discipline-specific methodology and research methods or modes of inquiry that arise from this methodology. In the next chapter, I am going to explain the role of international law as a constitutive aspect of war and armed conflict. But before doing so, it is necessary to look at how international law is used to make assessments and classifications. In order to determine if an applicable body of law is relevant to a given situation, it is necessary to understand what exists in the body of law and then make an assessment based upon the available evidence to see whether the law applies to the situation. The law of armed conflict is no different, and that is why 'it is necessary to assess first of all whether the situation amounts to an "armed conflict"'.[72] 'Classification', writes Elizabeth Wilmshurst, a professor of international law, 'provides the signpost to the body of law applicable in each situation'.[73] Understanding this method and purpose explains the attitude of Philip Alston, a former UN special rapporteur, to America's transnational war:

> Whether an armed conflict exists is a question that must be answered with reference to objective criteria, which depend on the facts on the ground, and not only on the subjective declarations either of States (which can often be influenced by political considerations rather than legal ones) or, if applicable, of non-state actors, including alleged terrorists (which may also have political reasons for seeking recognition as a belligerent party).[74]

There are three things at work here that are important to understand. First is the notion that international law gives us a set of 'objective criteria' with which we can judge the world around us. The second is that 'the facts on the ground' can be used to determine the existence of an armed conflict one way or another. The third is important for its absence: Who, or what, is making the judgement? This is where international law, and the practice of law, bleeds into the constitution of war. All lawyers are involved in making the same judgements, ideally from an unbiased position of neutrality, but some of them are advising states, others are working for NGOs, some are representing clients caught up in America's war and others are in the business of making public their independent analysis of the situation. All are important, but their position relative to the conflict differs, and some legal judgements are integral to acts of violence, while others are destined for discussion in books and journals.

There is no such thing as half an armed conflict—either one exists, or it does not. The two primary categories of armed conflict are international armed conflicts and non-international armed conflicts. In recent years, some legal experts have argued that the problems that transnational terrorism poses require us to rethink the divisions between war and peace, or between armed conflict and normal political life.[75] Since America does not appear to be heading in that direction, we can stick to the commonly accepted division.

So how do armed conflicts come to exist in international law? The problem is that the point at which international law applies to each type of conflict is different. Since international law is meant to apply whenever states use force against one another, even if they are loathe to declare this fact, the threshold for the existence of an international armed conflict is very low: '[a]lmost any use of armed force by one State against another will bring into effect an international armed conflict'.[76] Once the threshold conditions are fulfilled, an international armed conflict exists, and the *in bello* elements of the law of armed conflict applies. Given that violent border incidents are routine in some areas of the world, particularly in disputed border regions, the distinction between border incidents and international armed conflicts is often disputed; however, international armed conflict does not have a threshold requirement.[77] Instead, it is the intention to initiate an armed conflict that matters.[78]

But what about internal conflicts or conflicts that do not even involve states? Unlike international armed conflicts, non-international armed conflicts are defined in the negative in Common Article 3 of the Geneva Conventions as an 'armed conflict not of an international character occurring in the territory of one of the High Contracting Parties'. As such, they exist once violence passes a certain threshold, as well as once a group can be considered organised enough to be a party to an armed conflict, but the lack of clear definitions of these thresholds is a major problem. After all, violence that challenges the authority of the state is not always organised, nor is it necessarily intended to overthrow the state itself. Temporary breakdowns of public order are more common in some countries than others, but they can happen anywhere. In 2011, riots broke out across the UK, including in the capital, London. Rioters used violence, sometimes against the police, but the inability of the police force to quell the disorder did not mean that an armed conflict had broken out. The point at which an internal conflict rises to the level of an armed conflict, and how such conflicts are defined, were key questions that defined the era of international interventions in the post-Cold War world.

With the exception of purely naval engagements, international armed conflicts involve the infringement (or perceived infringement by at least one party) of territorial sovereignty. International and non-international armed conflicts can easily overlap, especially if a state intervenes on behalf of rebels, and this is a complicated area of law, with multiple standards that would bring a state into an armed conflict.[79] This highlights one element of armed conflict that is important to both categories: territorial sovereignty. This provides us with the 'mostly tacit underpinning to the laws of war: an implied geography of war' that limits the scope of any given conflict.[80] Armed conflicts (in the sense defined by contemporary international law) have always occurred in the context of a system of sovereign states defined by territorial borders. The territorial dimension is an important political and military consideration: limited cross-border operations are a normal outgrowth of non-international armed conflicts where the non-state adversary seeks shelter across territorial borders.[81] For present purposes, it is important to keep in mind two things about the status of an armed conflict. The first is that an international armed conflict can morph into a non-international one. Probably the most explicit example of this in recent history is the 2003 Iraq War, which was an international armed conflict between the US-led coalition of states and the state of Iraq, but subsequently became a non-international one following the downfall of Saddam's regime and the eruption of insurgency and civil war in the country. The second point is that armed conflicts can coexist without necessarily merging into a single armed conflict—a state can be fighting rebels in one section of its territory and a state in another. What we have to keep in mind, however, is that these two classes of armed conflict differ from one another in that they need to satisfy different criteria in order to be classed as an armed conflict.

Al-Qaeda is not a state. Therefore, any armed conflict between al-Qaeda and the United States would be classed as a non-international armed conflict under current legal frameworks. Nonetheless, understanding the crossovers and relationships between these two categories of armed conflict is important. One reason for this is that non-international armed conflicts can have (or threaten to have) an international dimension. Direct and indirect inter-state military assistance is a feature of non-international armed conflict, as is state support for rebels. Around a fifth of internal conflicts since the Second World War have featured troops from an external state, and between the end of the Cold War and 2004 'as many as 80 involved external actors providing support short of troops, in the form of supplies of weapons, financial assistance, or sanctioned use of a neighbouring state's territory'.[82] Rebels often cross borders, and when states follow them, this can result in an international armed conflict. Just as important is when rebels effectively control enough territory in a stable enough manner to secede. At what point does a civil war transition to an inter-state war? This is an important dimension of the legal classification of conflicts in the former Yugoslavia, which, through the jurisprudence relating to the ICTY, also provides us with an influential set of ideas relating to the existence of armed conflict.

The importance of the ICTY for present purposes is that its decisions on the status of armed conflicts have proved influential. A key case relevant to the classification of armed conflict, and its existence, is the case of Duško Tadić. Tadić was the first person to appear before an international war crimes tribunal since Nuremberg, for his part in the collection and forced transfer of civilians in the Prijedor massacre.[83] His importance here is that Tadić's defence team attempted to appeal his conviction on the grounds of jurisdiction, arguing that the ICTY had no authority to convict him. It is the ICTY's judgement of this appeal that matters, since this provides us with a generally accepted standard, according to which:

> an armed conflict exists whenever there is a resort to armed force between States or protracted armed violence between governmental authorities

and organized armed groups or between such groups within a State. International humanitarian law applies from the initiation of such armed conflicts and extends beyond the cessation of hostilities until a general conclusion of peace is reached; or, in the case of internal conflicts, a peaceful settlement is achieved. Until that moment, international humanitarian law continues to apply in the whole territory of the warring States or, in the case of internal conflicts, the whole territory under the control of a party, whether or not actual combat takes place there.[84]

Protracted 'armed violence between governmental authorities and organized armed groups or between such groups within a State'[85] implies a threshold of organised violence, of some degree of intensity, for some period of time, above which an armed conflict exists, and below which one does not. Naturally, this also draws attention to the level of organisation and capability required for hostile groups to become 'organised armed groups'. The type of armed conflict that a state is engaged in therefore matters: if civil wars (usually non-international armed conflicts) were treated in the same way as inter-state wars (international armed conflicts), then an armed conflict would exist the moment rebels began firing upon the forces of the state. As important, international armed conflicts extend to the totality of states' territories, whereas territorial control is taken as the criteria for internal armed conflicts.

Is the United States in a non-international armed conflict with al-Qaeda? There are two primary objections to this, centred on organisation and violence. This distinguishes armed conflict, and non-international armed conflict in particular, from internal disturbances and civil unrest.[86] One could argue that al-Qaeda is not sufficiently organised to count as an armed group (and therefore cannot be a participant in an armed conflict), since 'there are serious concerns about describing Al-Qaeda as a distinct and organized armed group, rather than a network of loosely affiliated groups sometimes reduced to little more than similar ideologies'.[87] The crux of the matter, however, is that the type, duration and intensity of the violence that occurs between the United States and al-Qaeda is relatively novel and does not appear to be similar in kind to the civil wars and guerrilla wars that critics of the US government's legal position have in mind when they discuss non-international armed conflict. This relates to a third objection: the relationship of armed conflict to territory. It is the idea of a deterritorialised armed conflict that appears to be fundamentally at odds with the concept itself, yet, as I will explain in the next chapter, this, and the other objections, arise from the social entities present in contemporary international politics.

I will examine the particular features of such determinations in the next chapter, but for present purposes the most important aspect of this to keep in mind is that non-international armed conflicts require an assessment in order to determine whether or not they exist. Who, or what, has the right to make such an assessment is important. While international law would like to see this as the exercise of impartial judgement upon objective facts, I think social constructivism provides the best perspective for understanding the US position that it has the right to make these judgements. If the jurisprudence of the ICTY demonstrates the definitional problems associated with armed conflict, the American case demonstrates the role of law in the absence or silence of formal institutions charged with providing such categorisation. It is, after all, how we get the idea of a transnational armed conflict.

The challenge of social constructivism

The shift from war to armed conflict does not change the fact that these categories of political violence are socially constructed, and that instances of these phenomena are also socially constituted by violent political hostility. This presents a problem for international law, which, as a discipline, is dedicated to the pursuit of neutral and objective analysis of international affairs.

This is not a criticism of international law, since this pursuit is understandable, in part because these standards or tests are necessary in the legal proccedings that are a fundamental element of international law. However, the idea of 'objective criteria' to determine the existence of something that is socially constructed highlights the tension between the concept of armed conflict in law and the changing social practice and definition of armed conflict. This change is implicit in the conduct of war itself—after all, how state militaries organise themselves, use violence and why they do so are all socially contingent and in a constant process of change, hence the academic and military study of military history, military revolutions and the conduct of contemporary and future wars.[88]

The fact that this issue is a problem reflects the particular predicament of contemporary states, where terrorist 'sanctuaries' provide respite for global campaigns of terrorism. In the years after 9/11, the phrase 'ungoverned space' gained some traction in the policy world and academia, describing areas of low or non-existent state authority.[89] The *de jure* authority of states has always exceeded their *de facto* authority. Academics such as Robert Jackson have studied this phenomenon for decades.[90] Yet such differences are inherent in all states, to some extent. Globalisation has changed the importance of low governance regions in the international system of states. Whereas they were once a problem (or intentional area of abandonment) for states and their neighbours, these areas now harbour persons that some states consider to be global threats.

Still, the notion of states waging war against transnational opponents disturbs many lawyers. Philip Alston points to the fact that:

> If States unilaterally extend the law of armed conflict to situations that are essentially matters of law enforcement that must, under international law, be dealt with under the framework of human rights, they are not only effectively declaring war against a particular group, but eviscerating key and necessary distinctions between international law frameworks that restricts States' ability to kill arbitrarily.[91]

The problem that is readily apparent regarding America's transnational war is that no consensus exists regarding the processes or legitimacy for determining the existence of war in the contemporary world. Even if we focus the question on whether the United States is, or is not, engaged in an armed conflict with al-Qaeda, America's insistence that this armed conflict exists is questioned by a range of people and organisations. This disagreement is not just about particular observations of the world around us; it is fundamentally about who gets to judge the existence, or non-existence, of a given armed conflict.

International law reflects the international system itself: there is no centralised authority to hold states to account. Moreover, there are multiple sources of international law. Custom and treaty are two important sources. Customary international law is very difficult to ascertain, since it is 'deduced from the practice and behaviour of states'.[92] As Malcolm Shaw writes:

How can one tell when a particular line of action by a state reflects a legal rule or is merely prompted by, for example, courtesy? Indeed, how can one discover what precisely a state is doing or why, since there is no living 'state' but rather thousands of officials in scores of departments exercising governmental functions?[93]

Assessing the existence of customary law usually involves examining state practice, or the routine customs and behaviours of states, in order to assess whether states view such actions as rule-bound activities. How one goes about doing so is a complex area of international legal law, but scholars and courts generally search for *opinio juris*—belief on the part of states that a given action is a legal obligation. From the perspective of social constructivism, it does not require a huge intellectual leap to see this as a process by which states construct rules of behaviour in the international sphere of a particular type.

The second significant source of law is treaty text. States agree treaties in a formal manner and expect one another to adhere to them. The law of armed conflict consists not just of common state practice but also binding treaties to which all states are obliged to adhere. Yet at the fringes, there are issues. One common problem in international law is that not all states sign every multilateral treaty, and even those that do sometimes express reservations upon signing, or differ in their interpretation of the treaty itself. Again, the interpretation of treaty law is a substantial area of international legal jurisprudence in and of itself. For present purposes, it is worth considering that the type of international law that this book is primarily concerned with, the law of armed conflict, is perhaps the most contested field of international law that exists. International commercial law, for example, is far more successful. One reason for this might be down to the fact that contemporary international commerce is a mutually beneficial activity that would be impossible without a stable and predictable legal framework. Although David Keen has pointed out that there is such a thing as 'useful enemies' with whom conflict is mutually beneficial,[94] and some elements of the law of armed conflict are also beneficial to both fighting forces, there is plenty of scope in war to break the rules in order to attain a military advantage over one's opponent.

Whereas the social construction of war and armed conflict is fluid and subject to normative change, the argument of those who dismiss the notion of an armed conflict between the United States and terrorist groups is that international law is not so flexible. Returning to the issue of whether the United States could enter into an armed conflict with al-Qaeda, some argue that al-Qaeda (like terrorist groups from previous years, or organised criminal groups) does not, and could not, constitute a legitimate opponent in an armed conflict. In contrast, anyone supporting the US government's position that an armed conflict exists implicitly accepts that al-Qaeda, despite its relative novelty, could satisfy the standards for organisation that would make it possible to identify it as a belligerent entity in an armed conflict. Rather than dismiss the notion out of hand, others opposed to America's war argue that al-Qaeda could be a participant in an armed conflict, but that the type of violence that occurs does not constitute an armed conflict—in particular, it fails to satisfy standards in law that define non-international armed conflict. However, this line of argument runs counter to the second prevailing narrative that highlights the scale of civilian casualties caused by targeted killings and drone strikes that 'belies the claim that the scope and intensity of the fighting is too low. The relevant scope of violence is not the fighting performed by the enemy; it is the total amount of fighting in the area.'[95]

The importance of law in the present context is not necessarily to ascertain whether the actions of the United States are legal or illegal, but the degree to which the idea of law-abidance now shapes US actions and military operations. Some lawyers see the role of international law as a powerful normative constraint on the power of states, while others see little else except rational self-interest.[96] But to view the role of law simply as a matter of right or wrong, or as a regulatory force on states, is wrong, at least with regard to the resort to force by states. Instead, we need to look at the role of the law of armed conflict in the way that states constitute war.

Conclusion

Armed conflict with a transnational opponent challenges the traditional understanding of what non-international armed conflicts are. It is clear that the US position is controversial, not least among scholars of international law. Further, the idea that the United States might be engaged in an armed conflict with a number of individuals regardless of the territory that the individuals find themselves in is should give us pause for thought. After all, that territory belongs to a state, and the use of targeted killings in the territory of another state brings us back to one of the principal problems of international politics that international law is meant to eliminate: international armed conflict and war.

The key elements contained in the definition of non-international armed conflict are constitutive aspects of war itself. Therefore, a core element of the disagreement is in effect what war should appear to be once constituted. For this reason, it is necessary to explain how politics, violence and the rules of war constitute war itself, and the degree to which this applies to America's conflict with al-Qaeda.

3

IN WASHINGTON'S SHADOW

'In these places where they have not attacked us, we are looking for a person, not a country.'

General James 'Hoss' Cartwright[1]

Introduction

War and armed conflict aren't natural phenomena, they result from the decisions taken by political actors and elites. If war is a bounded activity defined by rules, both stated and unstated, then how is it constituted? The previous chapter outlined one way of thinking about the role of law as a frame of observation and judgement. Here, I want to concentrate on an alternative perspective that America's transnational war highlights: the role of law in the constitution of war and armed conflict.

We know that the United States was at war with Japan when it killed Admiral Yamamoto because America had declared war, mobilised for war and engaged Japanese forces in battle.[2] Yet such legal declarations of war are now all but defunct.[3] It is too simplistic to state, as some have, that states no longer declare war. Instead, it is more accurate to say that the political and legal constitution of war has taken on a different form from our image of open declarations. This image is itself based upon a very particular understanding of war, and examples abound of past wars that were not accompanied by them.[4] This change reflects the change in both the international system and the United States itself. The fact that offensively declaring war is now illegal has not stopped states from going to war and engaging in armed conflict. In place of the stereotypical declaration of war, the political and legal articulations of states now take on different forms. The United States, in a constitutional sense, did not declare war on Iraq in 2003; it declared that Iraq was in breach of its international obligations to disarm via Congressional authorisation to use force.[5] We should note that whereas the US Congress declared war on Japan in 1941, in 2002 the US Congress authorised the president to use force against Iraq. This is worth considering in relation to the 2001 Authorization for Use of Military Force (AUMF) that authorised the president 'to use all necessary and appropriate force against those nations, organizations, or persons he determines planned, authorized, committed, or aided the terrorist attacks that occurred on September 11, 2001'.[6]

These authorisations and declarations exist because of political hostility, but they do not exist in isolation. Rather, it is the widespread application of law on their authority that constitutes war and armed conflict, at least in the United States.

America's war—in legal terms, armed conflict—with al-Qaeda was not constituted by a simple declaration. As this chapter now demonstrates, it was constituted by a change in America's political relationship with al-Qaeda, the application of the rules of war to al-Qaeda and the violence that was shaped by these rules. Ultimately, the example of America's 'third war', as analyst Micah Zenko refers to it, demonstrates that war is constituted by the subjective definitions that states make, in parallel with the violence that accompanies them.[7] Before we begin to look at the way America constitutes transnational war with al-Qaeda, it is important to consider the role of these factors in the case of Anwar al-Awlaki, an American citizen who was killed by the US government because of everything that I will discuss in this chapter.

Killing Anwar

Of all the controversies involved in the Obama administration's waging of transnational war, few have as far-reaching domestic consequences as the decision to define Anwar al-Awlaki as a legitimate target and kill him. Al-Awlaki was neither the first nor the last US citizen to be killed by an American targeted killing. Nonetheless, his case is the most well-known example and demonstrates many of the key issues of this chapter.

Al-Awlaki, an American–Yemeni dual-national citizen, was killed by an American strike in Yemen in 2011.[8] Whereas the earlier examples of targeted killings targeted people who were not American citizens, al-Awlaki's citizenship meant that the very possibility that he could be killed was very controversial, and to some ran counter to the idea of the cornerstone of the rule of law in the United States—the US Constitution. The US republic is founded upon the idea of limited government, and the Constitution of the United States and the Bill of Rights is supposed to restrain the government—and its agents—from depriving a US citizen of their individual rights, such as the right to life or liberty, without due process of law, overstepping the constitutional limits on the authority of the president. 'How,' writes Ross Douthat, 'did the man who was supposed to tame the imperial presidency become, in certain ways, more imperial than his predecessor?'[9]

The killing of Anwar al-Awlaki highlighted the range of opinions about the authority of the president and the executive branch of government in times of war, sometimes cutting across the partisan political divisions that characterise contemporary US politics. Rand Paul, a libertarian Republican senator wrote that this asserted authority 'does not apply merely to a despicable human being who wanted to harm the United States. The Obama administration has established a legal justification that applies to every American citizen, whether in Yemen, Germany or Canada.'[10]

Needless to say, the arguments that arose over al-Awlaki's life were by no means settled by his killing at the hands of the American state.

Al-Awlaki was not the first US citizen to be killed by a targeted killing. Kamal Derwish (also an American) was killed in the same 2002 strike that killed Abu Ali al-Harithi, the target.[11] Still, it was the notion that American agencies were intentionally targeting al-Awlaki, and that his name was on a 'kill list', that caused significant outcry in the United States.[12] Al-Awlaki was born in New Mexico, raised in Yemen during his teenage years, and returned to America to attend college in 1991. Graduating with an engineering degree, al-Awlaki became an imam.

Despite American authorities suspecting him of ties to the 9/11 hijackers,[13] he was a prominent Muslim figure who condemned the 9/11 attacks to the national media.[14] Al-Awlaki later left the United States for the UK, before travelling to Yemen, where he became involved with al-Qaeda in the Arabian Peninsula (AQAP). It is this involvement that led the US government to kill him, and it is the way the US government went about it that is pertinent here.

Barack Obama decided that al-Awlaki was a lawful target on 5 February 2010, although the possibility of targeting him had first been raised in 2007, under the Bush administration.[15] He derived the ultimate authority to use force against al-Awlaki from the 2001 Authorization for the Use of Military Force (AUMF), but this decision rested upon a significant amount of case law, as well legal opinions. Whereas the US government claims that it is at war with al-Qaeda and its associated forces, this supposed fact is disputed by a range of academics, lawyers and activists.[16] The political hostility between the United States and al-Qaeda, including the rhetoric of the War on Terror, exists in tandem with legal classification of their relationship as armed conflict. The existence of an armed conflict between the United States and al-Qaeda was an important element of the *habeas corpus* court cases of Guantanamo detainees.[17] The fact that an armed conflict exists between the two is stated in the first sentence of the Department of Justice white paper that sketched the legal status of al-Awlaki before he was killed. This armed conflict, and the authority afforded the president of the United States by the 2001 AUMF,[18] were key points of the legal opinions that declared him to be a lawful target of attack.[19] Lawyers—alongside policy advisors, the military and representatives from the intelligence community—were integral to the decision-making process that led to his death.[20]

The key issue that al-Awlaki's death highlights is the role that these legal judgements and opinions play in the constitution of war, and the degree to which they are made behind closed doors, away from public scrutiny. The legal memorandum that authorised al-Awlaki's killing was not open to public scrutiny before his death, yet the legal architecture that it drew from was. What al-Awlaki's killing highlights is the combination of legal interpretation and policy judgement that constitutes war and warfare.

The idea that the president has the authority to define US citizens as legitimate targets of attack without any kind of judicial process leaves many aghast. For David Cole, the killing of Anwar al-Awlaki highlighted the overlap between America's transnational war abroad and US democracy at home: 'As long as the Obama administration insists on the power to kill the people it was elected to represent—and to do so in secret, on the basis of secret legal memos—can we really claim that we live in a democracy?'[21]

An interesting aspect of al-Awlaki's killing is that it was litigated in US courts both before and after the event. The very question of whether al-Awlaki could be targeted by the US government led to significant media speculation and speeches by senior figures in the Obama administration that sought to clarify the legitimacy of targeting him. In *al-Aulaqi v. Obama*,[22] al-Awlaki's father, Nasser, challenged the US government's right to 'impose extrajudicial death sentences in violation of the Constitution and international law'.[23] After al-Awlaki's death, Nasser brought an action claiming damages from infringing the constitutional rights of al-Awlaki (and his son, Abdulrahman, who was killed separately).[24] Associated court cases filed by the American Civil Liberties Union (ACLU) and the Center for Constitutional Reform (CCR) also forced the government to disclose elements of its legal reasoning to the public.[25] The DOJ white paper mentioned above is one such document. While cases filed to remedy executive decision-making in war are not new, the individual targeting inherent in the way that America was waging its war on al-Qaeda seems to give rise to this kind of case-by-case challenge to its decisions.

The suits brought by Nasser were ultimately dismissed, but they highlight the way in which public and secret legal opinions constitute the existence of war. The public law and secret legal opinions that constitute the government's understanding of its legal authority are part and parcel of that conflict. Yet the politics of this is easy to grasp: the power to define a person as an enemy combatant is likened to a death sentence. As the ACLU frames the issue: 'The notion that the U.S. can execute its own citizens anywhere in the world, far from any battlefield, without a legal determination of guilt and without firm and public standards is repugnant to our democracy.'[26] In examining the constitution of war, it is therefore important to note that this refers to the institutional belief of the US government, rather than an objective truth. In a democracy, this institutional belief is unlikely to be accepted by everyone, nor, for that matter, is it likely to be accepted by other states or transnational groups. Nonetheless, the generation of such institutional beliefs, and the action arising from them, constitute war.

The existence of war, and al-Awlaki's status in relation to it, are key elements of the decision to kill him. Al-Awlaki was killed because the president defined him as 'the leader of external operations for al Qaeda in the Arabian Peninsula' and this membership made him a permissible target in America's war.[27] Multiple senior sources allege that he was—at the time of his death—a senior operational figure in AQAP, with ties to 'multiple plots to kill Americans and Europeans, all of which [he] had been deeply involved in at an operational level'.[28] Wars have complicated the issue of constitutional protections for US citizens for well over a century. One long-standing legal norm is that citizenship does not prevent Americans being treated as belligerents since '[c]itizens who associate themselves with the military arm of the enemy government, and with its aid, guidance and direction enter this country bent on hostile acts are enemy belligerents within the meaning of the Hague Convention and the law of war'.[29]

In some respects, the protection that the Constitution affords to those who commit treason is greater than that it affords to those who join a military force opposed to the United States.[30] But the issue of citizenship was very much an after the fact question until the development of ISR technologies and systems that allow states to identify their own citizens in an opposing force on a case-by-case basis. Consider the case of Gaetano Territo, a US citizen captured in Italy while serving with Italian forces in World War 2. Territo could quite easily have been killed in the conduct of operations, but it would have been impossible for the Allied forces to know who was, or wasn't, a US citizen in the forces that opposed them. Territo's citizenship was certainly an issue after his capture, but not prior to this event.[31] In comparison, the picture of a host of senior US government figures sitting in a conference call, weighing up whether or not it is legal to kill a US citizen is quite a different state of affairs, even if the normative principle—that joining an enemy military makes one a permissible target—remains the same.

As we return to the present, the difference between Territo and al-Awlaki was that the existence of the Second World War was not contested. Territo's case concerned the continuation of war powers after the cessation of hostilities, but not the existence of hostilities in the first place. What al-Awlaki's case highlights is the way in which the existence of armed conflict is something that states both judge and constitute. Law, policy and violence constitute war, but this constitution arises from the definitional element of war itself: political hostility.

The constitution of transnational war: politics

Some form of political hostility defines war. Without conflicting political aims between armed groups, the violence that characterises and constitutes war would not take place. The concept of non-international armed conflict does not reference these contrasting political aims, yet political hostility underpins all armed conflicts and wars. Although international law is state-centric, war is ultimately an activity of political communities and groups, not states, even though states are undoubtedly better equipped to wage war than any other non-state entity on the planet.

How states respond to transnational threats will be one of the defining features of security and conflict in the twenty-first century, in part because such groups were, for the most part, impossible to manage and organise to the same standard of operational effectiveness in the pre-digital world. Groups such as al-Qaeda have pre-digital antecedents. The immediate example is the international melting pot of resistance to the Soviet Union in Afghanistan in the late 1970s and 1980s, as is the case with ISIS in Syria and Iraq today, where over 15,000 foreigners have travelled in order to support a struggle against local states, thereby making the conflict in part transnational.[32] Yet similar 'war pilgrims' are a feature of wars past and present: the brigades of foreign fighters that supported the Republican cause in the Spanish Civil War are one example among many. One could look further back, before the era of national armies, to eras when states happily used foreign soldiers to fight their battles, but the further one looks, the less applicable the present-day norm of national militaries applies. We cannot truly compare the armies that existed before the nation state with the military forces being organised today by states, and the transnational groups of fighters that coalesce in places such as Iraq or Pakistan's border regions.

Al-Qaeda is a challenge to the Westphalian order, one 'imagined market state of terror' among many, as Philip Bobbitt describes the various twenty-first-century movements that aim to upend the system of territorial states.[33] The chances of al-Qaeda, or any other non-state actor, overturning the current world order are slim. Nonetheless, this political challenge is a significant element of the relationship between the United States and al-Qaeda—at least from the perspective of US policymakers. Al-Qaeda is inherently a transnational group, unlike the rebels, guerrillas or insurgents that have challenged existing states or political orders in previous eras. In the words of John Yoo, a prominent lawyer who worked for the Bush administration:

> In previous wars, such as World War II, the enemy was defined by citizenship; the enemy was Germany, Italy, and Japan. But al Qaeda is stateless. Our enemies don't wear uniforms, and they are not defined by national identity. Al Qaeda's members are citizens of countries with which we are at peace, including citizens of the United States itself and its allies, such as Saudi Arabia and Pakistan.[34]

Yoo is a controversial figure, not least because of his significant role in authoring the legal opinions that covered the use of torture, or 'enhanced interrogation'. Nonetheless, his claims that 'Applying criminal justice rules to al Qaeda terrorists would gravely impede the killing or capture of the enemy'[35] and that the United States 'must take aggressive action to defeat al Qaeda, while also adapting the rules of war to provide a new framework to address the new enemies of the twenty-first century' were far from unique during the Bush administration.[36] Yet the applicability of law to al-Qaeda and its members is not a binary issue. Rather, it is a question of what legal frameworks—national and international—apply to US actions against al-Qaeda, rather than if law applies at all.

The perceived and defined political relationship between the United States and al-Qaeda matters more than any attempt at an objective evaluation of the threat that al-Qaeda poses to the United States. Al-Qaeda can be defined as a transnational movement, group or network. All three descriptions serve to highlight elements that define al-Qaeda as an entity in international politics. As a movement, al-Qaeda is an embodiment of transnational jihadi belief and 'Al Qaeda training camps were the Ivy Leagues of jihadist education.'[37] The idea of al-Qaeda draws upon common threads of belief that motivate men and women from a range of backgrounds across the world who join jihadist groups. An element of perceived common cause (fighting for the establishment of an Islamic state or form of government) is present, even if groups like al-Qaeda and Islamic State (IS) vie for a symbolic leadership role of this movement.[38]

As a group, al-Qaeda is an organisation, with leadership figures, a semblance of hierarchy and a decision-making structure, even though all of these have been affected by the violent reaction of the United States after 9/11. Bruce Hoffman, a terrorism specialist, writes that since 9/11 al-Qaeda's 'core leadership was progressively eroded by death or capture and its operational capabilities progressively degraded' and that it 'also consistently expanded its ties with affiliated and associated groups—who often took the initiative in allying themselves with Al Qaeda—while continuing to plan and less regularly successfully execute terrorist attacks in a variety of countries'.[39] As a network, al-Qaeda is embedded in wider society, relying upon connections, licit and illicit, to sustain itself.

Defining al-Qaeda as a network, group or social movement has important consequences, since the choice of definition 'shapes the way that counterterrorism and policy professionals think about their adversary and, therefore, approach their efforts to counter it'.[40] This includes who the US government judges to be its enemies. In the context of this book, the 'true' nature of al-Qaeda, in objective terms, is perhaps less important than the US government's perception of al-Qaeda: a terrorist group with whom the United States is engaged in a war.

The division between enemies and non-enemies is one of war's integral limits, even if its characteristic feature is lethal violence. On the eve of the 2003 Iraq War, the US Marine Corps General James Mattis—a man given to somewhat blunt statements regarding the nature of military activity—captured this divide in his pre-invasion message to the troops under his command:

> When I give you the word, together we will cross the Line of Departure, close with those forces that choose to fight, and destroy them. Our fight is not with the Iraqi people, nor is it with members of the Iraqi army who choose to surrender. While we will move swiftly and aggressively against those who resist, we will treat all others with decency, demonstrating

chivalry and soldierly compassion for people who have endured a lifetime under Saddam's oppression.[41]

The distinctions Mattis makes are important—not only between the Iraqi people and the Iraqi army but also between the Iraqi army that fights, and those that put down their arms. Mattis thought of his enemy as a very specific subset of the overall population of the country in which he went to war, and he did not even conceive of the entire Iraqi military as his 'true' opponent. The situation with regard to al-Qaeda, on the other hand, is clearly different. First, we rarely—if ever—speak of al-Qaeda's 'people' in the same way that a population is connected to the military of their state. Secondly, the United States does not divide al-Qaeda into resistant and non-resistant sections: the entire organisation—and therefore its entire membership—is America's political enemy.

The issue of a state waging war on a transnational terrorist network is but one of a host of issues associated with the transition from nation states to market states.[42] The US military is composed of far more people than American nationals. The military itself is a pathway to US citizenship for immigrants, and it could not function without private military and security companies integrated into a wide variety of functions.[43] Still, in terms of authority, states matter. Due to the extensive use of contractors, the US military and the US intelligence community functionally include both non-citizens and civilians. Nonetheless the legitimacy conferred by the American state matters: many activities performed by defence contractors would be illegal if not sanctioned by the US government. As such, America's war against al-Qaeda is not only an example of a state facing a transnational foe, but of the transnational free markets working through the traditional structures of the nation state.

There is of course considerable resistance to the idea that the United States is at war with al-Qaeda, or that the members of this group should be treated as anything other than criminals. O'Connell is one of the leading proponents of the view that terrorism is a matter for law enforcement and criminal punishment. For this reason, she argues that, beyond 'hot' battlefields, law enforcement procedures should be used, and that terrorists should be arrested rather than killed via targeted killings. O'Connell's analysis of al-Qaeda clearly differs from that of the US government. One problem with O'Connell's argument is that she offers no compelling evidence that the law enforcement methods and standards expected in the United States (or globally) could be applied to terrorists or terrorist networks that purposefully position themselves at the fringes of state authority.

O'Connell's criticism relies upon the implicit idea that the law enforcement paradigm can be applied at anytime, anywhere.[44] Some disagree on the relative choice of law enforcement—Afsheen Radsan and Richard Murphy argue that 'Because terrorism poses a far greater danger than organized crime or narcotics trafficking, we must go beyond the law enforcement model for justice.'[45] The Obama administration argues that the choice favoured by O'Connell and others does not exist, and that there exist certain places where military means, such as targeted killings, are required to engage al-Qaeda. As John Brennan pointed out in a public speech:

> The reality, however, is that since 2001 such unilateral captures by U.S. forces outside of 'hot' battlefields, like Afghanistan, have been exceedingly rare … These terrorists are skilled at seeking remote, inhospitable terrain—places where the United States and our partners simply do not have the ability to arrest or capture them.[46]

An element of O'Connell's argument is that states always have a choice in their response. To a certain degree, this is true, yet power and public office are both constraints on individual autonomy. Private citizens aren't required to pay close attention to policy problems and can often stick to their personal principles without undue consequences. In contrast, public officials are often required to make hard policy choices that can conflict with their personal beliefs. The real issue is that the United States cannot control the actions of al-Qaeda, or the actions of groups like al-Qaeda. Moreover, al-Qaeda rejects the entire framework of rules and conventions that European states enshrined to contain political violence. The United States, it must be remembered, is an obstacle in al-Qaeda's way, not its ultimate target. As unrealistic as it may be, al-Qaeda's aim is to overthrow the existing order of states by using force to create theocratic Islamic states.

War is not a force of nature, though no political actor can control the existence of hostile entities. America's attitude towards al-Qaeda, at least among those in government, is presented in stark terms for the fact that the US government, and a significant section of its populace, saw 9/11 as an attack in military terms. Hostility to al-Qaeda predates 9/11: Richard A. Clarke, the former counterterrorism coordinator for the National Security Council at the time of 9/11, gave America's 1998 combined political and military plan for dealing with al-Qaeda the codename 'Delenda'.[47] This Latin word is a component of the famous phrase attributed to Cato, *Carthago delenda est* (Carthage must be destroyed). Yet the War on Terror was a policy choice, albeit one forced (to a certain degree) by the events of 9/11. It is not only political hostility between groups that constitutes war but the policy choice to employ violence within the frame of this relationship. At the same time, the United States is a democracy, one that espouses the rule of law. The US response to al-Qaeda reflects this, since in terms of America's war with al-Qaeda, legal concepts structure the existence of war, as well as guiding actions within it.

Law as constitution

The application of the rules of war is a constitutive aspect of war itself. But war is not constituted by the impartial judgements of lawyers trained in international law, as it is effectively constituted by states behaving as though these legal constraints matter and apply. For this reason, it is necessary to think about how law plays a role in the resort to violence and the use of force. In particular, it is necessary to think about how states constitute a state of war, or engage in armed conflict. In the US context, the foundation of its war with al-Qaeda is the 2001 AUMF, which gave the president wide-ranging powers to use:

> all necessary and appropriate force against those nations, organizations, or persons he determines planned, authorized, committed, or aided the terrorist attacks that occurred on September 11, 2001, or harbored such organizations or persons, in order to prevent any future acts of international terrorism against the United States by such nations, organizations or persons.[48]

As of 2016, there is a substantial degree of clarity about the US government's understanding of its legal authority, and where, when and why the law of armed conflict applies to its actions, and this clarity did not exist five years ago.[49] The basis of the US government's legal understanding is that America is in an armed conflict with al-Qaeda, though it reserves the right to use force in self-defence.[50] How, then, do these legal ideas contribute to the constitution of a transnational armed conflict?

The authority to define the application of international law is an exercise of power. Whereas the International Committee of the Red Cross and other NGOs have pressured states to apply the law of armed conflict to their internal wars, both declared and undeclared, this sovereign authority has often been exercised in non-recognition. This is conceptually similar to the defence strategy in the Tadić appeal—making the argument that an armed conflict does not exist.

Repressive states often use the language of war but refuse to apply the rules, although they are far from alone in this regard—denial of the existence of internal armed conflict and the subsequent applicability of international law is common. Political legitimacy is a key area of contest in uprisings and unrest associated with rebellions and civil wars. Insurgent or separatist groups define themselves as combatants, and one way of challenging this is for states to declare that no war or armed conflict exists. The final report of the International Law Association's Use of Force Committee on the concept of war and armed conflict noted that 'Until the 11 September 2001 attacks, states generally resisted acknowledging that even intense fighting on their territory was armed conflict. To do so was to admit failure, a loss of control to opposition forces, and could be seen as recognizing a status for insurgents.'[51]

Whereas states usually use this sovereign authority by remaining silent or declaring that an armed conflict does not exist, the problem the US case poses is that it involves the sovereign definition of the existence of an armed conflict. This is the same authority (in essence: defining whether or not an armed conflict exists) but exercised in a contentious manner. Lawyers may search for 'objective criteria' to determine the existence of an armed conflict, but the social construction of political violence means that this pretence of objectivity is an illusion, at best.[52] After all, who can judge the United States? As a permanent member of the UNSC, America's definitions of what is true or real are unlikely to be challenged by that institution, since it can veto any Security Council resolution, and it can functionally ignore any ruling by the International Court of Justice without fear of enforcement.

The United States, like two thirds of states, does not accept the compulsory jurisdiction of the International Court of Justice, and therefore only accepts the jurisdiction of the court on a case-by-case basis.[53] Jurisdiction is an important issue, since courts that have made important rulings on the existence of armed conflict, or the breach of the law of armed conflict, such as the ICTY, require jurisdiction in order to pass judgements that could overrule the decisions and opinions of states (albeit by extension from individual criminal trials). The United States goes to great lengths to preserve this independence; most notably, it has developed a system of agreements to ensure that its citizens are not transferred to the jurisdiction of the International Criminal Court.[54]

If this is the situation that gives the United States considerable latitude to apply the law of armed conflict (since international courts and organisations lack the functional capability to overrule its decisions in this regard), then we also need to pay attention to the role of law at the state and sub-state level. This is the idea that law informs the way in which the organs of the American state act, and this orientation towards al-Qaeda is a vital constitutive element of armed conflict.

The legal rationale that the American state is engaged in an armed conflict is found at a level below inter-state politics. It is internal to the state itself, and the three branches of the American government take the existence of this armed conflict as a fact. Congress has given the executive branch expansive authority to use force in the form of the AUMF, the Supreme Court has held that an armed conflict exists (classified as a non-international armed conflict),[55] and the executive branch, backed by private legal advice, publicly states that America is at war.[56]

The legal and political authorities that bind and guide the actions of the US government also serve to reinforce its corporate understanding that the United States is engaged in an armed conflict. Central to this body of law is the 2001 AUMF, which gives the president wide-ranging powers to do as he sees fit against al-Qaeda.[57] America is not at war— or in an armed conflict—because it merely says so, it is at war in part because the government organises and conducts itself as though an armed conflict exists. America's self-defined need to be 'law abiding' is a key feature of its campaign against al-Qaeda. Despite the fact that its opponents intentionally break or disregard legal constraints, America's response to al-Qaeda is shaped by its interpretation of, and adherence to, legal constraints.

The Bush administration clearly broke international law at certain points—notably in its authorisation of waterboarding and torture—but preserved for itself the self-image of lawful conduct.[58] From this perspective, the most important element of the torture debate is not the eventual judgment rendered, but the degree of effort that went into calibrating its supposed legality. Law and politics are inseparable. The very concept of the rule of law is political in nature, and adherence to the law (or lack thereof) by a society's government or its agents is by definition a political matter.

We can clearly see the influence and adherence to international law present in the structure of US institutions. The US military sets itself a standard whereby it should always use violence in accordance with the law of armed conflict and the just war tradition.[59] This is a core element of its self-definition of military professionalism—the rules, and adherence to them, define what it means to be a member of the professional military.[60] As part of this, the military does not make war, or commence armed conflicts, without direction from the executive branch of government, which must in turn seek Congressional approval for the long-term use of the US military in operations abroad.[61] Understood in this manner, the body of law and legal opinion that the US military relies upon to ensure its lawful conduct is integral to its exercise of violence on behalf of the United States.[62]

At the same time, the legal opinion of the US military is the most visible form of law at work. Different classes of presidential decision and legal opinion, such as executive orders and presidential policy directives, have evolved in an ad-hoc manner but carry the weight of executive decision and law, while still remaining confidential.[63] Moreover, if institutions such as the Office of Legal Counsel cannot give advice in secret, then the ability of any president to make effective decisions would be undermined, as the president would not be able to query the legality of action or have lawyers 'sign off' on an action without revealing the existence of a proposed plan of action. In the context of targeted killings, the individual and routine nature of the decisions made at this very high level alters the role of office of the president. While the president has always been responsible for war as commander-in-chief, this kind of case-by-case judgment means that '[t]he power of accuser, prosecutor, judge, jury, and executioner are all consolidated in this one man, and those powers are exercised in the dark'.[64]

How the US state communicates the fact that it is engaged in an armed conflict is a problem, especially since the existence of this armed conflict rests in part on secret legal opinions.

Warfare is usually a secretive endeavour, and processes of military justice, while a self-defined requirement of professional militaries, are hardly standardised the world over. Yet critics make an important point: even if other countries may fight in a secretive manner, it does not befit US democracy to fight secret wars, particularly those that target and kill US citizens. As Conor Friedersdorf pointed out in February 2012: 'official secrecy makes robust civic debate impossible ... Secrecy can be useful in foreign affairs. But if its benefits come at the cost of a citizenry that can no longer meaningfully decide whether its country's foreign policy is in accordance with its interests and values, the price is too high.'[65]

The US government is caught between trying to preserve traditional secrecy and convincing the public that an armed conflict exists. In this context, the public defence of targeted killings is an attempt to convey overarching ideas about America's current participation in an armed conflict. Details of America's transnational war are selectively leaked, often to favourable journalists, to generate public support in the absence of official explanations for drone strikes.[66] At the same time, the Obama administration has used the 1917 Espionage Act to prosecute a record number of whistleblowers, thus controlling the media narrative by instituting an environment where '[l]eaks to the media are equated with espionage'.[67]

Thinking of international law as providing 'objective criteria' to evaluate the existence of armed conflict understates the role that law—alongside the moral concepts that provide the normative basis for the rules of war—plays in constituting war and armed conflict itself. The law of armed conflict and the just war tradition act as organising principles for the use of force, and the way in which both states and non-state groups organise their armed forces is a constitutive element of war itself. With that in mind, we need to turn to how the American state has organised itself to wage war in accordance with the principles of law and ethics.

Policies of violence

While a state of war can be declared, warfare itself is constituted by organised violence, and armed conflict as a legal concept makes little sense without warfare. War, armed conflict and hostilities all require the threat of physical force or violence to be constituted as an identifiable occurrence or phenomena. Yet while certain elemental factors of violence are axiomatic (in that it kills and injures human beings, or in that it destroys physical objects), the actual implementation of violence is socially produced. Cultural factors shape the way in which societies conduct organised violence. In other words, what we observe as violence in the conduct of armed conflict is a product of the relationship between two culturally shaped ideas of how violence should best be employed to achieve strategic effect in order to achieve political goals.

O'Connell argues that states are able to make a choice between waging war and using law enforcement, and therefore 'criminal law, not the law of armed conflict, is the right choice against sporadic acts of terrorist violence'.[68] But this choice does not take into account the political character of a national security state whose legitimacy is founded on the protection of its citizens from external harm. O'Connell gives short shrift to the considerations that militate against the success of any law enforcement approach. That it might be impossible to arrest terrorist networks operating in areas of low state authority, and that they might be able to continue to coordinate and launch attacks from these areas, is secondary to O'Connell's perception of the rule of law. I will return to these issues in Chapters 4 and 5, not least because O'Connell's ideas require more discussion than I can give them in this context. For the purposes of the present argument, the important issue is that a choice exists but the political relationship between the United States and al-Qaeda, as defined by successive US governments, militates towards a specific goal: the destruction of al-Qaeda.

Why resort to the use of force at all? One reason is that al-Qaeda bases itself in low-governance regions. Some analysts refer to this as 'ungoverned space', although this term is a misnomer. Such regions feature plenty of governance structures that are primarily non-state in character, something that Ken Menkhaus refers to as 'governance without government'.[69] In recent years, academics such as Francis Fukuyama have turned to governance as the 'solution' to the myriad problems that non-state governed regions cause for states and the people located within them.[70] The idea that the problem of al-Qaeda could somehow be resolved by development of these regions is seductive, but as a policy choice it is unlikely to succeed. It costs a lot to extend the authority of states. Furthermore, given the character of some of the 'local' states involved, extending the reach and power of the state might be even worse for the locals.[71]

If inaction is not an option for the United States, then the least-worst option for communities in these areas might be a targeted killing campaign, rather than the extension of state authority. That is not a justification in and of itself, but these alternative options are worth considering alongside America's war. Enforcement of the 'law enforcement paradigm' first requires the extension of state authority. In Pakistan, this has resulted in punitive military campaigns aimed at eliminating existing armed groups that threaten this authority. Large-scale ground campaigns have dire consequences for local populations—Pakistan's 2009 Rah-e-Nijat campaign to clear South Waziristan of militants caused the internal displacement of hundreds of thousands of civilians.[72]

Despite being a conflict with a transnational opponent, inter-state politics defines America's war, since it must work with and through other states. The United States is so dominant in international affairs that in 1999 Samuel Huntington called it the 'lonely superpower', and it retains this status (albeit with China rising to parity at some speed).[73] Despite America's pre-eminence, fighting a war against a terrorist network also requires negotiations with the states on whose territory the terrorists operate. Examples of this abound. In 2010, WikiLeaks, an organisation dedicated to publishing secret government and corporate material, published a large number of US diplomatic cables.[74] Contained within these cables were communications with governments in Yemen and Pakistan on the delicate matter of authorising strikes against people in their territory.[75] These governments have allowed the United States to wage war within their territorial borders, albeit in official secrecy. Pakistan's ISI, for example, 'insisted that all drone flights in Pakistan operate under the CIA's covert-action authority—meaning that the United states would never acknowledge the missile strikes and Pakistan would either take credit for individual kills or remain silent'.[76]

America's war also overlaps with internal conflicts. This has created problems for the US assault on al-Qaeda and its affiliates. In 2010, an American strike killed Jabir Shabwani (alongside at least five others). Shabwani was thought to be a political rival to the Yemeni government, and US officials now believe that they were fed false information by their Yemeni compatriots in order to eliminate him.[77] Similarly, the first targeted killing conducted by America in Pakistan killed Nek Muhammad, a Pashtun militant whom Pakistan's government wanted dead, and the CIA killed him 'in exchange for access to airspace it had long sought so it could use drones to hunt down its own enemies'.[78] It is unclear at this point what the official internal legal justification for this strike was, but it likely exists. These questionable strikes hardly help America's case that it is fighting a clean war. Nonetheless, it appears impossible for the US government to wage the war it wishes to without such negotiation with local sovereigns.

The US campaign highlights issues associated with warfare at the fringes of state authority, but, more importantly, it also highlights the problems that transnational warfare pose to the international system of states. As 'building blocks' of legitimate authority, states and their territory are the lens through which warfare is analysed and theorised. A war between America and al-Qaeda takes place in the context of an international system of territorial states, of which America is one, and which al-Qaeda seeks to upend. Analysing this conflict in terms of low state authority gives an important perspective on the conflict itself, but as a second lens of analysis, the non-territorial nature of transnational terrorist networks defines this conflict as much as low state authority does.

Here, again, law matters. In particular, the Obama administration's adherence to the rule of law means that it has defended and defined two lines of lawful reason to use force—the existence of an armed conflict and acts of self-defence—both of which effectively target the same set of enemies under the 2001 AUMF. The published policy standards state that 'there must be a legal basis for using lethal force' and that 'the United States will use lethal force only against a target that poses a continuing, imminent threat to U.S. persons.'[79] The criteria that the administration uses are in effect similar to the policy choice description above, notably that '[a]n assessment that the relevant governmental authorities in the country where action is contemplated cannot or will not effectively address the threat to U.S. Persons' and '[a]n assessment that no other reasonable alternatives exist to effectively address the threat to U.S. persons'. This is the legal translation of policy choices characteristic of the Obama administration—the role of law in constructing the permissible spaces of force, and the processes for selecting options to use force.

A key element, however, is the way in which lines of authority are selected, as 'whenever the United States uses force in foreign territories, international legal principles, including respect for sovereignty and the law of armed conflict, impose important constraints on the ability of the United States to act unilaterally—and on the way in which the United States can use force'.[80]

This leads to the authorisation of force in self-defence, a fourth explanation for US violence in Pakistan's border areas. The use of force in self-defence against terrorists has been defended by law professors such as Kenneth Anderson, since the United States, like most other states, has traditionally asserted the legal right to use force in self-defence, notwithstanding armed conflict.[81] America can declare itself to be in an armed conflict with al-Qaeda, but also use force in self-defence against al-Qaeda. The difference between the two is that this gives rise to different legal justifications for the use of force that are inextricably linked to the idea of respecting the norms of international law. The 'unwilling or unable' legal test[82] serves as a legal procedural standard to determine whether force is justified to violate the sovereignty of another country, rather than the hazy language of 'ungoverned space'. Importantly, upholding these norms also means that the United States cannot admit to covert action,[83] which has fundamental consequences for the transparency of its targeted killings. This will be explored further in Chapter 7.

In light of the twin pressures of American strategic culture, and hostilities with a transnational opponent, it is possible to discern the reason for the violence in America's war differing in significant ways from conventional inter-state wars, or from civil wars and insurgencies. America's war is transnational, but it is also political to the extreme in that all US actions in this war need to take account of the political consequences of action in other states. These relationships are not stable, as evidenced by the particularly fractious events of 2010 and 2011. Not only did the US blame Pakistan's ISI for the public naming of the CIA's Islamabad station chief by Pakistan's government, but it also conducted the raid that killed Osama Bin Laden without giving notice to Pakistan's government beforehand.[84] Furthermore, America might be waging a war to destroy al-Qaeda, but it is not a decisive one, since al-Qaeda will never arrange itself in a manner amenable to American annihilation. But America remains focused on the destruction of al-Qaeda, whereas some commentators on US foreign policy argue that states like America should be conducting something of a 'global counterinsurgency' campaign.[85]

The objective of violence in counterinsurgency is not the destruction of the opponent, but to win over the population that supports them.[86] Although the United States supports this goal on a political and diplomatic level, its goals within its war are focused on disrupting and destroying al-Qaeda. Therefore, the violence that is conducted is almost always directed at members of al-Qaeda, or its affiliates, and explained as such (if explained at all). Since neither side is fighting for slices of territory, and have asymmetric strategic aims, we should not expect to see types of violence that reflect territorial warfare, or war that is waged to protect local populations. Instead, as the next chapter explains, we see forms of violence that reduce the scope of warfare to the level of individuals, while expanding the reach of war to follow them as they move in the low-governance regions of the world.

Law also shapes the policy decisions to use force. In the US legal system, the CIA and the US military can both lawfully kill people abroad, but the legal basis for this differs, as does the social legitimacy of both organisations. After all, although the CIA can be authorised to use force, the expected principal organisation in any armed conflict is the armed forces of the United States. Political violence is socially legitimated and the military's ability to use violence is seen as more legitimate than the CIA's. For an extended period of time between the 1975 Church Committee hearings and the 9/11 attacks, the CIA's primary role was intelligence collection and analysis, whereas today, '[t]he agency's main purpose is to go kill terrorists'.[87] In 2013, Obama indicated that he wanted to transfer control of US drones operations to the military, but this effort has apparently stalled due to internal resistance and Congressional oversight concerns.[88]

As a result, the United States now uses four different models—total military control (Iraq), the CIA running operations in Pakistan, the CIA and JSOC running parallel missions in Yemen independent of one another and a last model in Syria where Greg Miller reports that 'armed CIA drones can be fired only if they are operating under JSOC authority'.[89] This separation, Miller notes, is because 'administration officials now see the hybrid approach in Syria as a possible way to salvage at least part of Obama's plan. The agency will remain deeply involved in "finding and fixing" terrorism targets in collaboration with JSOC but will leave the "finish" to the military, at least in Syria.'[90]

Regardless of whether the CIA or military is ultimately responsible for ordering a strike, or actually conducting it, the authority and definitions that they use derive from the president. The complex legal questions of military inter-operability with the CIA, and the legal authorities of both to kill, sometimes mask the fact that both answer to the White House. In turn, the executive branch exercises this authority on behalf of Congress, subject to Congressional oversight and budgetary controls in the context of a transnational armed conflict sanctioned by Congress. The Navy SEALs that were 'sheep dipped'—operating under CIA authority rather than that of the military—for the purposes of Operation Neptune Spear did so in the context of this conflict,[91] as do the drones operating under CIA authority and military authority conducting strikes in a range of countries. Congress could, if it wished to, cut these intelligence and military activities off at the knees by denying them funding, or inserting provisions into Congressional legislation that specifically restrict the actions of the executive branch. As it stands, Congress has used its budgetary authority to stymie the efforts of the Obama administration to transfer the authority of lethal operations to the Department of Defense.[92]

The means of warfare is a principal issue, too. Warfare, and by extension war, depends upon available technology, yet the technology available today allows states to use violence in ways that do not appear, at first instance, to be warfare at all. Martin Libicki describes this idea that the 'very fact of warfare' might be 'completely ambiguous' as 'non-obvious warfare'.[93] Libicki's concept of non-obvious warfare highlights the role that ambiguity plays in interpretations of attacks and responses to them, both by participants and third-party states.[94] His argument that the very fact of warfare, and by extension, the existence of a war or armed conflict, could be completely ambiguous implies that there would be no way to know one way or the other. It is this ambiguity that troubles many critics of America's targeted killings. After all, if America is at war, shouldn't it be obvious? The rules of war, not to mention the national and international political constraints on war, are in part predicated on being able to confirm the existence of war. Targeted killings lie at the fringes of such ambiguous means of warfare, but this is in part explainable by the legal constraints preventing the president from admitting the use of covert action.

Again, we can point to key differences between contemporary targeted killings and the example of Admiral Yamamoto. To kill Zarqawi, the US military adapted its operational planning in order to hunt him down and capture or kill him. Unlike the Yamamoto strike, which was a one-off aerial interception, Zarqawi's death was the result of years of planning and operations designed to locate and neutralise him along with the core members of his group. Moreover, this operation was not designed to take out the top leadership figures alone. In the words of Stanley McChrystal, the American general who was tasked with leading the force that killed Zarqawi, the Americans intended to 'disembowel the organization [al-Qaeda in Iraq] by targeting its midlevel commanders … By hollowing out its midsection, we believed we could get the organization to collapse in on itself.'[95] In other words, the American theory for defeating AQI was predicated on its ability to identify individual members of the network and capture or kill them. Unlike the Second World War, where armies clashed, this resembled a deadly game of cat-and-mouse, with US airpower and Special Forces soldiers pouncing on jihadists whenever they could identify and strike them before their targets moved on to another safe house. At the same time, this operation took place within the context of a recognisable armed conflict. As different as the operations that killed Yamamoto and Zarqawi were, third-party observers would easily be able to identify the existence of the war and armed conflict in which they took place.

The same cannot be said for the strike that killed al-Harithi, or others like him.

The targeting of Zarqawi demonstrated a combination of concepts that feature in targeted killings—an emphasis on the lawful use of force, precision, surveillance that enables such precision, and a relatively limited use of violence. McChrystal's Special Forces teams were not there to take and hold territory or provide physical protection for people or buildings. They reduced warfare to the direct application of violence to their opponents. The ultimate American aim after the invasion was to provide security to the population of Iraq. This may have been misguided, since no-one appeared willing at the time to admit that a civil war was unfolding. Nonetheless, the concept of taking the fight to the enemy stuck. High-value targeting methods developed by the Americans in Iraq were also used in Afghanistan, even though some analysts doubted the efficacy of this way of using Special Forces.[96] It is the combination of the policy decision to use force, the means of using force and the role of law in both that give us contemporary American targeted killings.

Conclusion

The most tangible aspect of war is violence: the death and destruction that accompanies any conflict that has been defined as war in human history. Yet violence—although central to the concept of war—is a reflection of a hostile political relationship. Political enmity or hostility is a prerequisite for the organised forms of public violence that constitute war.[97] We cannot directly access such enmity, though in any political conflict worth referring to as war, there will be plenty of evidence for it in the form of speeches and other types of social legitimation made by political elites (among other actors in the political realm) seeking to create support for the resort to war. Declarations of war are not the be-all and end-all of formal state discourse. Remember that the last US Declaration of war (in its purest sense) was made against Romania in 1942, but this hasn't stopped generations of American political and military elites referring to America's many subsequent wars as such.[98] But this enmity is channelled and constrained by the rules of war—both legal and moral in character—that place limits (however weak) on the employment of violence. The rules of war define war itself, and, importantly for this book, arguments over the applicability or non-applicability of these rules are central to understanding the constitution of war in our world.

4

LAWFUL ANNIHILATION?

'Come at the king, you best not miss.'

Omar Little, *The Wire*

Introduction

Wars have both logics and limits, and sometimes the two are in conflict. The law of armed conflict is intended to place certain absolute limits upon the conduct of war, such as the wanton and pointless massacre of civilians. At the same time, it accepts the justified killing of civilians so long as it makes sense in the context of war itself, such is the logic of military necessity which 'explains rather than determines what is distinguished as military and why'.[1] If we want to understand the current state of America's war, then it is necessary to explore and explain how it has changed since 9/11.

The logical and normative tensions inherent in the law of armed conflict could be explained as 'killing well'. This is consistent with the twin traditions of Geneva and The Hague: seeking to limit the consequences of warfare, and regulating its conduct. You can kill a person in any number of ways, often inflicting death upon them in a horrific manner, but you are not allowed to cause them unnecessary harm, use weapons that do so, hurt them if they have surrendered or torture them. This leads to some consequences that can seem illogical: it is legal to try to kill a person with an explosion that will rupture their internal organs and shred their body with shrapnel, but it is generally held to be illegal to use a laser designed to blind someone.[2]

Beneath both traditions lies military necessity. This, as the Lieber Code (Union army regulations in the American Civil War) phrases it, is the 'necessity of those measures which are indispensable for securing the ends of the war, and which are lawful according to the modern law and usages of war'.[3] In contemporary American military practice, military necessity 'may be defined as the principle that justifies the use of all measures needed to defeat the enemy as quickly and efficiently as possible that are not prohibited by the law of war'.[4]

Since the new American law of war manual also states that necessity 'also justifies certain incidental harms that inevitably result from the actions it justifies',[5] this leaves human life measured in terms of military necessity, proportionality and the utility of force. In the words of Rupert Smith, 'when employed [force] has only two immediate effects: it kills people and destroys things'.[6] These 'terrible hardships of war', to quote Henry Sherman, a Unionist general in America's Civil War, are integral to warfare given that necessity is a human judgement, and one that lacks a defined upper bound. The language of necessity can be used to justify personal self-defence, collateral damage and genocide. The importance of law is that it prohibits some actions (notably genocide) but also provides a framework for reaching judgements in others.

A war without limits or limiting factors is inherently unstable. Thinking and acting in terms of pure military necessity, without some counterbalancing thought as to whether an action was at all proportionate, would quickly tend towards escalation on both sides. In Clausewitz's words, 'If one side uses force without compunction, undeterred by the bloodshed it involves, while the other side refrains, the first will gain the upper hand.'[7] For Clausewitz, the logic inherent in the use of violence against an opponent that could react and use force back would drive both sides to use the utmost force possible. Yet it is rare that this is true in practice. If it were, then the aftermath of butchery that we witness in contemporary conflict would be many orders of magnitude worse. Clausewitz identified multiple principles that logically lead to unchecked escalation. He saw that the overriding political need to constrain war was a modifying factor in both theory and practice.[8] In this sense, the rule of law, and the constitutive idea of law-abidance explored in the last chapter, serve to add another dimension of stability to this system, as it affects fundamental limits on the use of force both in policy/political terms, and also in military practice. For this reason, no explanation for the use of targeted killings would be complete without reference to the influence of law upon contemporary American strategic culture.

Law is integral to American military culture and there are strategic choices and consequences inherent in the shifting definitions of legal and illegal action. On an abstract level, the elements of strategy appear to be universal, consisting of, according to Sir Lawrence Freedman, 'deception, coalition formation, and the instrumental use of violence'.[9] But these underlying principles are contingent on historical and cultural circumstances. As highlighted in Beatrice Heuser's study of the evolution of strategy, these historical and cultural circumstances have long shaped the way humans think about war.[10] In the words of Harry Sidebottom, 'The way in which a society makes war is a projection of that society itself.'[11] Adherence to the law is now an integral part of this projection, as Jack Goldsmith points out: 'Through years of teaching by and training with lawyers, the military establishment became acculturated to law and came to see legal compliance as serving the important post-Vietnam goals of restoring honor and discipline to the military.'[12]

As the previous chapters have demonstrated, legal concepts permeate and define all aspects of military activity, up to and including decisions to go to war. This law abidance militates against excess but cannot prevent it. Where excess occurs for some reason, the normative principles of law abidance serve as a point that societies seek to return to.

The focus of this chapter is on the relationship between law and strategy. America's widespread use of targeted killings and capture/kill raids are a consequence of a particular alignment of political goals, strategic choices and interpretations of the rules of war in the digital age. The political relationship between the United States and al-Qaeda is key to understanding these factors, and it is this relationship that explains America's strategic choice to continue to use military force against al-Qaeda until, as Jeh Johnson [then Pentagon General Counsel] stated:

> so many of the leaders and operatives of al Qaeda and its affiliates have been killed or captured, and the group is no longer able to attempt or

launch a strategic attack against the United States, such that al Qaeda as we know it, the organization that our Congress authorized the military to pursue in 2001, has been effectively destroyed.[13]

The question, then, is whether this political aim is lawful, and how law shapes and permits this strategy of attrition through targeted killing. First, we need to consider how the purpose and conduct of wars can be categorised as legal and illegal.

Ends, means and hard choices

There are many ways in which the wars of the present day can be regarded as unlawful. The three that I will consider here are the political goals, the conduct of war and the strategic intent that links these first two.

Perhaps the best way to understand the conduct of the war with al-Qaeda is to take the US government at its word. The US government's stated aim of 'Disrupt, dismantle and defeat' is a political goal of complete victory. But what does complete victory against an entity like al-Qaeda mean? Certainly, it differs from the instrumental use of violence between states in the Clausewitzian mould. For Clausewitz, the aim of war was disarmament—destroying the opponent's ability and will to resist—in order to impose a desired political settlement upon them. Force, Clausewitz wrote, 'is thus the means of war; to impose our will on the enemy is its object. To secure that object we must render the enemy powerless; and that, in theory, is the true aim of warfare.'[14] But Clausewitz was writing about states with civilian populations that supported military forces. Destroying those military forces was the means of rendering the enemy powerless. How can that apply to a terrorist network?

Defeating al-Qaeda will require destroying the group rather than disarmament. A better understanding of the US aim comes not from Clausewitz, but from those who subsequently used his theories in the development of 'total war'. Total war crystallised in the industrial era, with nation states throwing the entire resources of state and society into war. Total war was also anti-Clausewitzian since it involved the subordination of politics to the conduct of war. The ensuing war aims that accepted nothing short of total victory would later result in the bloodiest conflict of the twentieth century: the Second World War.

The threat al-Qaeda poses is hardly comparable to the threat posed by Japan and Germany up to 1945, or the Soviet Union during the Cold War.[15] This aside, George W. Bush's language and rhetoric depicted the War on Terror in existential terms akin to the Second World War. This mind-set was reflected in the attitude of political and bureaucratic elites, infamously encapsulated in Cofer Black, then head of the CIA's Counterterrorism Center (CTC), who proclaimed that 'When we're through with them they will have flies walking across their eyeballs'.[16] Despite any changes in language, the war aim of the United States is something akin to total victory, since the US government intends to fight to the finish.

Casting our frame of reference wider, it is possible to see that 'total victory' is often the political aim of other types of war and political violence. Moreover, such total aims are often associated with the abandonment of pre-existing restrictions on conduct. After all, if victory is an existential necessity, then why bother following the rules?

The dirty wars of Latin America (and similar campaigns elsewhere) are an example of wars with such total goals. During the 1970s, military dictatorships in Latin America waged war on their political opponents in campaigns of state repression that were predicated on the erasure of internal guerrillas or 'subversive' elements of society.[17] We can also see similar concepts inherent in crimes against humanity such as genocide committed in order to 'defeat' cultures or groups by killing and destroying as many of them as physically possible. War crimes such as murdering civilians can be used in a strategic manner in order to serve overarching (illegal) political goals.[18] In short, total victory often requires a strategy and means that are predicated upon the intentional targeting of civilians.[19] At heart, these forms of war and armed conflict ignore the fundamental principle of distinction between civilians and belligerents. The erasure or mangling of such a distinction is crucial to understanding them.

America's war is not 'total' as understood by reference to earlier wars. The United States does not define al-Qaeda as a political or military entity representing a defined civilian population. This is demonstrated in the way that its members are categorised and classified in legal terms so as to determine whether they can be lawfully targeted.[20] The non-state nature of al-Qaeda means that it is in effect defined as a military entity in and of itself. Whereas other total wars were fought against social and political entities that included civilians by definition (nations and states or fractions thereof, populations defined by religious or ethnic characteristics), reducing al-Qaeda to a militant network re-casts its members as potential military targets. Distinction works by first individuating al-Qaeda from the societies its members operate from, and then examining which members are lawful targets. I will explain this concept in full in chapter six. It is necessary to mention this point here purely to contrast it with the erasure of distinction in dirty wars, where 'subversives' and other civilians are openly targeted.

The importance of this form of classification lies in its parallel to Latin America's dirty wars, which were characterised by the intentional targeting of civilians by government forces and included the use of detention and torture. An element of dirty wars is the abandonment of legal restrictions on conduct. Dirty wars are characterised by non-observance and wilful contravention of the rules and customs of war and 'a seeming absence of rule-bound arrangements. Certainly, the rule of law is likely to be absent. More probably, rule *by* law will represent the norm.'[21] When the means of waging such wars involved the direct targeting of civilians and the use of torture, disappearances and extrajudicial killings, these methods contravened strong prohibitions against such actions in both the law of armed conflict and the just war tradition.[22] Many people characterised the early phase of the War on Terror as a dirty war. The journalist Jeremy Scahill, for instance, even went so far as to title his book about the War on Terror *Dirty Wars*.[23] The important question is whether a war of purported annihilation using targeted killings is any more justifiable than one that also employs torture, secret detention facilities and extraordinary rendition. This difference, after all, is the one that the Obama administration seeks to define between its conduct and the actions of the Bush administration.

The American government seems to think that it is possible to fight a war with such extreme goals in a lawful manner. One person whose work disagrees with this is Carl Schmitt, a German jurist and political thinker. It is impossible to say what Schmitt would have made of warfare between a state and 'global partisans', but a considerable amount of his work and thought is pertinent here. In one of his last major works, *Theory of the Partisan*, Schmitt examined the problem posed by partisans—irregular forces whose political commitment is so strong that they disregard the legal constraints and conventions of international law. In certain respects, al-Qaeda is a twenty-first-century version of this political figure.[24] There are two central points in this work that are relevant to America's current war. One is Schmitt's characterisation of war in terms of political hostility, because '[m]artial theory always has to do with the discrimination of enmity, which gives war its meaning and character'.[25] For Schmitt, it is this political hostility that determines whether war can or cannot be governed by rules between participants:

> Every attempt at containing or fencing in war must involve the consideration that in relation to the concept of war enmity is the primary concept, and that the distinction between various kinds of war is preceded by the discrimination among various kinds of enmity. Otherwise, all efforts at containing or fencing in war are only a game, one that cannot resist the onset of real enmity.[26]

This is relevant to America's transnational war in two ways. The first is that states which define their political opponents in such a way that demands their eradication will not be bound by the restrictions of law. As importantly, Schmitt argued that modern partisans were defined by 'standing outside any containment' and therefore '[t]he modern partisan expects neither justice nor mercy from his enemy'.[27] In other words, the ideological hatred that partisans had for their opponents was so great that no-one could count on them abiding by the civilised rules of territorial states. This enmity works both ways. The notion that al-Qaeda must be obliterated shares hallmarks of what Carl Schmitt termed wars of absolute enmity, since they know no bounds. In comparison to such a war, 'the contained war of classical European international law, proceeding by recognized rules, is little more than a duel between cavaliers seeking satisfaction'.[28]

'Uncontained war' is an apt description of some aspects of US conduct in the early years of the War on Terror. Critics alleged that the US government had either suspended the rule of law, or stripped its supposed enemies of legal protections. This is a function of the power that the US government had over detainees at Guantanamo Bay. For his part, Schmitt's work equated sovereign authority in society with the ability and accepted authority to define the application of law. As Schmitt's famous opening statement explains: 'Sovereign is he who decides on the exception'.[29] Professor Judith Butler was one of the first to draw attention to the parallels between Schmitt's thought and the actions of the Bush administration. In a 2002 article in *The Nation*, she pointed to the treatment of people detained at Guantanamo Bay, which placed them 'outside the law, outside the framework of countries at war imagined by the law, and so outside the protocols governing civilized conflict'.[30]

Drawing parallels between the American state and Carl Schmitt is no small criticism. Schmitt himself was both illiberal and authoritarian— much of his mid-career work aimed at the liberal idea of the rule of law constraining sovereign authority.[31] To equate the actions of a liberal democracy with the thought of a man known as the crown jurist of the Third Reich is a serious charge. But this touches on an important issue, which is the relationship between political purpose and the conduct of war. A political purpose that obliterates distinctions between belligerents and civilians leads to the idea of a 'dirty war'. Like civil wars, which Schmitt equates with absolute enmity, the defining characteristic of dirty wars is the politics of absolute enmity that Schmitt describes.

'Dirty wars' are difficult to define. In a survey of the literature on the topic of dirty wars, M.L.R. Smith and Sophie Roberts found that although the concept was widely used 'perhaps to signify, something that is considered, if only intuitively, as particularly extreme or distasteful', there was not much coherence in its use as the term was applied to wars and conflicts as different as the Algerian war of independence, the Latin American wars of the 1970s and human rights violations in Chechnya after the Chechen Wars of the 1990s and early 2000s.[32] By drawing a loose distinction between the idea of a 'clean' war and a dirty one, they identified four elements that could be used to differentiate the two. In this scheme, clean wars track quite closely to the ideal of an inter-state conventional war as the four elements require the open constitution of war, conduct by accepted modes of war (informed by the rules, laws and conventions of warfare), that the fundamental principle of distinction between combatants and civilians is respected and that war takes place between states, and violence is aimed at people external to each state's society. The hallmarks of a dirty war, in contrast, which are 'likely to manifest within states rather than between states', include a lack of formal declaration of hostilities, non-acceptance of the laws and conventions of war (and the use of law as an instrument of force) and non-observation of distinction (as well as war being waged by paramilitary or irregular forces).[33] Overall, Smith and Roberts argue that a 'dirty war can be defined as a systematic campaign of violence directed against a portion of the civil populace where the perpetrators aim to conceal both the extent of the violence and the true extent of their involvement for the primary purpose of creating fear for political purposes'.[34]

In particular, the ideological distinctions that characterise political definitions of opponents in dirty wars share many of the linguistic features of Schmitt's absolute enmity. In Argentina, for example, a 'public discourse emerged in revolutionary pamphlets in which the military were called exploiters, worms, vermin and parasites of the people, while the revolutionaries were described in the national newspapers as savages, subversives, terrorists, nihilists, nomads of cruelty, and drifters of destruction'.[35]

The conundrum that we face is that while America's war with al-Qaeda shares many elements of this kind of enmity (public references to al-Qaeda by leading political figures in the United States usually range between disgust and insults), we do not necessarily see the same breakdown of law and legal distinctions between permissible and impermissible targets. The US response to al-Qaeda does not match the kind of warfare that Schmitt associates with absolute enmity. First, even when the United States broke some important rules—for example, the prohibition on torture—it did so while adhering to many more. Second, though the Obama administration still talks about al-Qaeda in terms that match the absolute enmity of the Bush era, it believes that it can fight this enemy in accordance with the rule of law. While America's war has certainly inflicted much death and destruction, we have not seen calculated and planned campaigns of widespread repression that eliminate the distinction between belligerents and civilians. To understand why, we first need to look at the influence of law on American strategy.

Grinding out victory

The United States does not have infinite resources, nor can it fully predict or control the actions of other states or significant political entities. For that reason, the people charged with America's governance have to think in strategic terms. Following from the idea of war as a social construction, culture affects American strategy in addition to factors such as available resources, and therefore is important to connect the political aims with the violence that arises from them.

The idea that culture influences strategic choices is not new. In *The American Way of War*, historian Russell F. Weigley argued that the United States possessed a unique strategic culture, which implied the existence of a unique US approach to strategy and warfare.[36] Central to Weigley's argument is that the modern American way of war could be expressed in two types of military strategy—annihilation and attrition—each of which had their own roots in American history. Resources mattered—Americans adopted attritional strategies in the country's formative years when it was resource poor, but shifted to strategies of annihilation when the country grew rich.[37] Although reductive, Weigley's account was persuasive, and his argument that America 'tended to opt for strategies of annihilation' was not seriously contested until 2002.[38] I am going to cover some of these arguments here to outline their relevance to my argument, which is that America's transnational war is best understood as a war of attrition that is now waged in strict adherence to existing rules.

Some have drawn upon Weigley's work, and the later work of Jack Snyder, to present America's 'strategic culture' as an explanation for America's strategic choices.[39] As part of this, the idea built up that the United States separated politics and war: when matters were turned to the joint chiefs of staff, politicians set the goals, but the conduct of war was an apolitical realm for the military to do as it saw fit. Taking Weigley at face value, the question of why the United States opted to 'end' al-Qaeda can be answered quite easily: America chose to treat the terrorist group as a military opponent, and wars of annihilation are the American way. However, this 'easy' answer does not tell us why America defined al-Qaeda as a military target, nor does it explain how, if America is committed to annihilating al-Qaeda, it could go about doing so. Moreover, Weigley's more recent critics, such as military historian Brian Linn, point out that his account of strategy is too reductive.[40]

Linn criticised Weigley's work in four ways: that Weigley drew the concepts of annihilation and attrition/exhaustion from the work of Hans Delbrück in a confused manner; that he failed to account for alternative strategies; that he did not account for contrary opinions to military annihilation; and that American actions could be characterised 'more by improvisation and practicality than by a commitment to annihilation'.[41] Of these, Antulio Echevarria argued that the first is the most important, as it is 'essentially the foundation for the other three' since the mistaken use of a binary framework led him to overfit events in American military history to suit it.[42] The importance of these criticisms is that they undermine the claim that America is pre-disposed towards strategies of annihilation. Echevarria's more serious charge is that 'the story of American strategic culture is one of elusive fictions' and that, by extension, this separation between warfare and politics does not exist in practice.[43] Echevarria backs up his criticism with a persuasive account of US warfare since the beginning of the republic, according to which 'the American way of war has been nothing less than political in every respect and in every period of its history'.[44]

If America's way of warfare is political, then it also reflects America's culture—namely its liberal values. This entails a particular way of thinking about war itself. I will explore the distinctions in liberal values in the next chapter, but the essence of this is well explained by Stephanie Carvin and Michael Williams as 'two conflicting imperatives' inherent in the need 'to protect itself and its liberal values at all costs' but 'to do so in a way that is acceptable to liberal/Enlightenment values'.[45] It is this tension that also serves to provide an explanation for the use of targeted killings.

With so many overlapping drivers for behaviour, it is clear that culture, and strategic culture, cannot explain all decisions to use military force, or the way in which force is used to achieve strategic ends. This should not, however, be taken as a dismissal of the important role that culture plays in strategy. One point to make is that culture is not stable over time. Weigley sought to define a particular US approach to war and warfare, but the very definition of what America was, and its role in international politics, changed over the period covered in his work.

All the same, there are limits to change—the arrangement of America's constitutional republic is such that each branch of the government retains some authority, and differences are often mediated through law. Law shapes US strategy precisely because the law confers legitimacy upon the president. Law, and the liberal values that underpin it, provide a lens for thinking about US conduct.

Law and liberal values are not static, and this is reflected in the essential continuities and discontinuities of the Bush and Obama administrations. Both administrations shared the common goal of destroying al-Qaeda. One way of dividing these administrations is to compare the early phase of the War on Terror, where torture was defined as lawful, and those interned at Guantanamo were denied the protections of the Geneva Conventions, with its later stages of targeted killings. True, torture is now a rejected policy, and the remaining Guantanamo detainees are being processed in military courts, even though the US government will only put a fraction of its total detainees on trial.[46] But we should exercise caution in drawing hard divisions between the administrations. After all, the status of those detained at Guantanamo was affected by multiple court cases and acts of Congress during the Bush administration.[47]

What I think is more important is a changing attitude towards the law between the two administrations. If the Bush administration overstepped the bounds, the Obama administration has attempted to reinforce them. Nowhere is this better encapsulated in the disuse of the phrase 'illegal enemy combatants'. This term was used by the Bush administration to describe people held under a Presidential Military Order.[48] In effect, the administration chose to describe those detained by the US military in a way that labelled them as participants in a war ('combatants'), that presumed they had broken the laws of war ('illegal') and that categorised them as an enemy of the United States. This made them subject, from the perspective of the US government, to the law of armed conflict—and therefore to military courts—but also denied them the protections afforded certain types of person, such as combatants, contained in this same body of international law.

If US strategy is political, it is also reflective of ongoing legal efforts. Due to lengthy court cases and political disagreements over the internment of prisoners at Guantanamo Bay, the term 'enemy combatant' fell into disuse. The Supreme Court even ruled that certain aspects of the Geneva Conventions did apply to detainees at Guantanamo Bay, which challenged the Bush administration's argument that they did not.[49] The status of individual members of al-Qaeda—or persons that the US state claims are members of al-Qaeda—differs depending on where they are, as well as the interplay of US laws and court cases, most notably those surrounding the detention of persons in Guantanamo Bay, as well as court cases over torture, rendition and targeted killings.[50] Early on in Obama's presidency, the Department of Justice withdrew the definition of 'enemy combatant' for the remaining Guantanamo detainees, a move that removed official sanction for the term.[51] But what does this change tell us, if anything, about US strategy?

What is clear is that both administrations paid considerable attention to the legal categorisations of persons. This is both for utilitarian reasons, as well as an attempt to preserve the principle of distinction. The titles of two articles published midway through Obama's first term as president by University of Texas law Professor Robert Chesney (who served on President Obama's Detention Policy Task Force) summed up the twin legal questions facing the American state: 'Who May Be Killed?'[52] And 'Who May Be Held?'[53] In other words, in what circumstances could the United States military detain a person or kill them? The key issue is that we cannot understand the massive expansion of targeted killings under Obama without also considering the degree to which the Obama administration's interpretations of the law also took certain categories of action off the table. Whereas legal and legitimate methods of intelligence collection can substitute for the information gleaned from waterboarding, there is no equivalent answer to the problem of military detention. If al-Qaeda must be destroyed, and must be destroyed in a lawful way, then the precise application of military force makes sense.

If strategic culture provides a general orientation to the world, it also provides a window into how America characterises its opponents. These characterisations matter because how 'the West responds to the new strategic actors in the making depends on how it perceives the strategic rationales of its new enemies'.[54] America's characterisation of al-Qaeda as a transnational terrorist network both constructs and permits the political goal of its destruction. Terrorists tend not to achieve their aims,[55] and states usually declare that a terrorist movement must be defeated or destroyed in some form, yet it is unusual for a state to seek to kill its way to total victory.

As much as governments attempting to crush terrorist groups are loathe to admit, many terrorist groups that pose a significant challenge have domestic constituencies that form a significant portion of the population of a state. Many of these national terrorist networks exhibit transnational features due to links to a wider ethnic or ideological diaspora.[56] The main uses of force, however, occur in a domestic setting, or at the borders of the state. Terrorist groups seek to shape and mobilise the opinion of domestic constituencies or communities to further their cause. The domestic nature of terrorist threats acts as a restraint on the use of force, particularly in democratic states where the rule of law is a significant factor in state legitimacy. States that use force risk political transformation (from a military coup or similar) as a result of overstepping the rule of law.[57] Regardless of whether it is true, al-Qaeda (or at least the portion of it that America uses military force against) is depicted as an existential threat.

Even though al-Qaeda's regional franchises are tied to the domestic context of the states that they operate within, the concept of al-Qaeda is often defined as a network without a defined community. The group perceives its 'own' community as Muslims worldwide, but America's rhetoric of war distinguishes Islam and Muslims from the violent jihadists of al-Qaeda. This depiction removes one of the primary restraints on state action in conflicts with terrorist networks, which is the opinion of such civilian constituencies. Andrew Exum and David Kilcullen argue that isolating al-Qaeda is more important than eliminating them.[58] The issue with al-Qaeda as a transnational opponent is that they are depicted as an opponent without a home population, at least not in terms of the local populations that Kilcullen and Exum refer to. In a sense, al-Qaeda is thought of as an army without a state or country. In practice, this is not true: al-Qaeda forms links with local populations, and members of al-Qaeda live in and around civilian populations.

If the Bush and Obama administrations are to be believed, the strategy of the United States is to eliminate al-Qaeda and its affiliates. The US use of targeted killings reflects this. Other states that use targeted killings do not necessarily share this strategic goal. Israeli politicians and policymakers know that targeted killings will not bring an end to Hamas, nor will they solve the problems arising from the ongoing occupation of Palestinian areas, even though 'Israeli governments have long used targeted killings as a last resort to achieve a sort of rough justice.'[59] Israel resorts to using targeted killings to disrupt terrorist networks, establishing what Thomas Rid calls 'deterrence beyond the state'.[60]

Alternatives to both these options exist. A decade ago, David Kilcullen argued that the United States should aim to disrupt transnational links between jihadi groups, rather than attempting to resolve the myriad conflicts that they are involved in worldwide.[61] But policies that reduce or eliminate the ability of terrorists to operate in local states is usually offered as a solution in place of targeted killings. In the long term, the United states aims to do this via 'building security partnerships', rather than by committing itself to providing ground troops and long-term military support in the form of counter-insurgency and stabilisation operations.[62] Although doing so could, in theory, achieve the desired goals, the experience of the past decade raises significant questions as to whether the United States has the resources or political will to achieve success through state-building or large-scale military deployments. This dilemma is summed up by Brian Michael Jenkins, a terrorism expert at the RAND Corporation: 'The challenge is how to deprive al Qaeda and its allies of safe havens without the United States having to fix failed states.'[63]

The characterisation of al-Qaeda as an enemy without a population is one way in which America's relationship with al-Qaeda is unique. The unique factor here is that although al-Qaeda no doubt possesses national and international links, America depicts its destruction as a strategic end in itself. This is in sharp contrast to the situation of Israel vis-à-vis its current political opponent, Hamas. The political relationship between opponents in many senses defines strategic goals and the use of force. It is why Israel's use of targeted killings is at best the preservation of political stasis, and America can in all honesty seek to 'disrupt, dismantle and defeat al Qaeda' with targeted killings and equivalent operations.[64] Consideration of US strategic culture therefore leaves us with more questions: Is this annihilation, or attrition? And do targeted killings even work?

Between decapitation and repression

How can we judge the success of American targeted killings? This is a considerable issue for people looking at targeted killings from a public policy perspective. After all, if there is little evidence on whether they work or not, how can experts advise governments one way or another? This question, like the existence of armed conflict, turns on the burden of proof: Does the US government have to provide proof that targeted killings work? Or is it up to the critics to disprove their efficacy? In the context of this chapter, both strategy and international law gives a particular spin to this issue: pointless killing in war is illegal since it does not satisfy the requirement of military necessity. If there is no point to targeted killings, then they are illegal by default. So what is America's strategic rationale that sustains their use?

The decisive use of military force is rare, even in conventional warfare. Attrition can kill terrorist networks just as it can exhaust formal armies. Conversely, terrorist networks are rarely vulnerable to decisive strikes, and the examples of this are predicated on particular hierarchical and centralised network structures, or those lacking popular support.[65] The key issue is whether the United States is waging a war of attrition using targeted killings as a tool, or tilting at windmills by seeking to 'cut the head off the snake', to use a common phrase regarding decapitation strikes. Is the use of targeted killings rational, or, in the words of Audrey Cronin, a leading expert on terrorism, has the United States let 'tactics drive strategy'?[66] The inherent problem of measuring military utility is that it is a subjective measurement, made against criteria that are open to interpretation. Whether or not violence is useful depends upon 'the overarching or political purpose the force was intended to achieve' as well as 'the choice of targets or objectives, all within the broader context of the operation'.[67] Violence in war is rational when it serves a political purpose, and, if the US government is to be believed, the purpose of its targeted killings is the defeat of al-Qaeda. To understand how the two fit together, we first need to look at the ways states defeat terrorist groups.

Cronin has engaged in a considerable amount work examining defeated terrorist groups. Her book, *How Terrorism Ends*, examines the 'end-game' of terrorist campaigns using a dataset of 457 terrorist groups to look at the processes and state responses that led to their demise.[68] The defeat of these groups, according to Cronin, can be divided into six different analytical frames. Terrorism ends due to decapitation, negotiations, success, failure, repression or reorientation. The aim of Cronin's study was to examine the various (and messy) endings of terrorist campaigns to see if they were relevant to America's conflict with al-Qaeda. Sometimes terrorists win, though this is rare, as 'attacks on civilians, by themselves, almost never lead to long-standing political results'.[69] If terrorist groups can channel their violence into legitimacy, or support wider political settlements, then their actions stand a slim chance of success. More often, they lose, since '[i]t is extraordinarily difficult to maintain the momentum of a terrorist campaign'.[70] Finally, some groups reorient themselves towards new goals—redirecting efforts towards criminal ventures, or escalating towards insurgency and conventional war.[71] Suffice to say, it appears highly unlikely that al-Qaeda will end up concluding a negotiated settlement with the US government.

What about the role of decapitation and repression? From Cronin's perspective, repression, defined as 'the state's use of overwhelming, indiscriminate, or disproportionate force, internally or externally (or both)', has a long history of success, despite the distaste that contemporary Western democracies have for such methods.[72] Whether repression ends a terrorist campaign 'comes down to perception and identity, a social-political tug-of-war for support that the state or regime usually wins, but at great cost'.[73] However, the kind of violence and force that constitutes repression is the same as the kind of violence that constitutes dirty wars, something that the Obama administration has forsworn.

Analysts and academics are divided on the utility of targeted killings. Most seem to agree with Cronin that 'while there have been vital tactical and operational gains as a result of taking out al-Qaeda operatives, decapitation of the top leadership is not a promising avenue for al-Qaeda's demise'.[74] Cronin was ultimately critical of the use of targeted killings, arguing that America's 'focus on killing the al-Qaeda leadership has proven strategically ineffective'.[75] Effectiveness, we must remember, is critical to justifying violence as lawful. Nonetheless, some subsequent studies have pointed out that targeted killings have disrupted the functioning of al-Qaeda,[76] although, again, this is contentious.[77] Cronin wrote *How Terrorism Ends* before the large-scale use of targeted killings during the Obama administration. Like many others, Cronin was arguing that targeted killings were an obstruction to preferable political solutions.

The problem with the binary distinction between decapitation and repression is that it does not accurately represent the options available to the US government, nor does it describe its use of targeted killings. For Cronin, 'Little can be said about the sixth scenario of decline [repression], the use of overwhelming military force, in ending al-Qaeda'[78] as 'the terrorist groups that have been destroyed through decapitation looked nothing like al Qaeda'.[79] The problem lies in the emphasis on 'overwhelming' and 'destruction'—this is the vision of violence, or a given policy, as a decisive act. Cronin argues that 'the drone campaign has morphed, in effect, into remote-control repression: the direct application of brute force by a state, rather than an attempt to deal a pivotal blow to a movement'.[80] This should remind us that most of the people examining targeted killings as decapitation are thinking of their use as a decisive measure. But what if they are not? What if targeted killings are instead framed as a tool of attrition rather than annihilation?

The image of decapitation is a series of strikes or arrests directed at top-tier leadership that cause an organisation to collapse or split into smaller organisations. This is the idea of decapitation as a decisive act. In contrast, military repression is the use of wide-scale military violence, both against an organisation and the civilian population that it forms a part of. America's use of targeted killings shares elements with all of the above, but neither the category of decapitation, nor repression, accurately describes its conduct. America's violence appears to target not just the leadership, but anyone who could be defined as a member of al-Qaeda or its affiliates. At the same time, American strategy appears to be predicated on doing this in a lawful way—fundamentally different from Cronin's examples of Russian repression in Chechnya and Peru's campaign against Sendero Luminoso (Shining Path).[81] So how should we characterise this?

Cronin's argument relies on two points: America's strategy is to destroy al-Qaeda through decapitation, and large-scale use of targeted killings constitutes repression. Between the concepts of decapitation and repression lies a third way of thinking about targeted killings as means of attrition warfare against terrorist networks. In this, targeted killings can be effective by exhausting an opponent's key resources: the knowledge and skill of veteran operatives. As highlighted by Daniel Byman's study of Israeli counterterrorism policy, targeted killings can also be used to hollow out the expertise of a non-state group:

> simply swapping one militant for another does not work. The number of skilled terrorists is often quite limited. Generators of terror such as bomb makers, trainers, document forgers, recruiters, and leaders are both scarce in number and require many months if not years to perfect their skills. If these generators of terror can be eliminated through arrests or killings, the organization as a whole is disrupted. The movement may still have many willing recruits, but it is no longer effective.[82]

The importance of Byman's observation is that the Israeli military did not seek to 'defeat' Hamas with targeted killings; instead, it opted to prevent its opponent from launching effective strikes in service of an overarching policy goal of stabilising and normalising the stalled peace process. This is an example taken from a different context than the one we are presently focusing upon, but I think it is more informative than the decapitation/repression binary. Israeli targeted killings demonstrate that the utility of targeted killings might be their contribution to political goals by wearing down and disrupting terrorist groups, rather than as a means of decisively defeating them.

The attritional role of targeted killings can be seen in their use against al-Qaeda in Iraq, where General McChrystal sought to 'systematically dismantle his network and capture insurgents who hardly appeared to be high-value targets'.[83] That McChrystal's Special Forces group, Task Force 714, managed to target and kill al-Zarqawi in the process is beside the point: they had to target the entire network in order to disrupt and destroy it. The problem is that the concept of repression melds two concepts: the annihilation of a political opponent with violence and the use of indiscriminate disproportionate force to do so. There are understandable reasons for this conflation. Marshalling the requisite amount of military force to stamp out a terrorist group, combined with poor intelligence and discipline, invariably means that indiscriminate force is impossible to avoid. As Cronin's work draws from a historical survey, there is little precedent for a repressive campaign that lacks discriminate uses of force. The examples that she highlights where indiscriminate force does not alienate key segments of the state's population are down to the fact that terrorists derive their support from communities that can be separated from the state's base without endangering its foundations.

The means of warfare available to the United States also seem to negate some of the drawbacks to military force that Cronin highlights. The Kurdish PKK withdrew across the border to Iraq in the face of Turkish repression, rendering such methods ultimately futile as a means of destroying the PKK itself.[84] In response to America's invasion of Afghanistan, al-Qaeda's 'core' withdrew to Pakistan. Unlike Turkey, however, neither the location's remoteness nor its position relative to political borders offers much respite. America cannot use conventional forces against al-Qaeda in Pakistan, but hundreds of drone strikes have demonstrated that it does not need to do so in order to target and kill people in Pakistan's territory.

Viewed as a means of attritional warfare against a transnational opponent, targeted killings make sense. From this perspective, the fact that networks do not fall apart when leadership figures are removed is beside the point—it is the overall capability of the network that is being degraded. Whether or not this will work is ultimately an open question. What we should consider, however, is that this is unlikely to change the underlying political conditions that give rise to al-Qaeda and similar groups. Therefore, it is probably wise to consider the criticism of Israeli counterterrorism offered by one former head of Israel's Shin Bet, Ami Ayalon: 'The tragedy of Israel's public security debate is that we don't realize that we face a frustrating situation in which we win every battle, but we lose the war.'[85]

Conclusions

Even if states want to adhere to the rule of law and the rules of war, using military force is difficult. The means available to states to root out violent terrorist networks and insurgent groups invariably involves harming civilians. But the remote 'turn' (to use Rorty's idea) purports to be a solution for this issue. For better or for worse, democratic states have managed to withstand the challenge of terrorist networks. To a certain degree, this may involve political compromise, both internal and between parties. The UK's 1998 Good Friday Agreement, which 'ended' the conflict in Northern Ireland, is a good example of the way in which states can come to terms with former terrorist groups. Lawrence Freedman writes that

> The IRA campaign over the three decades from the late 1960s can be seen either as a successful effort to extract concession from the British government, and unionists, or a long march away from initial absolutist demands … The critical negotiation for the leadership was less with the British government and the Unionists but those among their supporters who were aghast at what they saw as a sell-out and preferred to continue with an armed struggle, even though it could not succeed.[86]

Yet America is not fighting a nationalist terrorist group—it is seeking to eradicate a transnational terrorist network. The construction of al-Qaeda as a set of lawful targets in an armed conflict permits their destruction, and the idea that this group can in fact be destroyed using violence tends towards legitimising its annihilation. After all, while there is considerable disagreement over the status of individuals, al-Qaeda as an entity has few friends in the pantheon of states. This said, the political goal of annihilation admits a way of warfare centred on attrition, and this is where targeted killings make sense.

The rules of war are both moral and legal in character. The law of armed conflict/international humanitarian law cannot be truly extricated from the Christian just war tradition from which this (originally Eurocentric, but now global) body of law emanates. Christians do not, however, have a monopoly on justice. The perception that military conduct is immoral, however, can shape public opinions and presents a key challenge for governments attempting to legitimise the use of military force. President Obama's claim that America's war is both legal and moral goes beyond the law of armed conflict and the interpretations discussed thus far. The question, then, is: What kind of justice permits a transnational war of annihilation?

5

UNTO OTHERS

'Victims? Don't be melodramatic. Look down there. Tell me. Would you really feel any pity if one of those dots stopped moving forever?'

Harry Lime, *The Third Man* (1949)

Introduction

The concept of justice permeates the War on Terror: President Bush's first speech on 9/11, before the formal identification of al-Qaeda as the perpetrators, made clear that he intended 'to find those responsible and to bring them to justice'.[1] American preparations to strike at al-Qaeda in Afghanistan were initially codenamed Operation Infinite Justice, before being renamed Operation Enduring Freedom over concerns that the initial name might offend religious groups.[2] Speaking in the Whitehouse on 2 May 2011, President Obama announced the death of Osama Bin Laden at the hands of US Special Forces, stating that 'Justice has been done.'[3] The idea of justice may be integral to America's transnational war, but how do such values shape or constrain violence in this war?

Thus far, I have argued that American culture, especially its interpretations of law, are essential to understanding its transnational war. This is a legal view that a transnational war of attrition is lawful, so long as it respects the frameworks of international law and the principle of distinction. This account is, however, incomplete. In particular, it is missing an account of human rights law and the obligations that arise from it. Moreover, so far we have skated over the idea of liberalism, save for its requirement that liberal states are democratic and abide by the rule of law. In this chapter, I want to draw attention to two competing liberal visions of social relations and obligations—pluralism and cosmopolitanism—and the connection between these ideas, American interpretations of human rights law and America's transnational war.

If American legal interpretations and values construct and shape its war, then they also have a direct bearing on the people that America kills in the process of waging it. A good example of this is the US strike that hit a wedding convoy near Radda, Yemen, in 2013. This strike killed between twelve and seventeen people, between eight and sixteen of whom were civilians.[4] According to unnamed US sources, this strike was aimed at Shawqi Ali Ahmad al-Badani, a 'mid-level leader'[5] of al-Qaeda in the Arabian Peninsula who was apparently present in the wedding convoy, and wounded in the attack.[6] We have to keep in mind that the people killed in the attacks on men like al-Badani are far from alone. Ben Emmerson, a special rapporteur to the United Nations' Human Rights Council, identified thirty different US strikes that had injured or killed civilians.[7] Emmerson argued that the available evidence imposed 'a duty on the relevant States to provide a public explanation of the circumstances and the justification for the use of deadly force'.[8] The Bureau of Investigative Journalism, one of the organisations that track America's use of targeted killings, estimates that confirmed American strikes in Pakistan and Yemen have so far killed between 486 and 1,068 civilians.[9] One of the primary questions that needs to be addressed is how to regard these civilians in the context of America's war. After all, if America is at war with a transnational network, rather than a country or similar political entity, then how should we frame its relationship to civilians who are in essence bystanders to a transnational war?

For those who do not see US actions as war, America's use of violence against al-Qaeda is simply a series of widespread human rights violations.[10] True, the United States believes that the existence of its war precludes the applicability of human rights law for issues relevant to the conduct of war.[11] But what does this mean for those not participating in the war? Does America have any obligation towards them? For its part, the American government does not think it has extraterritorial human rights obligations.[12] This means that any legal obligations arising from its ratification of human rights treaties do not apply beyond the territory and jurisdiction of the United States.

The legal positions that the US government uses to constitute its war with al-Qaeda are rooted in normative concepts. Time and again, senior figures in the Obama administration have sought to outline the justice of America's continued war against al-Qaeda. Yet many see more continuity than change. After all, if the aim of this war is still the disruption, degradation and destruction of al-Qaeda, what separates Obama's war from the more maligned Bush administration's war? Whether or not these concepts conflict with the social and political norms that define liberal democracy and 'American values' is the matter at hand, and first we will need to look at how these values connect to the very real problem facing decision-makers: keeping the country safe.

Morality and national security

Is it immoral to wage a prolonged transnational war of extermination using targeted killings? Moreover, would any moral theory of such a war be incompatible with the liberal values of the American state? These questions constitute ways of thinking through an overarching problem: How should liberal states such as America wage war? Before answering these questions, we first need to consider the connection between law, morality and war.

The moral quality of American actions since 9/11 was justified by both George W. Bush and Barack Obama using the just war tradition.[13] The just war tradition provides the basis of discussion for moral discussion between Western states regarding the just use of force in international affairs, even if such discussions are usually expressed in terms of international law—such as self-defence—which shares many of the same principles. Although the rules of war are primarily expressed in legal terms in the present day, it is important to remember that the law of armed conflict originates in the just war tradition. The connection between law and morality is not straightforward. Some argue that law inherently contains moral, or normative, values, others that morality and law are separate from one another. The philosophy of international law is an important and rich field of debate,[14] but I do not intend to make a normative argument here (setting out what I judge to be the proper state of affairs). Instead, my focus is on describing the normative values that are inherent in America's war.

The just war tradition is in essence the ethics of violent political hostility. In the words of Charles Guthrie, formerly chief of defence staff for the UK's armed forces, and Sir Michael Quinlan, a former civil servant in the UK's Ministry of Defence, the just war tradition 'sets out a range of tests—criteria—that must be satisfied if war is to be morally justified'.[15] As important, however, is that a just war 'is a hostile response to injustice directed against the agents who cause it'.[16] Guthrie and Quinlan's use of the word 'criteria' is important in this context because although the set of criteria is accepted by most commentators and thinkers to represent necessary standards, how and why these standards should be satisfied is up for debate. These criteria are divided—like international law—into two branches: *jus ad bellum* 'concerns the morality of going to war at all' and *jus in bello* 'concerns the morality of what is done within war—how it is to be waged'.[17] We should note, however, that the just war tradition contains a number of non-reconcilable competing theories of justice (how one should consider these criteria, if at all) in relation to war. Theological explanations of justice differ from those provided by the concept of natural law, which again differs from those found in other strands of liberalism, such as cosmopolitanism.[18] These moral outlooks may each satisfy the rules common to the just war tradition, if not all of them, and perhaps for reasons quite alien to the adherents of another outlook. Nonetheless, the just war tradition is important because this framework of thinking about the ethics of war is widespread. What makes the just war tradition cohesive is that the questions and problems it analyses are inherent to most thinking about the ethics of war. The answers to the ethical challenges that war poses to both individuals and societies are fundamentally subjective, but since war gives rise to common and recurring issues, these subjective interpretations form a long-running tradition of thought. For those like Michael Walzer who are opposed to the idea that morality is entirely subjective, this shared ethical practice and debate is important, because, even fundamental social and political transformations within a particular culture may well leave the moral world intact or at least sufficiently whole so that we can still be said to share it with our ancestors. It is rare indeed that we do not share it with our contemporaries, and by and large we learn how to act among our contemporaries by studying the actions of those who have preceded us.[19]

Like law, the way in which people discuss and reflect upon the moral character of war—from pacifists who reject violence to ardent realists who reject moral limitations to political conduct—is in itself a demonstration of their moral values and standards. Ethical debates of all kinds are heated precisely because they touch upon deeply held values and our senses of self. Quinlan and Guthrie outline six criteria that need to be satisfied under *jus ad bellum*—just cause, proportionate cause, right intention, right authority, reasonable prospect of success, and last resort—as well as two criteria under *jus in bello*—distinction and proportionality—in order for a war to be justified according to the just war tradition.[20] In order for America's transnational war to be justified in the frame that Obama sets, it must satisfy these criteria but do so with a concept of justice that underpins US values—a liberal just war.

Further complicating the problem is the foundation of America's war: national security. Maintaining national security, where '[a] nation has security when it does not have to sacrifice its legitimate interests to avoid war, and is able, if challenged, to maintain them by war'[21] is often analysed in terms that dismiss the relevance of morality, or ignore it altogether. The rejection of the relevance of morality to political violence has a long pedigree. After all, Michael Walzer's landmark work on the just war tradition, *Just and Unjust Wars*, had to dedicate its first pages to considering moral realists, those people who insist 'that war lies beyond (or beneath) moral judgement'.[22] This echoes the political realism of Machiavelli, who counselled that '[a] prince, therefore, so as to keep his subjects united and faithful, should not care about the infamy of cruelty,'[23] and that '[t]he prince should nonetheless make himself feared in such a mode that if he does not acquire love, he escapes hatred, because being feared and not being hated can go together very well'.[24] In other words, the efficiency of rule and actions taken to protect the state should take precedence over fear of the morality (or judgement thereof) of said actions.

Nonetheless, it is important to distinguish moral realists from amoralists. As Bernard Williams points out, it is very difficult to think of a person without any connection to morality. Instead, those who proclaim themselves amoralists usually display a very particular, self-interested set of morals.[25] Indeed, such a person 'is capable of thinking in terms of others' interests, and his failure to be a moral agent lies (partly) in the fact that he is only intermittently and capriciously disposed to do so'.[26] The difference here is the idea of war as a special political state, with its own ethical category. For moral realists, of the type Walzer describes, war is a sphere of human activity to which no rules can apply.

Walzer's argument against realism is a product of his moral framework. For Walzer, realism is wrong because it gives 'a general account of war as a realm of necessity and duress, the purpose of which is to make discourse about particular cases appear to be idle chatter, a mask of noise with which we conceal, even from ourselves, the awful truth'.[27] Yet even if war is in some senses a special sphere of human activity, Guthrie and Quinlan are right in stating that 'Every human activity must be open to moral examination.'[28] More important is the fact that quite the reverse of moral realism can be observed in the American case. As I have argued, the concept of justice, and ethical judgements, have played an important role in the policy decision to go to war with al-Qaeda, as well as the character of political hostility America demonstrates towards this opponent.

A second challenge to the just war tradition comes not from those who deny the applicability of ethical frameworks to war but from those who consider that war should be treated no differently from everyday ethical dilemmas. This is the 'revisionist' account of the just war tradition that has gained significant traction in recent years. The importance of this account (or set of criticisms of the just war tradition) is that it is fundamentally rooted in liberal ideals. In essence, revisionists take an individual's rights as the starting point of enquiry.[29] This account is rooted in cosmopolitan understandings of liberalism. I will explain what I mean about this at length later in this chapter, but for now it suffices to say that this account rarely (if ever) draws distinctions between individuals, except via their actions. Combatants and non-combatants, important categories in both law and ethics, are therefore given far less weight, and are instead expressed in terms of moral obligations to others, and moral wrongs performed by individuals. This leads key theorists associated with this movement, such as philosopher Jeff McMahan, to take positions at odds with traditional understandings of justice in war. McMahan's most notable argument is that combatants fighting an unjust war are little different, in moral terms, from murderers.[30] Needless to say, this is at odds with the just war tradition that describes combatants as moral equals.

So where does this leave us? The first point to make is that the concept of a just war for national security is not a contradiction in terms. Moral principles and justifications construct the idea of national security—the concept cannot be disentangled from the social values of a given polity. Arnold Wolfers highlighted this intrinsic relationship between values and national security as far back as 1952:

> Those who advocate a policy devoted to national security are not always aware of the fact—if they do not explicitly deny it—that they are passing moral judgment when they advise a nation to pursue the goal of national security or when they insist that such means as the accumulation of coercive power—or its use—should be employed for this purpose. Nations like individuals or other groups may value things not because they consider them good or less evil than their alternative; they may value them because they satisfy their pride, heighten their sense of self-esteem or reduce their fears. However, no policy, or human act in general, can escape becoming a subject for moral judgment—whether by the conscience of the actor himself or by others—which calls for the sacrifice of other values, as any security policy is bound to do. Here it becomes a matter of comparing and weighing values in order to decide which of them are deemed sufficiently good to justify the evil of sacrificing others.[31]

Rooted in the notion of national security is protection of the nation and the national way of life—both concepts that are intimately tied to the *jus ad bellum* criteria of self-defence. In this sense, the justifications for violence offered by both the Bush and Obama administrations are important precisely because they reflect on the character of national life that they seek to defend. As an aside, we should note that Latin America's dirty wars waged on the grounds of national security were primarily internal conflicts, with coercive violence directed at the internal population to eradicate 'threats' to the nation. Conversely, America's war is ostensibly directed outwards, in defence of the nation, its moral nature reflective of the nation itself, rather than an authoritarian government dictating moral values to the population. These are crude differences to draw, and they certainly understate the degree to which democratic political elites attempt to impose moral values on their democratic polities. Despite this, the moral justifications of the Bush and Obama administrations for the use of force against al-Qaeda reflect the nature of the democratic market state that Philip Bobbitt depicts—these moral claims legitimised actions against al-Qaeda in response to the population's wishes, not as an imposition upon them.

The relevance of the just war tradition is that it provides a good starting point for thinking about the ethical questions of war and how they contribute to its character. People advance competing normative theories of justice and morality with vigour (and sometimes venom) precisely because they address significant aspects of the human condition and define politics and society. Liberal societies thrive on this difference of opinion, since 'liberalism requires for its social embodiment continuous philosophical and quasi-philosophical debate about the principles of justice'.[32]

In the present day, the dominant strand of discussion on theories of just war is post-Christian liberalism, despite the plurality of cultures and thinkers that constitute the tradition.[33] Different ethical approaches limit the morally permissible reasons for war, the political aims of war, and the way war is conducted. Although liberal states have waged total war, the total annihilation of an opponent would seem to be *prima facie* impermissible—a problem since this is America's stated war aim.[34] Yet liberalism is a broad church, within which there are numerous different identified strands of moral thought and reasoning, such as deontologists that seek clear rules of moral behaviour, or consequentialists that look to the consequences of choices to determine the relative justice of an act.[35] What follows, however, is a descriptive account of the ethics of America's war and how it holds together as an ethical theory. The importance of this account is that it reinforces normative values and political relationships rooted in the idea of nationally-defined political communities, as opposed to cosmopolitan values that promote the idea of humans as members of a single community.

The importance of ethics

Why are ethical considerations important? Like law, morality serves a judgemental role as well as a constitutive one. The moral arguments are also integral to international politics. In this sense, the difference between the ethical statements of President Obama vis-à-vis George W. Bush 'is meaningful in so far as it indicates a shift towards a more prudential and minimalist understanding of the right to war in international society'.[36] Given the partisan nature of contemporary US politics, criticisms that deride the moral choices of the incumbent president are both frequent and expected. War also serves as a moral frame. The debate over the specific moral wrong of torture occurred within the broader moral context of America's war with al-Qaeda. Most of the ethical problems, questions and quandaries relate to state responses to terrorism, given that al-Qaeda's acts of terrorism break most widely held ethical norms.[37] In this sense, the ethical frame of war sets the stage for engaging with the rights and wrongs of specific ethical issues arising from policy problems and events. The idea of a 'War on Terror' made the unthinkable a topic of discussion and debate. It's difficult to separate the ethical debate over the use of torture after 9/11 from the prior framing of the 'War on Terror'. Highly controversial opinions, like Alan Dershowitz's defence of state-sanctioned 'torture warrants', need to be understood in the context of this wider moral framing.[38]

Shared ethical frames constitute and define political actors.[39] Ethical considerations and debates, like the debate on the ethics of torture in the early stages of the War on Terror, therefore shape and define the political realm. Ethical critiques, like the one Obama himself implicitly directed at the administration of his predecessor, serve to shape the contours of future action. Obama's contention that '[i]nstead of strategically applying our power and our principles [after 9/11], too often we set those principles aside as luxuries that we could no longer afford'[40] served to distance himself from torture, while defining torture as unjust by US standards, independent of international ones.

If shared ethical frames constitute and define political actors, then we should consider shared moral limits within a political group when analysing their interactions with other groups. While societies cannot control their power relationships with others, these moral principles often shape interactions between political groups. The idea of a 'real'

119

political realm detached from morality—often attributed to realists through poor readings of political realism—is a straw man. Classical realist thought was threaded with explicit and implicit moral judgements. Hans Morgenthau's classic of realist thought, *Politics among Nations*, dedicated entire chapters to the role of morality in constraining political power.[41] Although one finds the language of amoralism in discussions of national security, in the American case there is an undeniable imprint of moral thought and reasoning to its approach to protecting both the state and population. One should not forget that the 'classical' proponents of realist thought struggled with the inherent tension between US values (as opposed to those of communist Russia) in a world where the development and acquisition of nuclear weapons was seen as integral to the survival of the state. Reinhold Niebuhr expressed this tension best in the opening to his book *The Irony of American History*:

> We are defending freedom against tyranny and are trying to preserve justice against a system which has, demonically, distilled injustice and cruelty out of its original promise of a higher justice ... Could there be a clearer tragic dilemma than that which faces our civilization? Though confident of its virtue, it must yet hold atomic bombs ready for use so as to prevent a possible world conflagration. It may actually make the conflict the more inevitable by this threat; and yet it cannot abandon the threat.[42]

America is currently in a similar situation: though confident of its virtue, it feels compelled to wage low-level war across the world, so as to forestall attacks that would otherwise murder its citizens. One point Morgenthau makes that is highly pertinent here is that these moral rules create self-imposed restrictions, even in the worst cases:

> if we ask ourselves what statesmen and diplomats are capable of doing to further the power objectives of their respective nations and what they actually do, we realise that they do less than they probably could and less than they actually did in other periods of history. They refuse to consider certain ends and to use certain means, either altogether or under certain conditions, not because in the light of expediency they appear impractical or unwise, but because certain moral rules interpose an absolute barrier.[43]

Philip Bobbitt argues that as the basis for state legitimacy changes there is also a shift in the moral character of the state. In the transition from nation states to market states, the 'moral role of the State as a protector' transforms from the protection of the nation, to protecting its way of life, so as to enable engagement (and profit) in the global system of markets.[44] Here, ethics in part defines the relationship between government and citizens. Underpinning this moral basis is the notion of consent: that democratic states have a moral duty to govern by consent, as well as to uphold the possibility of government by consent.

It is at this point where we can draw together a second vision of morality, not only as something that constitutes actors, but one that also shapes their agency and actions. Liberal societies see themselves as peaceful, but as the writing of Niebuhr and others demonstrates, liberal values also give moral force for the use of violence. Some critical theorists go further, arguing that liberalism does not necessarily end in peace: the logic of liberalism lends itself to war.[45]

A similar note of caution regarding the relationship between ethics and war is also offered by Carl Schmitt. For Schmitt, moralising about war was far from a useless activity. But as Schmitt saw it, this moral discussion doesn't limit or ameliorate war, to the contrary, it has the effect of worsening the effects of war itself as moral distinctions of 'just' and 'unjust' invite annihilation as a goal.[46] This is part of a wider critique of the concept of just wars contained within his body of work. Important to us is the notion that the re-emergence of just wars threatens the delicate legal bracketing of war between nation states that Schmitt considers to be the best form of international order.[47] In this sense, ethics challenges the legal regulation of force in the international sphere.

Liberalism is neither pacifist nor militarist by default. This liberal ambivalence towards violence is also inherent in the just war tradition where, even though violence is wrong, it is sometimes necessary where justified. As A.J. Coates writes:

> In opposition to the amoral and wholly pragmatic approach of the 'pure' realist, the just war theorist insists on the moral determination of war where that is possible, and on the moral renunciation of war where it is not. In opposition to the militarist, the just war theorist consistently affirms the moral primacy of peace over war, resisting the cult of violence and the drift into total war to which militarism in both its open and covert forms is prone. In opposition to the pacifist the just war theorist resists the blanket moral condemnation of war and of all things military, affirming the potential moral instrumentality of war and the virtues of an imperfect and often precarious peace.[48]

Even so, liberal states consider themselves to be different from other states (and, it must be added, morally superior to them as well). All societies demonstrate some kind of ethical code. The central question, then, is how liberal states justify the use of force—the liberal basis for just wars. What can liberal states—such as America—justify in the name of national security, while still defining themselves as liberal?

The United States is waging a transnational war of annihilation against al-Qaeda, using targeted killings and Special Forces raids to do so. At the same time, the Obama administration has set overarching limits upon its conduct—arguing for explicit adherence to the law of armed conflict and rejecting torture—and has evoked the language of morality and values to justify this. The speeches made by the Obama administration in the defence of targeted killings do form a cohesive moral position.[49] For Carl Schmitt, Obama's positions would appear to be a contradiction in terms, since, for Schmitt, just war tends towards the abolition of limits. Schmitt 'claims that the notion of just war assumes that one party has morality on its side and that, consequently, the opposing party is morally defective'.[50] Due to this, Schmitt argues, the language of just war does away with the careful positive law restraints that ensure the equality of combatants and thus, given the goal of annihilation, the self-imposition of limits displayed by the Obama administration makes little logical sense.[51] In Walzer's legalistic interpretation of the just war tradition, combatants are morally equal on the basis of the legal right to make war,[52] as opposed to the Christian tradition that 'regards just war as basically punitive', so 'it cannot logically espouse a general doctrine of the moral equality of combatants'.[53] Liberalism explains some of the tensions inherent in America's war—a war of annihilation waged with the most precise means possible, a war against criminalised political enemies who are nonetheless recognised as fellow humans—but this is a particular form of pluralist liberalism that recognises the existence and importance of separate communities, rather than a cosmopolitan form of liberalism that is concerned with fairness towards individuals independent of social or political ties.

Humanitarian warfare

Ethical attitudes form a significant part of the social constitution of war, but this is in tandem with international law. The relationships between participants in a war are constituted by both legal and ethical relationships, and the way in which international law is interpreted or applied by a state has both an ethical and political dimension. Nowhere is this more apparent than in the US attitude to international human rights law and its relationship to war and armed conflict.

Inevitably, any ethical debate takes place in parallel with international law and the law of armed conflict, which incorporates many principles from the just war tradition. Nonetheless, the concept of a 'just war' has waxed and waned in international law.[54] This said, international law is not as flexible, nor as subject to change, as an ethical tradition.

Given that the just war tradition is contingent upon a society's culture and politics, this has led over time to numerous theories of justice that might seem strange today. The evolution of shared normative understandings means that the norms of the past sometimes bear little relationship to the same concept in the present day. For example, in contrast to the contemporary world, where self defence is often seen as the inherent right of both individuals and states, Grotius qualified this right, arguing that 'It may happen, on the contrary, that because the Aggressor's Life may be serviceable to many, it would be criminal to take it from him'.[55] One important element of the present day ethics of war is that all humans are recognised as having equal moral significance. This is because of both individualism—the idea that individuals are equal—and humanitarianism—the idea that humans are obliged to care for one another.

The rules of war serve a dual function in that they create a framework that legitimates and permits the use of political violence, while also seeking to curtail unnecessary harm. In this duality, the principle of military necessity is bound to the principle of humanity—the protective aspect of international law. This recognition of humans as equals deserving minimal standards of protection means that some categories of action that were previously justified in ethical terms are unjustifiable in the present day. For example, the use of theological morality by the Spanish in their conquest of the new world is at odds with liberal ideals that posit freedom and equality between humans, not least because it threatened resisting populations with slavery.[56]

What is important about the present day is that we now have a common global understanding of humans as equals, as well as the concept of human rights. Even though interpretations of the term are markedly different, and many states commit human rights violations, this is a core global legal and ethical framework. The humanitarian dimension to the law of armed conflict also serves as a general protection, first expressed as the Martens Clause in the preamble to the 1899 Hague Convention: 'in cases not included in the Regulations adopted by them [state parties], populations and belligerents remain under the protection and empire of the principles of international law, as they result from the usages established between civilized nations, from the laws of humanity and the requirements of public conscience'.[57]

Additional Protocol I to the 1949 Geneva Conventions (which America has not signed) expresses this as: 'In cases not covered by this Protocol or by other international agreements, civilians and combatants remain under the protection and authority of the principles of international law derived from established custom, from the principles of humanity and from the dictates of public conscience.'[58]

Although the role and scope of this clause is in part designed to be open to interpretation, as it relates to disagreements between small and weak powers, the general principle is that natural law concepts should protect all engaged in an armed conflict, and that the 'principle of humanity and the dictates of public conscience have been restraining factors on the freedom of states to do what is not expressly prohibited by treaty or custom'.[59] Yet while the principle of humanity is a vital component of our contemporary ethical understanding of war (i.e., that humans are equal), it is the ethical relationships described by human rights law that are my primary focus here, not least because these describe structures of obligations between individuals and states.

When the United States invaded Iraq in 2003, its moral aim was not to wipe out the Iraqi nation but to depose Saddam Hussein and remove the Baathist government from power. As part of this effort, members of Iraq's armed forces, from conscripts to the elite Republican Guard units, were considered legal and morally permissible targets of attack. The civilians, usually referred to as 'non-combatants' in the just war tradition, were impermissible targets of attack, although standard interpretations of the just war tradition permit harming or killing civilians in the course of attacking a military objective, subject to the constraints of necessity and proportionality. Yet before the invasion, when no armed conflict existed, these kinds of categories of person did not apply. What, then, was the relationship between Iraqi citizens and the American state? In the contemporary world, this depends upon the duties and obligations that states have to protect the human rights of individuals, be they citizen or non-citizen, located within the state's territory or abroad.

If the modern law of armed conflict is markedly different from its pre-1949 origins, so, too, is the modern law of peace. Nowhere is this more apparent than in the rise of international human rights law as a widely accepted set of obligations between states and individuals. Of course, the idea of political rights is hundreds of years old. The US Declaration of Independence, a foundational element of American society, features the language of rights in the 'self-evident' truths 'that all men are created equal, that they are endowed by their Creator with certain unalienable Rights, that among these are Life, Liberty and the pursuit of Happiness'.[60] However, these nascent political ideas of equality and consent-based government differ from the contemporary regime of human rights law. Human rights, encapsulated by the Universal Declaration of Human Rights in 1948, require 'recognition of the inherent dignity and of the equal and inalienable rights of all members of the human family is the foundation of freedom, justice and peace in the world'.[61]

The idea that all humans have rights, arising from their equal status as human beings, is the cornerstone of international human rights law. It is encompassed in a wide variety of treaties that have created both global and regional human rights regimes. America, for its part, is a signatory and state party to the International Covenant on Civil and Political Rights (ICCPR) and has signed the International Covenant on Economic, Social and Cultural Rights (ICESCR). As a state party to the ICCPR, the United States recognises that '[e]very human being has the inherent right to life'[62] and a number of other rights. Again, the interpretation of treaties matters. As previously noted, the United States does not think its ICCPR obligations are extraterritorial; in other words, it does not believe that its obligations to respect the rights of its own citizens, or people within its jurisdiction, applies to citizens of otherstates outside US jurisdiction. This stance has been brought into question by a large number of legal opinions and court rulings.[63]

The importance of extraterritorial obligations is that they describe ethical and political relations between states and individuals alongside legal ones. While legal obligations do not necessarily arise from ethical obligations or duties, legal obligations imply ethical ties. The legal position of the United States describes a world in which it is conscious of the rights of non-US citizens but has no obligation to uphold them or to respect them. The US position is state-centric—it sees it as the responsibility of other states to protect the rights of their own citizens. This is in contrast to states that consider their ICCPR obligations to extend beyond their borders—for these states, they have an obligation to respect the human rights of other states' citizens.

What happens to rights when the shooting starts? The traditional view is that the law of armed conflict, as the specialised body of law (*lex specialis*), supersedes the general set of applicable rules. The understanding of human rights arising from the 'human rights revolution'[64] of the late 1970s is very different. The 'humanization of humanitarian law' means that 'the law of war has been changing and acquiring a more humane face', and developments in the law of armed conflict have introduced the notion of individual rights arising from law of armed conflict treaties.[65] Human rights law and the law of armed conflict still start from very different normative standpoints,[66] and the UN Human Rights Committee's idea that they might apply simultaneously has been criticised.[67] But, crucially, courts have determined that some elements of states' human rights obligations extend to armed conflict situations abroad. For instance, in *Al-Skeini and Others v. the United Kingdom*, the European Court of Human Rights held that the UK had violated its ECHR obligations for failing to investigate the deaths of five civilians in Basra.[68] This builds upon considerable case law in the ECHR relating to similar matters.[69] The United States, however, is not subject to the ECHR's jurisdiction, and some authors have noted that legal activism by courts in this area is likely to 'increase the gap between legal theory and state compliance'.[70]

In sum, the United States is waging a transnational armed conflict, cognisant that all humans have rights, yet asserting that it is not obliged to consider those rights in the context of said armed conflict. In view of the US military, human rights law is superseded by the existence of armed conflict, and that human rights law creates obligations between states and their own populations, not between America and the populations of other states.[71] This stands in contrast to the emerging pattern of human rights law and norms in Europe, as well as the relatively mixed regime that regulates Israel's use of targeted killings.[72] Arguing that human rights law does not apply to US conduct is not quite the same as arguing that human rights do not exist—'strangers at a distance' still count as human.

Unto others

In terms of international politics and war, one of the key differences is the way in which community is conceived of and constituted by these moral differences. Here, we should consider the resulting differences in weighted obligations. The cosmopolitan ideal that all humans are equal, or, in the words of Raimond Gaita, that they share 'a common humanity', presses for a notion of justice that ignores society and is universally applicable.[73] On the other hand, a notion of ethical obligation that is founded in national differences differs from cosmopolitan ideals in a significant way. The importance here is that cosmopolitan ideas of politics and ethical practice are inherent in many key areas of normative debate in the present day. The idea of there being a 'responsibility to protect' the citizens of other countries from their own governments, or that 'human security' demands that we should consider the security from the perspective of individuals, share this same understanding. These ideals and values exert force in international politics to the extent that such arguments affect the actions and policy choices of states. Given that they resonate with liberal ideals of human rights, they exerted considerable rhetorical force in the late 1990s and early 2000s. However, cosmopolitan ideals faced considerable resistance from political pluralists, those who are intensely cautious of the cosmopolitan idea that shared universal values exist, and that these values should be accepted by all. Fundamentally, a distinction can be made between cosmopolitans who take individual human beings as the central actor in international relations, and pluralists who take societies (however defined) as the fundamental unit of concern. The importance of this clash is that although the United States is a liberal democracy, its current campaign is rooted in a pluralistic idea of rights and shared values, rather than cosmopolitan ones.

There is a distinct variation in the degree of obligations owed to other individuals present in cosmopolitan theory. The egalitarian principle can be interpreted as requiring radical equality between individuals (that is to say it is unjust to aim for anything other than a perfectly equal planet) or it can be interpreted weakly. In her book on cosmopolitanism and just war, Cécile Fabre utilises a weaker form of egalitarian argument to form a cosmopolitan theory of just war.[74] The reason for engaging with Fabre's work here is that she intentionally uses 'plausible, relatively minimalist theory of cosmopolitan justice' as a basis for cosmopolitan just war, one that contains markedly weaker obligations between individuals than other cosmopolitan theories would produce.[75] It is the fact that this very weak cosmopolitanism cannot be reconciled with America's war that leads to the conclusion that America's war is irreconcilable with cosmopolitanism, and therefore best described as being constituted by pluralist liberalism.

The reason that America's war is antithetical to cosmopolitanism is that it is, from a cosmopolitan point of view, markedly unjust to 'distant strangers', as Fabre refers to individuals beyond the immediate political community. The structure of obligations that Fabre envisions is one where:

> citizens and public officials are under a duty of justice to (respectively) support and implement just institutions, laws, and policies, and not to support or implement unjust ones, for the sake of distant strangers; they are also in their daily life under negative duties not to take part in structured and organized practices the effects of which are similarly harmful to those individuals. However, they are not under a positive duty of justice (as a duty of assistance) to act accordingly, in their daily life, in the interstices of the law—by, for example, giving money to Oxfam as remedy to their community's failure to operate resource transfers towards the very deprived abroad. Nor are they under a negative duty of justice, in their daily life, not to take part in unstructured practices the effects of which are severely harmful to distant strangers.[76]

War, we should remember, is a 'structured and organised practice', and one that is distinctly harmful. America's war, we should also remember, is harmful to a great many strangers, at remarkable distance from the United States itself. One of the primary injustices in America's transnational war is that civilians are harmed. This harm differs from previous wars, since al-Qaeda does not, by definition, have a civilian population in the same sense that a state does. How, then, are we to consider the moral relationship between these persons that have nothing to do with America's transnational war, and the United States itself?

Even the weakest form of cosmopolitan justice, detailed by Fabre, recognises that a negative duty exists to prevent active harm against 'strangers at a distance'. The transnational nature of America's war with al-Qaeda means that most civilians lie beyond its immediate scope. Al-Qaeda is envisaged as a belligerent with no civilian population, strictly speaking. Therefore, many of the civilians present in the regions that America attacks are not only impermissible targets, but effectively lie outside the political scope of the armed conflict, if not physically removed to a safe distance from people that America considers to be legitimate targets. In moral terms, these civilians are effectively bystanders to armed conflict.

How does this difference in moral thinking translate into limits upon warfare? John Brennan's speech in defence of targeted killings articulated four 'basic principles of the law of war that govern the use of force': necessity, distinction, proportionality and humanity.[77] It is the last of these that is most important to analyse. Brennan stated that 'targeted strikes conform to the principle of humanity which requires us to use weapons that will not inflict unnecessary suffering'. The focus on humanity is due to the importance of international law, as well as liberal ideology, and differences over what constitutes 'humane warfare' is the matter at hand. Wars have always been fought by humans, but liberals attempt to justify them with reference to the language of individual rights and duties. Liberalism does not always constrain—cosmopolitan understandings of human rights underpin the concept of the 'right to protect' that provided the moral and political argument to breach the sovereignty of states that seriously abused their populations.[78]

In order to understand different liberal ideas of just war, it is necessary to examine the process by which the two core principles of liberalism, liberty and equality, constitute the political realm of liberal societies. It is also necessary to recognise fundamental tensions that arise from different interpretations of these terms—of the production of liberal justice—and how this leads to markedly differing views not only of what is right but how the relations between individuals, societies and states should be conceived. Two dimensions of opinion are important here: the tension between ideas of absolute value (such as Immanuel Kant's categorical imperative—'act only in accordance with that maxim through which you can at the same time will that it become a universal law')[79] and value pluralism (best expressed by Isaiah Berlin—'the ends of men are many, and not all of them are in principle compatible with each other').[80] There is also a tension between those that theorise justice at an atomic individual level and those that consider justice as being constituted by society—that 'men cannot physically survive alone, but much more that they only develop their characteristically human capacities in society'.[81] The latter difference arises from reactions to John Rawls' landmark work, *A Theory of Justice*, and his notion of 'justice as fairness'—the so-called 'liberal–communitarian debate'.

Rawls is rightly famous for providing an account of justice measured in equality. It is, however, one that erases individual identity implied by his 'veil of ignorance' by which means fairness is achieved. Rawls asked us to consider the allocation of goods and the ordering of society in an impartial manner, without regard to who we ourselves might be, as a means of arriving at agreed and shared principles of justice.[82] It is this idea of impartial justice and universal values, combined with the idea of human equality, that gives rise to the cosmopolitan view of the just war tradition introduced above. Cosmopolitanism reflects a particular way of thinking about ethical obligations that is rooted in both procedural justice (obligations between persons) and centred on abstract individuals.[83] One of the key criticisms that communitarian thinkers make of this kind of individualistic approach to ethics is that it neglects the social dimension of ethics by undermining community and political life, and that it therefore cannot properly describe or account for communal relationships and obligations.[84] This deletion of the social layer and re-imagination of ethics as instrumental relationships between individuals is important to consider, particularly since war is fundamentally a social practice.

Rawls' work developed from his initial concern with justice for individuals in response to criticism from communitarian thinkers— who consider justice to be rooted in societies, communities and particular traditions—to account for social entities and society. Rawls translated his theory of justice as fairness into the political realm in his later books, *Political Liberalism* and *The Law of Peoples*, arguing that two principles of justice are:

a. Each person has an equal claim to a fully adequate scheme of equal basic
rights and liberties, which scheme is compatible with the same scheme
for all; and in this scheme the equal political liberties, and only those
liberties, are to be guaranteed their fair value.

b. Social and economic inequalities are to satisfy two conditions: first, they
are to be attached to positions and offices open to all under conditions
of fair equality of opportunity; and second, they are to be to the greatest
benefit of the least advantaged members of society.[85]

This translation from societal theories of justice to inter-societal
justice matters. Despite the fact that John Rawls' original concept of
justice as fairness appears cosmopolitan in nature due to its focus on a
universal theory of justice, he acknowledged the differences that
existed between societies, as 'the highly nonideal conditions of our
world with its great injustices and widespread social evils' meant that
societies that chose to live fairly would have to do so shoulder to shoulder with those that do not.[86]

What is key to Rawls' contention here is that 'good' liberal societies
organised according to his principle of justice would exist shoulder to
shoulder with unjust ones. This acceptance of difference is something
of an anathema to cosmopolitan thought. After all, what of the individuals trapped in oppressive social conditions? Although differences
exist between cosmopolitan thinkers, their core shared principles militate against such acceptance of injustice, as Fabre explains:

> Whichever kind of cosmopolitan one is, however, one will subscribe to the
> view that human beings are the fundamental units of moral concern and
> have equal moral worth, irrespective of group membership (cultural,
> familial, ethnic and national). Cosmopolitan morality is thus individualist,
> egalitarian and universal."[87]

Rawls noted the consequences of this worldview for international
relations. In his words, cosmopolitans:

> imagine a global original position with its veil of ignorance behind which all
> parties are situated symmetrically. Following the kind of reasoning familiar
> in the original position for the domestic case, the parties would then adopt
> a first principle that all persons have equal basic rights and liberties.
> Proceeding this way would straightaway ground human rights in a political
> (moral) conception of liberal cosmopolitan justice ... On this account, the
> foreign policy of a liberal people—which it is our concern to elaborate—

will be to act gradually to shape all not yet liberal societies in a liberal direction, until eventually (in the ideal case) all societies are liberal.[88]

Rawls criticises the totalising implications of this cosmopolitan world view because in his view liberalism requires a pluralist world view—the acceptance of the views and beliefs of others—since 'we cannot know that non-liberal societies cannot be acceptable'. Therefore, in his view, the task for liberals is to reconcile their liberal societies with a world that contains non-liberal societies.[89] For Rawls, the right to self-defence, possessed by all 'well-ordered societies', was open to interpretation by each such society since 'they may interpret their actions in a different way depending on how they think of their ends and purposes'.[90] This non-universal rationale for using force does not appeal to cosmopolitans. In particular, cosmopolitan theorists tend to look to organisations above the level of the state for justice,[91] and this once again points to the UN being the legitimate authority to authorise war.

For cosmopolitans, justice is global—therefore, a transnational war to defend the polity of a single state would be impermissible—whereas for pluralists such as Rawls, the notion of a state seeking to protect its own liberal order from 'disordered peoples' could constitute a just cause. From this perspective, the United States is justified in annihilating al-Qaeda only for so long as the organisation continues to pose a threat. Beyond that, any excess killing would be disproportionate. This, again, appears to mirror US strategy outlined in the previous chapter.

Needless to say, for the American state, nationality matters. The Obama administration (like the Bush administration that preceded it) does not mete out justice impartially, but seeks to preserve US society and its domestic liberal order. As Rawls notes, 'The ultimate concern of a cosmopolitan view is the well-being of individuals and not the justice of societies.'[92] Yet given that war is a social activity, it is difficult to reconcile the two.

Liberalism does—counter to Schmitt—imply limits on the means of warfare. Key to this is how the 'other' or outsider is perceived. Theorising about justice unto others is found in theology, as well as foundational works in the Western canon of philosophy. Liberal theorists take the just war tradition and think it through in terms of individual rights and relations. The notion of fairness and equality sustains an ethical model of war in which all participants have rights, so long as their cause is just, and that moral wrongs or harms done are seen to be done between participants. In this regard, liberal interpretations of just war tend towards exactly what Carl Schmitt thought they would: a situation of moral imbalance between individuals. Recent reimagining of just war theory from the perspective of liberal individualism rejects the central principle of the moral equality of combatants. Rawls argued against such imbalances, stating that:

> Well-ordered peoples must respect, so far as possible, the human rights of the members of the other side, both civilians and soldiers, for two reasons. One is simply that the enemy, like all others, has these rights by the Law of Peoples. The other reason is to teach enemy soldiers and civilians the content of those rights by the example set in the treatment they receive. In this way the meaning and significance of human rights are best brought home to them.[93]

Where both pluralist and cosmopolitan theories agree is that non-combatants should be spared on the basis of their humanity. Indeed, this principle is at work in America's war. One could argue that never before in the history of warfare has a state dedicated as much time and effort to preventing the deaths of non-combatants, while simultaneously attempting to wage a war. That is not to say that America does not kill civilians, or that it is blameless for civilian deaths, but that the US attitude towards civilian deaths is that they should be prevented not because civilians are 'innocent'—in the theological sense associated with Christian doctrines of just war—but because they are humans who have not done anything that makes them liable for targeting. Indeed, America's war, even if it is conducted with a goal of annihilation, appears to undermine Schmitt's central concern—that restraints on war would be abandoned—as some liberal theories of justice allow for a perceived moral inequality between the two sides, while retaining specific limits on means and methods of warfare.

America's legal opinion regarding the implementation of international human rights law implies that no legal obligation exists where armed conflict exists. From a pluralist perspective, the just war tradition requires that attacks should be proportionate and that excessive harm should be reduced to the minimum possible, but beyond this, neither the American state nor its armed forces have responsibilities for 'strangers at a distance', at least not in times of war. The Obama administration is at pains to point out that America reduces the number of civilians harmed to the minimum possible using precision methods of warfare. Still, this idea that America owes no obligations to individuals due to the existence of an armed conflict cannot be reconciled with cosmopolitan ideals. From a cosmopolitan perspective, the justice of continuing such a war would have to be examined with due regard to the negative duty owed to the millions of people affected by America's war in Pakistan, Yemen and beyond. Given the prominence of states and societies in pluralist thought, this interpretation of human rights law is far easier to reconcile. Since these obligations can be construed as being between a state and its citizens, and the state having no obligations to individuals who belong to other societies, the negative consequences to these individuals is of less concern. As such, it is easier for a pluralist to justify the continuance of American killing.

There is no barrier in law or the just war tradition to the annihilation of opposing military forces, subject to the constraints of military necessity and proportionality. The liberal impulse that war should be conducted with as little harm as necessary, and that killing be performed without undue suffering, is a hallmark of both pluralist and cosmopolitan liberalism. However, the moral implications of the transnational dimension to America's war with al-Qaeda are at odds with cosmopolitan theories of just war. Even if a cosmopolitan theorist were convinced of American justifications on the basis of self-defence through the lens of national security (a stretch, for cosmopolitan thinkers), the moral implications of waging a remote war on this basis does not stand up to scrutiny. If we take individuals as our primary unit of moral concern, the harms and potential harms inflicted to the citizens of other states would vastly outweigh the potential harms averted by continuing to use force. In contrast, pluralist accounts of justice can tolerate this, since from this inter-societal perspective it is not assumed that a state owes obligations to individuals from other societies that need to be taken into account in any analysis of just war.

Conclusion

The war America is waging fits within the structure of the just war tradition, but it demonstrates a particular variant of liberalism that many would disagree with. This is important for a number of reasons, some of which were examined in this chapter. One is that liberal morality permits more violence than most contemporary liberals would care to admit. Critical examinations of the just war tradition itself highlight the way in which this mode of moral reasoning permits violence against a vast range of people, even as it purports to limit said violence.[94] But the just war tradition is important—moral realism fails to recognise the constitutive role of moral reasoning in the concept of war itself. Yet liberal morality is a broad church, and US conduct falls firmly into the camp of the pluralists. This has consequences. Favouring pluralist theories of justice over cosmopolitan ideals affects American 'soft power'. Soft power—'the ability to shape what others want'[95]—without resorting to 'hard power' (the threat or use of military force) is an alternative to coercive foreign policy since, as Joseph S. Nye argues:

> the attractiveness of the United States will be crucial to our ability to achieve the outcomes we want. Rather than having to put together pickup coalitions of the willing for each new game, we will benefit if we are able to attract others into institutional alliances and eschew weakening those we have already created.[96]

By embracing (or re-affirming) pluralist theories of justice, America weakens the claim that there exists any form of universally applicable standard for justice in the international arena. This may in time prove to be a problem given that the liberal order of states is predicated on standards of conduct largely drawn from the values of European states that originated the current international system. The United States has traditionally defended human rights in the international arena, as well as advancing Western norms of behaviour that require acceptance of human rights. The tension between cosmopolitan and pluralist ideas can be seen in the arc of Obama's presidency. Writing in Foreign Affairs as he sought the nomination to be the Democrat candidate for the Presidency in the 2008 elections, Obama set out his vision, that '[t]his is our moment to renew the trust and faith of our people-and all people-in an America that battles immediate evils, promotes an ultimate good, and leads the world once more.'[97] The problem is that this universal rhetoric that echoes cosmopolitan ideas is at odds with pluralist values that might accept the existence of 'immediate evils'. The problem for Obama is that the cosmopolitan discourse is at odds with his foreign policy choices that reflect a far more cautious—and plural-ist—set of values. The gap between rhetoric and reality reflects the difficulty of effectively communicating pluralist ideals. Although it is hard to determine the effect this has on American soft power, the con-tinued circulation of images of civilians killed by US strikes, alongside allegations of injustice that accompany them, certainly dent America's image in the world. Perhaps the greatest contribution that this offers to debates on global ethics is that actions in conformity with the just war tradition are not automatically perceived as 'good' by the global audi-ences that America seeks to persuade. Furthermore, as cosmopolitan interpretations of human rights gain ground in the Western world, the pluralist values that the United States demonstrates will begin to drive a wedge between the country and its most natural allies. It is for this reason that US values are vitally important—after all, forming and sustaining a coalition of states willing to take action against terrorism was the high point of American diplomacy immediately after 9/11. The United States squandered this goodwill in the run up to the 2003 Iraq War, foreclosing the possibility of sustaining this coalition, and isolating some of its natural democratic allies, such as France. Adhering to a set of values that places a wedge between America and its closest allies may weaken its alliances that remain, or foreclose the possibility of new coalitions forming.

6

INDIVIDUATED WARFARE

'To know them means to eliminate them'
Col. Mathieu, *The Battle of Algiers*[1]

Introduction

Targeted killings are best understood as a form of transnational warfare. However, despite the claimed precision of targeted killings, this practice of warfare has consequences for everyone. It is a form of warfare that contains an inherent tension in that it seeks to reduce war to the level of individuals, yet relies upon global infrastructure, pervasive intelligence collection and international political ties. This tension is, again, best understood by taking into account the role of legal concepts and thought in the production of this form of warfare.

America's targeted killings are unique because of America's reach and scale. Although subject to the constraints of international politics—I doubt America would kill members of al-Qaeda in Russia or China—the United States has demonstrated the ability to select and kill at a distance that far surpasses the scope of any comparable campaign of selective killing by other states. One of the consequences of America's war is that civilians in very different geographic regions find themselves—through no fault of their own—caught between US forces and people that America considers legitimate targets. Furthermore, the lack of stationary ground forces means that intelligence collection issues can result in US strikes on incorrect targets. Remember that Reprieve's study of US targeted killings highlights that many civilians get killed in these strikes.[2] A transnational war waged with remote strikes may be incredibly precise, as its supporters claim, but the geographical boundaries of this war are ill-defined, such claims of precision are hardly a comfort for the civilians that are injured or killed in the process. But to understand how and why US forces end up killing civilians on this scale in places far removed from America itself, we need to look at the means of warfare: How and why is America able to project violence in this way?

In Chapter 1, I sketched an outline of the relationship between culture and technology. Just as law, strategy and politics influence the purpose and conduct of war, so, too, does technology. Novel technologies, and the changing use of existing ones, enable new military operations—and novel forms of warfare—but the use of technology is often shaped by military culture and social factors.[3] Most of the technology that America uses to conduct targeted killings already existed before 9/11. Hellfire missiles were originally developed to destroy armoured vehicles, not pickup trucks carrying terrorists. Again, in Chapter 1, I explored the 'revolution in military affairs' that effectively provided the baseline technologies now used to hunt and kill members of al-Qaeda. Material objects cannot fully explain what we currently see as targeted killings, but aside from being used against a transnational opponent, what exactly is novel about American targeted killings? The answer lies in the organisational mind-set that this kind of activity requires, and the intangible threat of imminent violence that it creates.

Individuated warfare

Targeted killings are more than a collection of technologies arrayed against a new type of opponent. To fully understand them, we need to explore the relationship between technologies, systems and ideas. Remote violence and Special Forces raids are the visible hallmarks of America's transnational war. Yet, as the Zarqawi case study demonstrated, targeted killings require not only drones and surveillance but a way of thinking about, and operating against, networks of individuals.

INDIVIDUATED WARFARE

American targeted killings are often described as remote warfare. The problem is that this term is used to cover everything from NATO's bombing in the Kosovo War to Special Forces raids like the one that killed Osama Bin Laden. This kind of variety should not surprise us, since, as we have seen in the previous chapters, war is constituted by a number of elements that inform the practice or conduct of war itself. The problem is that remote warfare does not add much in terms of clarity. Western militaries equipped and trained to wage inter-state wars have always adjusted their doctrine and operational behaviour in order to fight irregular opponents—a difficult task given that this often requires altering deep-seated organisational culture and practices.[4] This brings us back to the way we frame American targeted killings. If remote warfare covers both traditional bombing campaigns against states and drone strikes on individuals, then the concept is of little use for present purposes since both activities are quite different. If we take remote warfare to mean distance, then it seems strange to include Special Forces, who are trained to kill at close quarters.

Another way of thinking about remote warfare is in terms of extreme asymmetry: the inability of Serb forces to actually fight back against NATO, the little chance that the truck stands against the hellfire, the odds against your escape or survival if JSOC knock down your front door in the middle of the night. Just as political asymmetry defines transnational war, asymmetries of capability define transnational warfare. But all wars are asymmetric to some degree, even when they feature massed armies fighting one another in a conventional manner there will be degrees of asymmetrical capability or intent. Defining and analysing asymmetry, however, is difficult. What do we mean by asymmetric warfare?

One way would be to look at the effort expended by either side. It is difficult, if not impossible, to reduce this question to comparable figures given the scale of organisations, systems and technology involved, at least on the American side. Nonetheless, given that America has reoriented its intelligence community and substantial components of its global military capability to defeating al-Qaeda, its investment of money and work-hours surely dwarfs that of its opponents. Given the secretive nature of al-Qaeda, it would be even harder to come up with a reliable figure for their commitment, but it is unlikely to be even in the ballpark of American spending on its intelligence community and military.

At the same time, money isn't everything. Asymmetrical political goals, commitment and resources also give rise to asymmetric strategies. Insurgency and guerrilla warfare are useful comparisons in this regard. Counterinsurgency operations often feature an asymmetry of guerrillas seeking to exhaust a state, with state forces attempting to find and defeat the guerrillas. The tactical asymmetry of America's war in Vietnam was borne of these higher-level asymmetries. At the same time, the creation of a positive asymmetry in favour of your own side is at the core of military practice. Nor should we think of such asymmetry as skewed in a single direction. Israel had a decided advantage in armoured vehicles in the opening stages of the 1973 Yom Kippur War, which Egyptian forces countered by arming their infantry with anti-tank weapons.[5] For this reason, we should be wary about thinking of the asymmetries in America's war in a single dimension. The image of helpless individuals being picked off by hellfire missiles is by far and away the dominant conceptual frame of this conflict, but it is the organisation and activity that enables these kinds of strikes that defines it. This works both ways. Despite the fact that the visible element of al-Qaeda's activity, violent attacks, is now sporadic, that is not to say that the group is not actively planning to commit further large scale acts of violence.

While asymmetries of capability and intent are important, what defines targeted killings, and the operational methods of conducting them, is the way in which it reduces warfare to the individual and personal level. Rather than thinking of targeted killings in terms of people under the shadow of drones, we should consider the scattered networks existing under the glare of the American state. This is what I term 'individuated warfare' and others have used similar concepts to address this issue.[6] Individuated warfare is the result of a number of overlapping influences. Individuated warfare arises when warfare is conceptualised in terms of killing, not combat. It is what happens when a rule-abiding state gets very good at targeting and produces the kind of apparatus required to employ force against non-traditional opponents.

All of this takes place in the context of technological innovation. The nature of innovation is disputed—the people who study it disagree over how to frame the processes of innovation as well as how to judge technology as innovative.[7] Nonetheless, we tend to think of innovation in terms of new material objects or ideas, re-purposing existing technologies or the development of new systems and social structures for improving their use. One technology that will feature quite heavily in this chapter is the ongoing revolution in digital information and communications technology (ICTs). The word 'revolution' is prone to misuse. This is because it is often difficult to disentangle cause from effect in the relationship between societies and the technologies that they use. Do technologies shape human society, or do human societies (and their social values) drive the development of technology? This is a debate between technological determinists who believe the former and social constructivists, who believe the latter. What matters for present purposes is that digital ICTs are a 'general purpose technology'[8]—a vital part of the social and economic systems that enable human societies the world over. That is not to say that this general purpose technology determines a given direction of travel or trajectory, but simply that it exists and many people make use of it for the benefits that easy, cheap and global communications can bring.

Individuated warfare is only possible because the United States is now able to process vast stores of information to identify purported members of al-Qaeda and act against them. Drones are an efficient means of doing this, and their use for similar kinds of missions are important, but I am more interested in the wider bureaucracy and its orientation towards picking out individuals as participants in war. Without the technology that enables the identification (or purported identification) of individuals as members of al-Qaeda, or other legitimate targets, this type of warfare would be impossible. It is wholly possible to conduct a targeted killing campaign with knives and guns, but identifying people as members of a terrorist network in near-real time, halfway around the world, requires sophisticated communications networks, intelligence, surveillance and reconnaissance (ISR) capabilities, as well as data storage and close cooperation between soldiers and intelligence analysts.

What unifies this entire system is a particular mind-set or orientation towards a given goal. Interpretations of the rules of war inform the training of military forces and the development of organisational routines designed to ensure adherence to those rules.[9] Different interpretations of the applicable rules, or of their validity, can result in markedly different practices. Rather than thinking about the combination of technology and practice, it will be useful here to borrow a perspective from Ursula Franklin, a philosopher of technology, and consider the idea of technology as practice.

Franklin argues that technology 'is a system. It entails far more than the individual material components. Technology involves organization, procedures, symbols, new words, equations, and, most of all, a mind-set.'[10] It is this mind-set that is important, as it arises as much from the cultural factors that I have identified throughout this book as the 'material components' like Predator and Reaper drones. In this sense, targeted killings are more than the act of killing individuals; it is the act (and practice) of thinking about opponents as individuals, and organising activity around this idea.

To restate my case at the outset of this book: the mind-set associated with targeted killings does not arise from the material object of a Predator drone. Instead, we need to think about the systems that support and include this platform, as well as the ideas and social concepts that guide their use. We therefore need to focus on the organisations, processes and ideas that enable acts of violence. The question is whether this kind of violence falls outside what we can call warfare.

Combat and killing

One of the core questions about targeted killings is whether they can even be described as warfare. Given the extreme asymmetry in resources and capability to commit violence, at what point does warfare become so uneven that 'war' ceases to make sense as a category of analysis? The answer to this question really depends on whether one defines warfare in terms of combat or killing. These two are inseparable to a certain degree, since combat requires killing, but the reverse is not true: killing does not require combat. It is easy to reach for instinctive definitions that completely separate the two, such as, for example, a comparison of the image of soldiers fighting one another to the image them massacring civilians. The problem is that the two blur together, and technology plays a role in this. After all, if an aircraft kills someone from tens of thousands of feet above the earth, does that still count as combat?

For some, war and warfare are predicated on 'combat', and for this reason, a war conducted by targeted killings is not worthy of the name.

'Outside of armed conflicts involving the United States in Afghanistan, Iraq, and Somalia', writes O'Connell, 'Al-Qaeda's actions and U.S. responses have been too sporadic and low-intensity to qualify as armed conflict.'[11] This is one of the reasons why drones are seen to pose a special problem in terms of both asymmetry and intensity: a war could be waged by one side that is never at risk of serious harm, at least in the region that killing actually occurs. As one-sided as night raids by Special Forces can be, they still involve danger and risk for the soldiers on the ground. Even though we know little about the numbers involved, there are plenty of examples of botched raids in the news. Even where raids achieve their objective, such as the one that killed Osama Bin Laden, accidents occur. Famously, one of the helicopters involved in the Bin Laden raid crashed at the start of the final phase of the operation. But, again, we should be wary of focusing upon platforms, as targeted killings are better defined by everything that leads to an individual act of violence rather than by the specific mechanism of violence itself.

The problem that targeted killings pose is that they produce a pattern of violence and killing that is quite distinct from combat and battle. It is this difference that leads lawyers like Philip Alston to question whether this violence 'rises to the level necessary for an armed conflict to exist'.[12] Others depict this difference in slightly more abstract terms. Gregoiré Chamayou, a French academic, argues that drone warfare is about predation, tracing a line from his work on manhunts—and how humans hunt one another—to the state that hunts humans with Predator drones.[13] In this line of criticism, American violence is not war—as commonly understood—but acts of predation. Chamayou writes that

> the radical imbalance in exposure to death leads to a redefinition of relations of hostility and of the very sense of what is called 'waging war.' Warfare, by distancing itself totally from the model of hand-to-hand combat, becomes something quite different, a 'state of violence' of a different kind. It degenerates into slaughter or hunting. One no longer fights the enemy; one eliminates him, as one shoots rabbits.[14]

Should the rules of war cover what can be termed a transnational manhunt, or, less charitably, a game of 'global whack-a-mole with terrorists'?[15]

As we have seen, there is a strong normative bias against allowing states to use the rules of war, and its framework of legitimation, where it does not need to use violence. Allowing states a free hand to 'expand the notion of non-international armed conflict to groups that are essentially drug cartels, criminal gangs or other groups that should be dealt with under the law enforcement framework', would, in the words of Philip Alston, 'be to do deep damage to the IHL [international humanitarian law] and human rights frameworks'.[16] Considered thus, the critique of transnational war considered in the first part of this book overlaps with, and is reinforced by, critiques of transnational warfare and targeted killings. If America does not need to wage war, and the way in which it metes out violence is so imbalanced as to fall outside the definition of war, then targeted killings are murder and human rights violations, not warfare. In short: no combat, no war.

The rules that justify killing in war originate in times where it was nearly impossible for a combatant to kill an enemy in battle without running the risk of getting hurt or killed themselves. By deploying expensive technology, the United States can now kill people while risking only the odd crashed drone in return, and perhaps suffering the occasional al-Qaeda-inspired or directed attack on American territory. Do, or should, the rules apply when armed conflicts carry no more risk for one side's military than shooting fish in a barrel? I think so. This is because war and warfare consists of regulated killing, not specified modes of combat.

Chamayou's work is worth consideration because it highlights one of the aspects of America's war that creates unease—how one-sided does warfare have to become before it ceases to 'count' as warfare? The problem of judgements that in essence relate the fairness or parity of warfare is that the history of warfare is replete with instances of one-sided violence. One quite famous example is the Battle of Cannae, where the Carthaginian General Hannibal not only defeated a larger Roman army, but slaughtered it with minimal losses by first enveloping it, and then killing the survivors as they fled.[17] It is worth bearing in mind that for all the supposed equality of combatants, the military leaders who dominated the industrial era considered such one-sided butchery to be the pinnacle of military skill.

The idea that predation somehow differs from war is seductive, but it ignores the development of war fighting in general. Technology is in part responsible for these issues as it enables individuals to kill at an extreme distance. So, too, is culture: adopting 'post-heroic' methods of warfare requires altering perceptions of right conduct in war where the means of warfare are judged by the lack of collateral damage and measures taken to protect ones own forces from harm.[18] Force protection is not limited to targeted killings; it is a key political consideration for Western interventions abroad.[19] Drones are an extreme example of the separation of military personnel from personal danger, but they are also part of a longer story of mediated violence. Means and methods of warfare are rarely static, particularly since the Industrial Revolution due to the pace of technological development and change. Consider that today's military commanders now have to account for air superiority, or the protection of space-based assets, as a result of technology developed in the nineteenth and twentieth centuries. While some may view the ability of militaries to fight without exposing their personnel to the risk of death as being problematic, this is the way in which militaries have long sought to wage war. After all, in the words of the oft-repeated quote attributed to the Second World War American General George Patton: 'no son of a bitch ever won a war by dying for his country. He won it by making the other poor dumb son of a bitch die for his country.'[20]

Targeted killings therefore force us to recognise that at heart the rules of war are about the regulation of violence, and they do not explicitly require violence to take place as combat. If they did, then a large number of military practices, such as the use of indirect artillery fire and the use of remote sensors, would result in unlawful activity. Such a situation would border on the absurd, if only because the many techniques and technologies developed since the nineteenth century have made reversion to pure forms of direct combat impossible—indirect warfare is now a permanent fixture of war.[21] This is an odd consequence, in the grand scheme of civilised warfare, since the kind of cloak-and-dagger killing that is typically performed by the underdog in an irregular war is something that Western states have often railed against. International law is also structured to render underhand forms of killing illegal—for example, the ban on perfidy.[22] This is not to say that combat is outdated or outmoded, but that some states are now capable of using force and killing in a way that exists beyond common understandings of combat. In this sense, predation is perhaps the acme of military professionalism, rather than a radical departure from wars of the past. Still, the combination of means and method produces a highly asymmetrical relationship as yet unseen in the history of warfare. States have previously developed missiles that can be fired from half a planet away, but the notion of picking out individuals from half a planet away in 'split operations' strikes many, including myself, as qualitatively different.[23] Certainly, we can find continuity in almost all aspects of technology and practice that define American targeted killings. But this law originates in physical warfare between opposed armies. The problem is not so much the misapplication of the rules of war, but the way in which they can now be applied with the aid of novel technologies and systems. What, then, enables the American state to set about destroying a network of terrorists? It begins with information.

Find, fix, finish, exploit, analyse

Intelligence, bureaucracy and logistics are key dimensions to warfare that are usually overlooked in cultural depictions of war. Armies cannot function without information about their operating environment; nor can they fight without food or ammunition. Organising and providing these resources in an efficient manner takes time and effort. In his memoir, General Stanley McChrystal, the man responsible for the Special Forces campaign that killed Zarqawi, wrote that reorganising the way his forces operated was essential to the effort to kill Zarqawi. In McChrystal's words, 'It takes a network to defeat a network.'[24] However, McChrystal's flat network of force elements working as peers was situated within the hierarchical bureaucratic structures of the US military. Still, McChrystal's hybrid military force structure worked better than its predecessor, the question is how and why it did so.

The main idea behind social networks is that the relations between individuals are as important as the individuals themselves: 'the unit of analysis in network analysis is not the individual, but an entity consisting of a collection of individuals and the linkages among them'.[25] What McChrystal wanted to do was effectively a violent form of social network analysis: identify members of a network, capture or kill them, and in the process identify relations that point to as-yet unknown members of the network. The overall aim is to 'kill' the entity by degrading or disrupting the relational ties that hold it together. McChrystal's problem was that his own organisation (which can also be viewed as a network) was too slow at doing this. By reorganising the relationships of his own social network, and improving its connection to other networks (be they intelligence agencies or military units), he was able to speed up this process and achieve his immediate goal: destroying AQI.

The key to understanding McChrystal's mind-set is targeting and the military targeting cycle. Returning to the distinction between warfare as killing and warfare as combat, targeting processes are the bureau-cratic method of producing violence and they lend themselves more towards thinking of warfare as the application of violence, not as com-bat.[26] Although militaries obviously act on the spot as circumstances change, targeting cycles are typically twenty-four to seventy-two hours long for the simple reason that ensuring the availability of assets for a given military operation takes time and effort.[27] For McChrystal, this timescale was too long, since the members of AQI had a vested interest in not being identified or found, and would therefore react to the opera-tions of the US military in an attempt to stay alive. This kind of competi-tive adaptation to circumstances can be found in a variety of similar situ-ations, such as drug cartels reacting to counter-narcotics operations,[28] but it hardly requires academic theory to understand on an intuitive level. Most people would understand that if the US military is hunting you, your best chance of survival is probably to keep moving.

What McChrystal was working against was the inherent anonymity of informal opponents. Surveillance is one of the defining features of irregular warfare, since terrorists and guerrillas rarely separate them selves from the civilian population in the way that state militaries do. Specific symbols of participation, such as the donning of a uniform, serve to separate and identify members of the military from the pub-lic.[29] That said, surveillance is integral to most forms of warfare— observing patterns of enemy activity is a feature of all but the most ritu-alistic acts of collective violence, such as Aztec pitched battles.[30] What separates surveillance of irregular opponents from surveillance in con-ventional wars is the need to identify members of the opposing force/ group as a first step. In the words of Michael Flynn, who served as the director of intelligence of the Joint Special Operations Command under McChrystal: 'Today's enemy is a low-contrast foe easily camouflaged among civilian clutter.'[31] The conventions of inter-state warfare require that their military forces distinguish themselves from the civilian population;[32] however, revolutionary or insurgent forces rarely do this, and it is uncommon for irregular opponents to do so until they have established some form of territorial control. The first problem for state forces in all such conflicts is to distinguish their opponents from the general civilian populace without symbolic guides like uniforms, conventional patterns of military activity (conventional warfare) or defined military equipment such as tanks to aid such identification processes.

The ability of states to identify their opponents should not be taken for granted. It is a difficult activity to undertake with any degree of precision given the paucity of available information. But what is important is the attempt to do so, and the influences on this kind of activity. I have already pointed out how law influences US strategy, and this forecloses the kind of wide-scale direct targeting of civilian populations that characterise state terror, repression and dirty wars. Some states, faced with the problem of irregular or clandestine opponents, resort to strategies where human rights violations and war crimes are integral to success.[33] This requires an abandonment or suspension of the rule of law. For example, in the Battle of Algiers, the French security forces indulged in widespread detention of civilians and committed routine acts of torture in order to glean information on the Front de Libération Nationale (FLN).[34] Given the impossibility of perfectly identifying clandestine opponents, states are faced with the choice of operations that err on the side of caution, or those that will inevitably target a sizeable section of the civilian population. In the case of dirty wars, they are in part defined by the fact that civilians deemed 'subversive' are defined as legitimate targets of attack or detention, even when they take no part in violent operations. Widening the aperture in this way increases the number of people that are going to be killed, but it will still fail to result in perfect targeting. As the Argentinian General Luciano Benjamín Menéndez stated: 'We are going to have to kill 50,000 people: 25,000 subversives, 20,000 sympathisers, and we will make 5,000 mistakes.'[35] Politics and strategy inform these decisions— the military regimes of Latin America were content to target sections of their own population for the purposes of 'national security'—yet even though America kills numerous civilians while waging war on al-Qaeda, the entire concept of this campaign is predicated on the direct targeting of al-Qaeda and its affiliated networks. The rule-abiding character of the Obama administration means that the American state is seeking to attack al-Qaeda and 'associated forces', with senior legal figures such as Harold Koh noting that the administration 'needed to carefully and consistently police the line between lawful and unlawful killings'.[36]

Policing the line requires the American government to adhere to the law of armed conflict, which means that it can, or should, only target individuals that are part of the networks with which they are in an armed conflict. Identifying individual members of clandestine networks with the minimum of disruption to the civilian populace is therefore the name of the game. Of course, there are other ways to go about the same activity. Where states decide to target supporters of insurgent or terrorist groups, mass arrests can sometimes catch important targets, but these tactics are geared towards mass repression, not picking apart a network person by person.[37]

How do you identify a terrorist network without causing considerable collateral damage and disruption to the civilians that they live among? Given that a civilian population is in essence a large social network that contains a myriad number of networks overlaid and connecting to one another, this task could be thought of as identifying a network within a network. In other words, McChrystal and Flynn needed to individuate the AQI network. To do this, they added to the traditional targeting cycle of 'Find, Fix, Finish' and developed the concept of 'F3EA' (standing for Find, Fix, Finish, Exploit, Analyse). This concept requires forces 'to find a target amidst civilian clutter and fix his exact location'.[38] Needless to say, 'finishing' the target involved lethal (or possibly lethal) action by Special Forces and other military assets. In F3EA, the exploit and analyse stages of this otherwise traditional cycle were emphasised. McChrystal wanted to eliminate 'blinks', moments where his forces were unable to keep tracking their targets, which were caused by frictions between JSOC and other intelligence partners, and hamstrung the exploitation and analysis of intelligence. In doing so, it gave JSOC a better chance of turning each 'finish' into an opportunity to identify further potential targets in a timely manner.[39] F3EA places a premium on aerial ISR assets such as drones.[40] This is in part because it requires constant 'unblinking' surveillance in order to function—people move, and they can be quickly lost in urban environments. This was a lesson that US forces learned at their cost in the hunt for Zarqawi, as journalist Chris Woods' interviews with drone pilots makes clear: cars are difficult to track, buildings get in the way, and al-Qaeda adapted to the new reality of drones overhead. It was only once the United States was able to mass ISR assets on a target that they could overcome these physical limitations. At one point in the hunt for Zarqawi, he escaped a strike by leaving a car in the brief period in which the drone pilots had lost track of the vehicle.[41]

If we think back to the discussion of decapitation operations in Chapter 4, the shift of emphasis here is clear: despite the centrality of Zarqawi to AQI, it was the ability to routinely identify members of the network at speed that was key to defeating them. By making the exploitation and analysis of lethal operations the 'main effort', F3EA shifts the emphasis of military operations to intelligence collection. Flynn's use of the term 'low-contrast enemy' indicates a concept of the enemy as small self-organising networks that 'remain low contrast until time to strike and then quickly blend back into the population'.[42] Rather than targeting a support network of civilians and supporters, F3EA envisions ripping apart these networks by using each offensive operation as a means of identifying other members of the network. Again, this resembles a violent form of social science, namely the 'snowball sampling' or 'chain referral sampling' method, whereby social scientists rely upon the help of initial study participants to identify others. JSOC raids were therefore not ends in themselves, but a chance to collect more intelligence. Here, the use of Special Forces to conduct raids is clearly more effective than stand-off kills using aerial platforms. This kind of military activity is in many cases closer to lethal police action than the battle and combat that typifies war in the popular imagination. That is not to say that this type of activity is 'not war', but that it exemplifies war waged between states and non-state actors where the state sticks to an interpretation of the rules of war that does not expand targeting to the 'civilian infrastructure' of a target group.

But McChrystal and Flynn were working against one cohesive section of al-Qaeda, in a single geographic space, at one specific moment in time. How, then, does this help us understand the use of targeted killings in places like Pakistan and Yemen? The example is important because it gives us a window into the military mind-set—how organisations like JSOC view al-Qaeda. But that does not necessarily cover Pakistan, since we cannot count on the CIA to follow the exact same procedures as the military.[43] It is fair to expect that both are working in accordance with the US government's published policy guidance on targeted killings, but these standards do not shed additional light on the categories of persons.[44]

The reason this is important in a general sense is that the core activity—picking out a terrorist network from the civilians it coexists with—is the key process of targeted killings. This is reflected in the similarities between the F3EA concept and the similar standardised processes that drive the use of targeted killings in a transnational context.[45] Moreover, the capability to conduct targeted killings relies upon the same infrastructure, regardless of the overall bureaucracy in charge. Yes, there is evidence that the CIA and the US military had different standards for acceptable civilian casualties, but then these standards are policy choices and political in nature—they are set by the White House.[46] The US military varies the level of acceptable civilian casualties depending upon the type and importance of individual operations or conflicts.[47] The net result is that there is more similarity than difference between the two. The CIA and the military are two different (and sometimes overlapping) branches of government waging the same war with more or less the same intent: destroy al-Qaeda with the minimum amount of collateral damage and destruction.

With this in mind, we can see that drone strikes and Special Forces raids are the tip of the iceberg. The heavy lifting is in many senses the intelligence collection and analysis that provides the backbone to America's use of targeted killings. What differentiates America's campaign is not only its scope, but the degree to which it is a product of the digital age.

Digital surveillance

Much has been made of the 'unblinking stare' of drones like the Predator and Reaper. Critical theorists like Chamayou have dedicated entire chapters to understanding this 'all-seeing eye'.[48] While it's true that drones do provide a special capability of persistent surveillance this needs to be seen in the wider context of the 'digitalisation' of society, or 'the way in which many domains of social life are restructured around digital communication and media infrastructures'.[49] The use of Special Forces to hunt and kill or capture non-conventional opponents is hardly new. And the same clearly applies to warfare conducted against guerrillas or insurgents. If we want to identify the novel elements in America's use of targeted killings, then it is necessary to think about the global switch from analogue to digital information communication technologies. In this sense, the combined information processing capabilities of the US military and intelligence community matters more than what can be seen through a single sensor platform.

It is hard to understate the impact of the digital revolution on war and warfare. Without digital ICTs, Predators and Reapers would not exist; nor, one suspects, would al-Qaeda. A transnational terrorist network could not exist in the same form in the pre-digital era. Moreover, digital intelligence collection and analysis is the backbone of targeted killings, just as it supports all forms of police and military operations in the present day.

Part of the problem is that we now live in digital societies, and much of this technology is now prosaic and mundane to the point that the degree to which it enables our day-to-day lives is often taken for granted. There are two principal changes that I want to focus upon here: the new scales of information processing enabled by digital ICTs, and the new forms of surveillance inherent in the widespread adoption of digital ICTs.

To understand the new scales of information processing, we can compare America's contemporary targeted killing campaign with American intelligence assistance to South Vietnam during the Vietnam War, known as the Phoenix Program. The program, which took place on the cusp of the digital era, was an attempt to identify and target the civilian support networks of Viet Cong. Given that this overall activity often resulted in the torture or murder of those identified as helping the opponents of South Vietnam, this activity was controversial, to say the least. Yet the CIA were not the ones killing people; instead, they were providing the information processing capability to South

Vietnam's security forces. The ability to store large volumes of information in card systems enabled the cross-referencing of this information to identify potential members of the Viet Cong's support network as a follow-on from early 'anti-infrastructure operations'.[50] Phoenix also demonstrated the political sensitivity of such data—the recognition that Viet Cong support was much larger than the public estimates of its strength caused bureaucratic and internal political tensions.[51]

This system was rudimentary by today's standards. In a pre-digital era, all information had to be stored, searched and analysed by human beings, although some automated data-retrieval systems existed, for example in the Combined Intelligence Centre, Vietnam (CICV).[52] By comparison, when JSOC found a mobile phone in a raid in Iraq, it could transmit that number to the NSA, who were able to query a computer database that held records of every mobile telephone call in Iraq (since the networks had been switched back on) in order to identify patterns of calls and connections between that phone and others that might belong to other members of AQI.[53] Without these organisational connections, computerised databases and methods of analysis, the kind of campaign that McChrystal ran against AQI would have been impossible. Without similar capabilities, targeted killings directed at members of al-Qaeda would also be impossible.

From this perspective, one of the most important technologies behind targeted killings, though we do not generally consider it as such, is the use of computerised databases. The computer database has become such an important and commonplace part of everyday life that we often fail to consider quite how revolutionary it is. Before the invention of the computerised database, all data was stored in complex physical file systems, where the bulk of work was performed by the user of the file system.[54] If the CIA wanted to provide their counterparts with information in Vietnam, then someone had to physically retrieve that information and cross-reference it by hand. That takes time and effort, and limits the overall speed of an organisation. All organisations have a limited pool of available personnel, and time spent retrieving information detracts from the time available to analyse, process and communicate information to counterparts.

The advent of computers allowed for digital storage, but it did not change the essential relationship between the human user and the system itself. Furthermore, the human users of databases had to know how the information was stored on the system in order to use them. This meant that a user had to know how the data within a given data retrieval system was stored in order to find it. The transition to digital storage was important, but the real change was in the reduction of knowledge required to access it. This shift dates to 1970, when an IBM engineer, Edgar F. Codd, proposed a 'relational model of data' as a way of storing data as values in tables that could be queried by users, without users needing to know the relations between data points, or memorising the structural trees within which data was stored in physical databases.[55] In the present context, relational databases matter because they allow for the storage and efficient retrieval of information at a scale far beyond that which is possible in analogue physical libraries and archives. By the 2000s, relational database management systems (RDBMS) underpinned the digital age. Large companies such as Oracle (whose initial incarnation Relational Software, Inc. developed the first commercial RDBMS in 1979), IBM and Microsoft provided the capability for governments and companies to store and access large volumes of information.

Large-scale databases were not new, of course, since census surveys by states, tax records and so on have been common state practice for decades, if not centuries in some places. The digital revolution, however, made the storage and retrieval of information cheaper, and more effective. In the 1980s, commercial marketing companies began to build up large databases of information about people, which they could then use to target marketing at persons they thought would buy given targeted products. The digitisation of these databases (which enabled many to be constructed without loss in the first place) also enabled companies to add additional data as it was acquired, and it also meant that anyone with access to more than one database could cross-reference them. If this sounds similar to the stories that you may have read in the media about the volumes of personal data collected by technology companies like Google and Facebook, that is because all these companies have built business models on the collection, analysis and sale of data about people and populations. Database marketing companies were perhaps the first to demonstrate that it was possible for private organisations to acquire levels of information about society itself that even governments could not collect. By way of example, as of 2012, Acxiom Corporation—owners of one of the largest marketing databases—held information on about 500 million active consumers around the world, each person tracked by about 1,500 individual data points that taken together gave the company some idea of who they were and what they might want to buy.[56]

What has helped, of course, is the general transition from analogue modes of communication to digital ones. Since digital communications systems require databases in order to function as infrastructure, this has had the near-automatic effect of creating huge databases of personal information. This means that the political importance of signals intelligence, or the gleaning of information from communications and communications systems, has transformed in the contemporary world. We now live in an era where intelligence services routinely access the civilian communications networks that constitute the internet, a practice that the former head of the UK's GCHQ, David Omand, refers to as 'digital intelligence'.[57] But this also means the ability to access scales of information unheard of in previous eras. We live in the era of 'big data' where companies like Google process 'more than 24 petabytes of data per day, a volume that is thousands of times the quantity of all printed material in the U.S. Library of Congress'.[58] Signals intelligence collection in the context of global digitisation could be used to identify patterns of interaction, which, in turn, could identify networks of individuals within populations. Large volumes of collected information, combined with new computing hardware and techniques for processing them, extended the ability of statisticians to derive meaning from excessive quantities of data. Given the amount of data produced by society, the capture of a fraction of this data in digital form dwarfs the amount of information that could be collected by intelligence agencies in the past. Recent examples of this include GCHQ's Tempora programme, which gave the UK intelligence agency 'access to 10 gigabits of data a second, or 21 petabytes a day'.[59] Furthermore, the digitisation of information allows computer programmes to do the heavy lifting of processing and comparison in order to identify patterns that human beings would be unable to spot or process.

Returning to the example of AQI, it is obvious that a central element of American success was the ability to leverage digital intelligence to their advantage. The NSA's tracking of mobile phone calls in Iraq enabled Special Forces to hunt down AQI and Zarqawi.[60] The NSA had access to a dataset that could be queried to identify the call records or communications patterns since the restart of cellular networks after the fall of Saddam. This meant that the past activity of a found phone could be cross-checked against existing information about AQI. These kinds of call record logs are impossible to maintain in analogue systems without specific targeting. The digital aspect is therefore important, as Stephen Graham and David Wood argued in 2003, since the use of automated surveillance systems 'enables monitoring, prioritization and judgement to occur across widening geographical distances and with little time delay' and 'it allows the active sorting, identification, prioritization and tracking of bodies, behaviours and characteristics of subject populations on a continuous, real-time basis'.[61]

Looking beyond Iraq, it is clear that this kind of digital surveillance has a transformative effect on the American ability to map and identify its opponents in places its own forces are unable to reach. Waging war against terrorist networks integrated with civilians at the fringes of state authority places limits on intelligence collection. Even if the United States, or its local allies, wanted to round up civilians, they lack the means to do so. Whereas American efforts in Vietnam under the Phoenix Program had the assistance of a state that could detain and interrogate people, that same authority is not applicable in places such as Pakistan or Somalia. The existence of Yemen's ongoing civil war places a fundamental limit on the state's reach and authority, even before the recent onset of violence that saw the president flee the country in March 2015.[62] For this reason, human intelligence—intelligence derived from human sources and informants—is limited. As Daniel Byman points out, 'SIGINT [signals intelligence] often provides reach where HUMINT [human intelligence] cannot: getting a spy to tribal parts of Pakistan, for example, is exceptionally difficult, but SIGINT is able to reach there.'[63] As a result, intelligence collection involving observation, in a variety of forms, or surveillance, is one of the primary means of identifying potential targets. Predator and Reaper drones are the most tangible and visible aspect of American surveillance, but their primary role appears to be in providing a specific form of information—where a person or object is at a given place and point in time. Much of the intelligence used to identify members of al-Qaeda falls under the broad definition of signals intelligence. As societies have increased their use of computers, a greater and greater proportion of information that might be used to identify citizens, and their intentions, is now amenable to bulk collection and analysis.

Timeliness is important, and digital information can be compared in both unprecedented volume and speed. Although real-time pattern analysis and person-tracking, of the type found in science fiction stories like *Minority Report* (later a film) and television programmes such as *Person of Interest* depict capabilities that are far too precise and accurate, intelligence agencies are developing institutional practices that seek 'activity-based intelligence'—patterns of life and action that can identify individuals. Activity-based intelligence 'is an analysis methodology which rapidly integrates data from multiple INTs [intelligence collection disciplines] and sources around the interactions of people, events and activities, in order to discover relevant patterns, determine and identify change, and characterize those patterns to drive collection and create decision advantage'.[64] In the next chapter, I will expand on the different types of information available, and the degree to which extrapolations from data and intelligence are vital in understanding American claims about precision, but for time being, the different modes of intelligence collection are more important. The difference between current American targeted killings and similar forms of warfare that have gone before lies in the volume of data that can be collected and its transformation into useful intelligence. The consequence, however, is that this assembled activity is for the most part intangible, yet these decisions translate into violence. In combination with the transnational nature of America's war, this means that violence becomes both immediate and difficult to observe in broad geographic regions where drones and Special Forces operate.

Remote and imminent violence

If the concept of physical remoteness fails to explain much of what is novel about American targeted killings, it also impairs our ability to recognise the consequential scope of this kind of warfare. Some actions can be differentiated in terms of distance. Whether someone fires a weapon from Creech Air Force Base in Nevada, or sitting in a cockpit above their target, or while standing directly in front of them, is the analytical frame that the concept of remoteness and physical presence draws us into. But what about the 'legal memos locked in a D.O.J safe', to quote a former director of the CIA, General Michael Hayden, that result in the deaths of bystanders half a world away?[65] Would it make a difference if these constitutive elements of American action were physically present at the scene of violence? Some argue that the problem of remote warfare is that it physically removes a person from the location of violence, and therefore changes how they make life or death decisions. While valid to a degree, the greater problem is the perpetual threat of imminent violence—the way in which the threat of violence becomes an imminent, and impossible to perceive, threat to people in wide geographical regions. Aerial platforms and missiles give states the capability to use violence over large regions, but the effective reach of this capability is determined by available intelligence. The particular issue here is that coupling aerial platforms with large datasets, and the bureaucracies required to analyse them, creates a new kind of capability, one that enables states to reach out and target individuals at a distance as a matter of routine. This is not to say this is illegal; quite the opposite, it is because this is justifiable under the law of armed conflict that this becomes a sustainable condition.

America's current transnational use of targeted killings differs from previous forms of irregular warfare since they largely remove American forces from immediate danger. The reliance upon drones to conduct violence also means that the people charged with the final act of killing find themselves very close, albeit in the form of virtual telepresence. The decision-makers are present, even when they are sitting in a ground control station half a world away. But physical remoteness doesn't necessarily mean emotional disconnection. The military personnel charged with launching ballistic or cruise missiles sometimes don't even know the target of their weapons, let alone view them. In contrast, drone pilots report emotional intimacy that comes from hours spent surveilling targets, sometimes as a prelude to attacking them.[66]

This closeness is a product of the military practices designed to reduce the risk of collateral damage and perform battle damage assessments,[67] as well as the operational requirement to collect intelligence after a strike, which means that drone pilots spend copious amounts of time 'on station' in a virtual sense. So much so that they often spend far longer watching their targets than a pilot in a manned aeroplane that may only have minutes 'on station' in a position to fire.[68] John Brennan, speaking as Barack Obama's senior advisor for counter-terrorism, noted that 'compared against other options, a pilot operating this [drone] aircraft remotely might actually have a clearer picture of the target and its surroundings, including the presence of innocent civilians'.[69] In this sense, although physically removed, drone pilots are far more present at their location than equivalent pilots would be.

Despite the physical distance of the operator, drones (and the intelligence apparatus that enables them) create the perpetual threat of violence in their operational area. The same is also true of Special Forces raids. Therefore, instead of physical presence, it makes more sense to consider the imminence of warfare.

The particular issue of disembodied war-fighting goes hand in hand with the issue of imminent violence. This, it must be remembered, is in marked contrast to earlier forms of irregular warfare. When states go to war with insurgents and guerrillas, their opponents can always strike back at the state's operatives, or at state assets that the state wishes to protect. The vulnerability of the state's buildings and employees to random attack is a powerful tool of insurgents and guerrillas.[70] Balancing the need to protect state forces against the need to employ them in offensive operations is integral to counterinsurgency doctrine.[71]

Remote forms of warfare remove some direct forms of violence such as the predation of soldiers in armed groups on nearby civilians,[72] but it does not necessarily decrease the imminent threat of violence to civilians in general. The violence and destruction that a hellfire missile can wreak is tiny compared to the overall American arsenal. Moreover, Predators can only carry two such missiles, although MQ-9 Reapers can carry up to sixteen.[73] The problem for civilians in these areas is that America's campaign appears, from the ground up, to be capricious. The possibility of violence, however limited, remains imminent, and when delivered from air platforms, civilians feel threatened as possible targets over a wide geographic range. The wedding party killed near Radda (discussed in the last chapter) is but one example of civilians suffering from this imminence who were probably unaware that they were minutes or seconds from being killed but no doubt conscious of the possibility, given ongoing American operations in the country. For this reason, the imminent but uncertain threat of violence is a fact of life in many of the areas where America conducts targeted killings.

Militaries at war understand that death is both a possible and probable outcome of their enterprise. When lawyers speak of the law of armed conflict, members of state armed forces with combatant status can lawfully kill, but may also be lawfully killed. This relationship 'illustrates the downside of combatancy: A lawful combatant enjoys the combatant's privilege, but also is a continuing lawful target.'[74] In theory, all service personnel face exactly the same threat of being killed at any time, but in practicality, this has never been the case. The Second World War was global in scope, but there were still areas of the world that were relatively untouched by its conduct. All types of war typically involve civilians and neutrals who, even if a state wished to kill them, are located in districts so remote that any practical effort to do so is futile. In other words, though for the most part people involved in wars may be liable to be killed at any time, most of their lives are spent without any immediate or foreseeable threat of violence.

Not so with drones. It's clear that there is a gap between America's actual use of drones in Pakistan and Yemen, and the perceptions of their use. Nonetheless, civilian perceptions of America's activities matter, and they have consequences. A number of surveys have now reported data that points out that persons 'living under drones' (to use the title of one New York University study) suffer from psychological effects due to the constant use or presence of drones.[75] Like most wars, the actual danger of violence is relatively slim, but the threat or prospect of violence is a cause of stress and psychological harm, even if studies demonstrate a 'direct correlation between the degree of trauma and the amount of psychological problems'.[76] I will consider this question in greater depth in Chapter 8, but for the time being we should note the role of technology in this, since the idea that a state could occupy 'a geographical space by a foreign power through the constant presence of airborne military force' is relatively new.[77]

Campaigns of state repression cultivate fear as a means of control. Making people disappear seemingly at random is not simply about eliminating political opposition, but about inculcating fear and subservience into sections of the population that might otherwise support them.[78] American targeted killings are not intended to terrorise populations, but the means of killing—armed drones—still inculcate civilians with a fear of these craft.

There are ways of interpreting this fear as forms of legal transgression even if, as Eliav Lieblich points out: 'while positive IHL is unequivocal about the need to prevent or at least minimise civilian harm, it does not tell us—beyond the obvious—what this harm is'.[79] Lieblich points out that 'incidental mental harm' is a particular blind spot—that the restrictions on causing mental harm are ill-defined or non-existent in international law. Whereas the intentional spreading of terror and fear is prohibited, the consequential terrorisation of civilians by the existence of armed conflict and violence is not.[80] Fear of death or injury is one of what the Civil War-era American general William Tecumseh Sherman referred to as the 'hardships of war'.[81] Even if it is not directly prohibited by the law of armed conflict, the fact remains that the precise and targeted methods used by the United States, even if they are not as precise as the Americans claim, still reproduce this hardship at a distance, regardless of precision.

For societies that lived in fear of a nuclear exchange for the duration of the Cold War, these nuclear weapons were an imminent threat to everyone. Although not in direct, existential confrontation, nuclear weapon states still point nuclear weapons at one another. Writing this book in London, I am conscious of the fact that there is probably a nuclear weapon somewhere in the world with pre-set coordinates that would kill me if used. Such fears are allayed in part by the lack of an overarching political confrontation between nuclear weapon states. The same cannot be said for those living in areas beneath drones.

The threat posed by America's war is not restricted to regions where it employs violence. The information processing capability of the US military and intelligence community allows it to wage transnational war, but also gives it unparalleled reach. Recent material published by a former NSA contractor Edward Snowden gives some idea of the scale of information that intelligence agencies are now able to collect and share.[82] Despite the lack of available detail, it seems clear that digital surveillance represents a significant shift of power from the private citizen and society towards the state. The mediation of many previously analogue activities to the digital sphere not only makes it easier for intelligence agencies to collect information and intelligence but it also makes it harder for their targets to avoid such collection. The cat-and-mouse activities of intelligence agencies and their subjects now affect the entire world—efforts to break encryption and introduce security flaws into ISPs weaken the overall protection of all internet users.[83] In the words of Bruce Schneier, a leading expert on computer security, the NSA has subverted the internet 'at every level to make it a vast, multi-layered and robust surveillance platform'.[84] Without this form of intelligence collection, not only would war against transnational terrorist networks be impossible, but it would be harder to target domestic criminal networks and traditional state opponents and terrorist networks, although all three are increasing their use of encrypted communications that states find difficult to intercept and understand.[85]

What we can therefore say about America's war on al-Qaeda is that, unlike the Phoenix Program, it has transnational consequences, including upon the American public. Maintaining the traditional freedom of action of intelligence agencies in the digital era means the implicit extension of state power due to the nature of computer networks and their exploitation. This reflects the interplay between culture and technology. Computer systems contain inbuilt rules and structures, which may be invisible to the end-user, but are often a design feature, rather than a mandatory requirement of computer systems.[86] Human-crafted rules are inherent in the messy process of translating analogue observations into digital data for the purposes of storage and comparison. Yes, sensors are biased to some degree, since one might only sense certain types of data such as heat, movement, or telephone calls. But code reflects the operating imperatives of the user. For example, software can include hard-coded digital translations of the legal restrictions on intelligence collection. The NSA is barred from collecting data on American citizens in many circumstances by the 1978 Foreign Intelligence Surveillance Act.[87] Nonetheless, it has the authority to collect data where authorised either by a court order or by a presidential order reviewed by the attorney general.[88]

The systems that collect and store digital intelligence cannot make the same kind of judgements that humans do. For this reason, the designers and programmers of these systems have to ensure to some degree that they do not collect information in an illegal manner. Given that computer systems need to process information independent of direct human supervision, this means that legal constraints have to be translated into computer programs. One upshot of this is that the protections of citizenship become dependent upon probabilistic assessments built into computer code. The strict restrictions on intelligence activities relating to US citizens, for example, translates into the use of systems whereby 'at least 51 percent confidence in a target's "foreignness"' is enough to warrant data collection.[89] These kinds of judgements are inevitable in processing large volumes of digital data, but even so, a 51 per cent chance of being correct seems little different from flipping a coin. This dimension of America's war lies mostly beyond the scope of this book, but it is necessary to highlight this in the course of examining the consequences of American targeted killings. Of course, America's intelligence community exists independent of its conflict with al-Qaeda, but there is little doubt that its current shape and purpose has been driven by American policy since 9/11.

Conclusion

American targeted killings reduce warfare and violence to the individual level, but the reach of American capabilities leaves the imminent threat of violence hanging over large geographical regions. As I have explained in this chapter, this is a by-product of the way the United States seeks to degrade and destroy al-Qaeda by identifying and killing members of this group.

As I have demonstrated here, American targeted killings are anything but remote and impersonal, as they rely upon huge volumes of intelligence collection and processing. When one considers the amount of effort and resources that go into a single targeted killing, it is clear that this is one of the greatest asymmetries involved in the entire activity. This is not, however, the end of the story. What this points to is the critical role that information processing and knowledge formation plays in American targeted killings. As we have seen, this emphasis on information processing and legal categorisation is due to cultural constraints and the need to adhere to the rule of law. This points to two important issues. The first is the role that this intelligence production plays in adhering to the law of armed conflict, while the second is the way that this conflict relates to the civilians caught between the United States and al-Qaeda.

7

KILLING THROUGH A MONITOR, DARKLY

... if the scanner sees only darkly, the way I myself do, ... we'll wind up dead this way, knowing very little and getting that little fragment wrong too.'

Philip K. Dick, *A Scanner Darkly*[1]

Introduction

It is impossible to escape identity when thinking about war, as how a society regards and identifies its opponents is part and parcel of any resort to political violence. Opposing societies are often personified. With some justification, warring societies tend to identify political and military leaders as figureheads for enemy nations or states. Therefore, it should not surprise us that upon killing Osama bin Laden, the leader of al-Qaeda, US President Barack Obama addressed the world and stated that 'The death of bin Laden marks the most significant achievement to date in our nation's effort to defeat al Qaeda.'[2] But even though the specific circumstances of bin Laden's death were remarkable—American Special Forces teams raided the Abbottabad compound where he was hiding in Pakistan without contacting the Pakistani government, which caused outrage in Pakistan—the wider circumstances of his death were not. For years since 9/11, America had been identifying, then capturing or killing, members of al-Qaeda and groups affiliated to it.

The particularities of law aside, war divides human beings into categories of people that may be killed and those that should be protected. A person may be killed because they are a combatant, or because they are directly participating in hostilities, whereas civilians 'enjoy general protection against the effects of hostilities'.[3] Grey areas such as the killing of civilians as a consequence of attacking a military target—referred to as 'collateral damage'—blur the boundaries somewhat, but this binary division between people (and objects) that can be attacked and those that cannot underpins the rules of war.

Combatant and civilian are legal terms of art as well as words that denote a set of moral characteristics. The connection between individual human beings and these categories of status in the context of war and armed conflict is important, but in a certain sense this connection is often assumed in discussions regarding the legality or morality of killing in war. Often, it appears that a combatant 'is' a combatant, just as a civilian 'is' a civilian, without due regard to the processes of observation and judgment that leads human beings to come to such conclusions. Legitimate violence in war requires active judgement: although the pressures of close combat may involve violence committed on reflex, the vast bulk of literature concerning the law and morality of violence focuses upon situations in which choices are made. The core normative principles of distinction, proportionality and necessity are all matters of human judgement.[4]

The categories implicit in the rules of war constitute identities that are often in tension with identification—either self-identification or third-party identification. Irregular warfare highlights this gap. For example, in Northern Ireland, members of the IRA believed themselves to be soldiers, and therefore deserving of the treatment accorded to soldiers in times of war—particularly since they were treated as common criminals and prosecuted as such by the British government when captured.[5]

Overlapping and coexisting legal frameworks give rise to multiple identities. Anwar al-Awlaki was one man, but he had many legal identities at once: as a person whose human rights must be respected, as a US citizen with Constitutional rights, as a Yemeni citizen with rights owed by the Yemeni government, and, as the Americans argue, as a person who fulfilled the criteria for legally permissible killing in the context of an armed conflict.[6] These overlapping legal frameworks restrict the US government, and its agents, from using lethal force against a person in very different ways.

How states identify people is therefore a critical issue. Processes of identification, and the assignment of an identity, is an integral part of the process that ends in a drone strike or Special Forces raid. In the present day, the US government has developed a 'Disposition Matrix'— a targeting list to track terrorist targets and keep track of the range of available options to either kill or capture them. The collected judgements that place people on this list, alongside the legal judgments of the US government's senior legal staff that identify that person as satisfying the criteria of a lawful target, allows them to be targeted by American forces should they be able to reach them.[7] As we have seen in the previous chapter, this kind of analysis and sorting is integral to American targeted killings. The 'AUMF CONOPS Approval process' (henceforth, 'AUMF process') that takes a median time of 35.5 days to approve the categorisation of a person as a permissible target is integral to the overall activity.[8] This process, however, occurs behind closed doors. Hina Shamsi from the ACLU criticised this process because 'we cannot be assured that the people in the government's death database truly present a concrete, imminent threat to the country'.[9] Uncertainty and the lack of such assurances are integral to the way the United States is currently waging its war on al-Qaeda.

Identity and processes of identification are inherent in a set of criticisms about the American use of targeted killings. Prevailing themes, such as the killing of civilians[10] and children,[11] are linked to other specific criticisms—that the United States 'is repeatedly missing its target', that it is wrong to classify people as 'military age males' in battle damage assessments instead of treating them as civilians,[12] because 'how can it know whether those killed are civilians?'[13] Furthermore critics allege that the US interpretation of the law relevant to defining individuals as lawful targets is wrong or sometimes relies upon 'legally inadequate signatures'.[14] A further issue is the differentiation between 'personality strikes' and those that are targeted at people identified as lawful targets, whose exact identity is unknown, so-called 'signature strikes'.[15] Inherent in all of these is a tension between the supposed objectivity of the categories defined by the rules of war and the subjective processes of identification that classify people as belonging to them. How militaries and states negotiate this tension—a problem far wider than transnational warfare and targeted killings—is the underlying object of criticism in the debates regarding targeted killings. These targeting processes are undoubtedly exercises of power, and the act of identifying a person as a permissible target is an exercise of power.

Identity and warfare

The controversy over the American use of signature strikes revolves around identity—who are the people that America is killing, and on what basis is it judging them to be lawful targets? Much has been made of the difference—real, theorised or imagined—between 'normal' attacks, targeted killings and the targeting method known as either a 'signature strike', or a 'terrorist attack disruption strike'.[16]

Signature strikes are also referred to as 'pattern of life' killings. That is, by observation and reference to a large variety of intelligence, the US military and the CIA identify certain patterns of life as being hallmarks of persons that they define as legitimate military targets. In other words, if a person's activities fit a given pattern associated with, say, being a member of a belligerent group, then the American government considers it legal and legitimate to kill them. Some, like Glenn Greenwald, consider this to be plainly illegal:

> How can any minimally rational person continue to walk around defending Obama's drone kills on the ground that they are killing The Terrorists or that civilian deaths are rare when even the government, let alone these defenders, often have no clue who is being targeted and then killed?[17]

The notion that it is lawful to kill a person without knowing exactly who they are is, to people who think this way, a gross breach of the fundamental principle of distinction. Signature strikes, however, are only one aspect of a more general problem that is apparent in the use of targeted killings and highlighted by the transnational nature of America's war. This is the intersection of identity, knowledge and rules of war, and the way in which these interact to authorise violence. In practical terms: Who is it lawful for a belligerent to kill in a war? What must be known about a person in order to categorise them as a lawful target and what role, if any, does their identity play in the process of targeting?

The rules of war produce the concept of status—categories of person who may, or may not, be the object of direct attack. Referring to this type of 'status-based' killing, Samuel Issacharoff and Richard H. Pildes note that the US military killed Admiral Yamamoto because he was a member of an opposing army.[18] However, they also argue that 'we are ... now moving to a world which implicitly or explicitly requires the individuation of personal responsibility of specific "enemy" persons before the use of military force is considered justified'.[19]

In other words, something more than status is now required in order to legitimise the use of 'all exertions of military power over enemies', which requires far more detail about their identity.[20] In this, Issacharoff and Pildes are partly correct—judgements about responsibility on an individual level do appear to factor in the decisions made by senior government lawyers as to whether a person can be targeted.[21] Yet the need to individuate personal responsibility is not a reflection of a change in the law, or legitimacy, but is instead a product of the kind of war that America is waging. A person's name, their family connections or friendship circles—all the elements that constitute their personal identity—are not essential for identifying them as a lawful target if they are wearing a uniform in an inter-state armed conflict. Conversely, such connections and fragments of identifiable information about a person may be the only way of identifying them as a member of a terrorist or guerrilla network. Even if legal categories remain stable, the character of the parties involved in a conflict will in part define what military commanders need to know in order to authorise attacks.

Part of the problem is how we think of, and conceive, decisions to use force that rely upon identification. Military advantage, integral to judging military necessity and proportionality, is defined by the type of war being waged. In the same sense, our idea of what constitutes an armed force is related to wars of the past, even though forms of state military organisation have demonstrably changed in the past 200 years. Rupert Smith writes that:

> Our understanding of war is based in large measure on the old paradigm of interstate industrial war: concepts founded on conflict between states,

the manoeuvre of forces en masse, and the total support of the state's manpower and industrial base, at the expense of all other interests, for the purpose of an absolute victory.[22]

We can contrast this with other types of warfare. For example, in the seventeenth century, European rulers 'outsourced their military responsibility and military authority' to fight wars 'based upon complex calculations of potential profit, systems of credit, and extensive networks of subcontractors'.[23] Nonetheless, Smith is correct with regard to our present shared image: modern conventional wars remain the prevailing idea of war and warfare, even if these industrial wars co-existed with asymmetric and colonial wars that often bore little resemblance to those he was writing about in this description. The difference between industrial warfare and America's present-day conflict is the level of personal information required to ascertain membership of a belligerent group.

The crux of the problem is the difference between the phrase 'a person who is identified as a terrorist by' and 'a person who is a terrorist'—whether identity or status is an objective truth, or the product of subjective observation and judgement. As Valentin Groebner puts it:

> 'Identity' thus refers today to several things at once. First, it refers to an individual's subjective self-definition, that is, to the identity of the self. Second, it stands for the heteronymous or external description of a second-person singular, that is, a person's distinguishing marks and classification. Finally, 'identity' is used to assign an individual to a particular group, to a set of collective features that the individual either represents or would like to represent.[24]

The law and ethics of war depend upon the categories of status to which a person belongs, and these categories are akin to Groebner's third class of identity. The foundational principles that govern the conduct of war—distinction and proportionality—are both predicated upon categories of status.

Distinction in contemporary positive and customary law means that parties to an armed conflict must distinguish between military targets and impermissible targets. This presupposes two general categories by which a person or object could be defined, but the complexity of international law is such that some precise categories only exist in certain types of armed conflict, whereas others transcend the particular type of armed conflict.[25] When discussing distinction, however, these categories of status are often described in objective terms—that a person 'is' a civilian or combatant, rather than being someone commonly identified 'as' a civilian or combatant. In practical terms, unless a person communicates information about their status (such as by wearing a uniform), we inhabit a world where people are forced to make judgements based upon the available information in order to identify someone as having a given status. It is for this reason that wearing a uniform is a requirement for combatant status in the law of armed conflict.[26]

Uncertainty and the lack of available information, commonly termed the 'fog of war', is usually blamed for identification errors. However generating uncertainty is inherent in war and warfare—military practice requires keeping an opposing force off-balance. Uncertain opponents hesitate to act, and exploiting such hesitancy can lead to decisive advantages at the tactical, operational and strategic levels. Despite this, one of the defining features of lawful combatants is that they are not meant to disguise their identity. While they are able to use ruses and camouflage, they are not meant to pretend that they are civilians, and have to distinguish themselves from the civilian population.

One accompaniment to Smith's idea of industrial war is that this form of warfare makes it possible to state that someone 'is' a soldier or enemy belligerent. Wars involving formal state armies fighting each other en masse give us stable categories as well as accepted regimes of identification. At a symbolic level, the practical organisation of industrial-era militaries as well as their use of uniforms meant that a combatant's private life and identity is not required in order to work out whether they had the status of combatant, and hence whether they could be killed or not. Irregular warfare, however, involves a specific type of uncertainty generation—where participants deprive their state opponents of the ability to identify them as participants in an armed conflict. This is quite understandable—the power imbalances inherent in guerrilla or insurgent conflicts mean that, if the state's armed forces were able to pick out its opponents, they would quickly win. Asymmetric wars therefore typically lack a shared basis for identifying participants by design—state definitions of membership in an armed group will not match the identity of the opposed group. Moreover, guerrillas, insurgents and terrorists usually organise themselves in such a way that they cannot be easily identified, at least until they are able to defend themselves from direct attacks by military forces.

The fluid nature of identity serves to differentiate between different forms of violence that are described as targeted killings. At a basic level of abstraction, Abu al-Harithi and Admiral Yamamoto died for the same reason: both men belonged to groups with which America considered itself to be at war. At the same level of abstraction, identity played the same role of providing US forces with a single, personal, target of attack. Yet such a level of abstraction erases the important differences that the role of identity played in the two attacks. This is both the way in which the targets considered their own identity, as well as the way that they identified themselves to their opponents. Yamamoto did not seek to hide his identity, even though he took sensible precautions in wartime to prevent the US Navy from discovering his location. While some members of al-Qaeda might serve as public figureheads, most are conscious of the fact that being identified as a member of al-Qaeda is dangerous in and of itself. As a side-note, al-Harithi's killing also highlights the role of new forms of information such as biometrics: a CIA officer had to be sent in to collect the forensic samples that could verify the identity of the dead.[27]

The discontinuities between the two cases outweigh the continuities that link them. The same applies to other military uses of targeted killings, or state violence that amounts to a targeted killing campaign. The best way of explaining this difference is to explore the differences between the legal status of both men. In military terms, Yamamoto was a combatant because he was a uniformed member of the Japanese Navy; however, al-Harithi, if he had a status in the law of armed conflict, would be a civilian who was directly participating in hostilities. The problem is that this latter category of person is very contentious, beyond the specific issue of targeted killings.

This leads us to the matter at hand: To what degree, if any, can a person's 'pattern of life' identify them as belonging to a category in the law of armed conflict? To answer such a question, we first need to distinguish between a person 'as' a combatant, and a person 'identified as' a combatant. This requires thinking through the role of identity in a wider sense than restricting discussion to who 'is' and who 'isn't' a legal target in warfare. Furthermore, it means doing so in the dark, so to speak, since the nature of targeted killings means that the information that constitutes a military's knowledge about the people it kills is often secret.

The social construction of direct participation

Understanding American targeted killings—and its use of force against al-Qaeda in general—requires an appreciation of the American interpretation of the law relevant to targeting irregular opponents as well as the difference between America's interpretation and other interpretations of the applicable rules. Although treaties, or 'black letter law', are static without renegotiation, customary international law, and the interpretation of treaties, occurs in a social context, both national and international—categories that are produced by the social practice of sovereignty.[28] As I have already explained, America's interpretation of the applicable law is sometimes at variance with other states, and is often at variance with the interpretations of its critics.

As the United States defines its war with al-Qaeda as a non-international armed conflict, the categories of permissible target—and therefore legal identity—differ significantly from international armed conflict. Much of this revolves around the issue of what it means for a person to 'take a direct part in hostilities'[29] in the context of a non-international armed conflict. The status of combatants is defined in positive terms—combatants gain the legal privileges associated with being a combatant by joining the armed forces of a state. In contrast, the legal identity of non-state groups is negative in character since they remain civilians, albeit ones that lose the protections that the law of armed conflict affords civilians. The individuals that take up arms against states in non-international armed conflicts do not gain a formal legal status, instead as individuals they are defined by their collective loss of protections associated with being a civilian. Since civilians enjoy general legal protection from attack (and the many other harms of war), the status of non-state armed groups is that of persons who have lost the right to the protections associated with civilian status.

This is a necessary simplification of a technical legal issue, but one that has wide-ranging implications. Many of the relevant issues are found in the difference between the US Department of Defense's recently published Law of War manual[30] and the guidance published in 2009 by the International Committee of the Red Cross on the notion of direct participation in hostilities.[31] Mapping the difference between America's position and those of its critics is extremely difficult due to America's non-signatory status with regard to a number of treaties, such as Additional Protocol I to the Geneva Conventions (1977), as well as the American government's refusal to accept the ICRC's findings in its wide-ranging study of customary international humanitarian law.[32] The essence of the disagreement is that America identifies people as participants in an armed conflict in a different way.

The US interpretation of international law does not recognise the 'revolving door' concept of protection for civilians who choose to participate, and, similarly, its interpretation of the law of armed conflict does not contain a presumption of civilian status.[33] The revolving door concept is based on the idea that civilians only lose the protection associated with their status when they 'take a direct part in hostilities'—after they stop taking part, they enjoy protected status once more. The presumption of civilian status, that '[i]n case of doubt whether a person is a civilian, that person shall be considered to be a civilian', is part of the API, which America is not a party to.[34] Taken together, these differences create quite different practical requirements for war. The interpretation, antithetical to America's, would require a military commander to positively identify a person as directly participating in hostilities before targeting them for attack, without there being any doubts as to their identity. Both these positions use the same language, and rely upon the same set of treaties, yet the significant differences between interpretations demonstrate the role that social ideas play in the constitution of categories of permissible targets under the law of armed conflict.

The ICRC view on non-international armed conflict is that the concepts of civilian, armed forces and organised armed groups are mutually exclusive.[35] Civilians are 'all persons who are not members of State armed forces or organized armed groups of a party to the conflict'.[36] Organised armed groups are distinct from a non-state party to a conflict and 'comprise both fighting forces and supportive segments of the civilian population, such as political and humanitarian wings'.[37] The ICRC does note, however, that 'the informal and clandestine structures of most organized armed groups and the elastic nature of membership render it particularly difficult to distinguish between a non-State party to the conflict and its armed forces'.[38] For the ICRC, a 'continuous combat function' is the 'decisive criterion' for determining whether a person is a member of an organised armed group, where 'a person assumes a continuous function for the group involving his or her direct participation in hostilities'.[39]

Beyond this organisational connection, however, the ICRC's guidance incorporates significant protections for civilians that participate in armed conflicts. For example, it states that civilians driving ammunition trucks away from active fighting should still be counted as civilians, and so too should civilians that choose to act as voluntary human shields.[40] In this, the ICRC guidance notes that 'The treaty terminology of taking a "direct" part in hostilities, which describes civilian conduct entailing loss of protection against direct attack, implies that there can also be "indirect" participation in hostilities, which does not lead to such loss of protection.'[41] In short, there are activities that constitute participation in hostilities where civilians retain protection against direct attack. The ICRC defines direct participation in hostilities in the following way:

> In order to qualify as direct participation in hostilities, a specific act must meet the following cumulative criteria:
>
> 1. the act must be likely to adversely affect the military operations or military capacity of a party to an armed conflict or, alternatively, to inflict death, injury, or destruction on persons or objects protected against direct attack (threshold of harm), and
> 2. there must be a direct causal link between the act and the harm likely to result either from that act, or from a coordinated military operation of which that act constitutes an integral part (direct causation), and
> 3. the act must be specifically designed to directly cause the required threshold of harm in support of a party to the conflict and to the detriment of another (belligerent nexus).[42]

The ICRC's notion of what constitutes direct participation in hostilities does not apply to most forms of participation in an insurgent, guerrilla or terrorist network/movement. In this sense, a great many people who play an essential role in sustaining organised armed groups would not be classified as taking a direct part in hostilities, thus ensuring that civilians performing these actions were protected against attack. Furthermore, the ICRC conceives of direct participation as having temporal limitations, such that a civilian's protection against an attack is 'temporarily suspended' when they take direct part in hostilities, but that they regain this protection once the specific act is completed.[43] This '"revolving door" of civilian protection is an integral part, not a malfunction, of IHL'.[44] So not only can many people involved in these groups not be targeted, but even those who commit violence can only be targeted for a period of time related to a given attack or act.

The ICRC's functional approach to defining group membership is not shared by the United States. Instead, the recently published Law of War manual classifies persons as belonging to non-state armed groups according to formal or functional criteria.[45] Formal criteria for membership include actions such as 'taking an oath of loyalty to the group or the group's leader' alongside the formal actions such as wearing a uniform or being identified as a member on documents produced by the group.[46] Importantly, in cases where members 'seek to conceal their association with that group', the manual points to functions or behaviours that can be used to identify formal membership such as accessing the group's private facilities, travelling along 'specific clandestine routes used by these groups' or travelling with group members.[47] This is alongside widely held functional activity such as taking direct part in hostilities. The United States defines functional membership— wider than actions relating to the notion of direct participation defined by the ICRC—as follows:

> An individual who is integrated into the group such that the group's hostile intent may be imputed to him or her may be deemed to be functionally (i.e., constructively) part of that group, even if not formally a member of the group. The integration of the person into the non-State armed group and the inference that the individual shares the group's intention to commit hostile acts distinguish such an individual from persons who are merely sympathetic to the group's goals.[48]

Even before exploring variance in the concept of direct participation in hostilities, it is clear that the difference between the ICRC's and America's position on the classification of people who belong to armed groups will produce quite substantial differences in who may be targeted.

Of particular importance is the emphasis in the American approach on inferring group participation from available information using both formal and functional criteria, whereas the ICRC's purely functional approach to group participation forecloses this type of reasoning. For this reason, the ICRC's guidance was criticised by a number of senior legal figures. One criticism of the ICRC's guidance, offered by Kenneth Watkin, is that the purely functional approach to identifying members of organised armed groups by identifying a continuous combat function based on the ICRC's definition of direct participation in hostilities excludes a great number of people who would be vital to the operation of a contemporary irregular armed group.[49] The ICRC's guidance, Watkin notes, would prevent states from lawfully targeting most persons involved in developing and deploying improvised explosive devices, since it includes 'individuals who purchase, smuggle, manufacture and maintain weapons and other equipment "outside specific military operations" in the category of civilians'.[50] Nils Melzer, on the other hand, has defended the ICRC's criteria:[51]

> there are essentially two solutions [to the problem of defining what constitutes direct participation in hostilities]: First, the notion of 'organized armed group' can be overextended to include *all persons accompanying or supporting that group* (i.e., regardless of their function); an excessively wide approach which would completely discard the distinction between 'direct' and 'indirect' participation in hostilities inherent in treaty and customary law. Alternatively, the notion of 'organized armed group' can be limited to those persons who represent the *functional equivalent of 'combatants'* in the regular armed forces.[52]

This disagreement between the interpretations of the United States and the ICRC has little effect on how non-state actors organise themselves. Its importance lies not in determining actual involvement in armed conflict, but how categories of permissible targets are socially constituted and constructed. This extends to the protection offered by the 'revolving door' protection of direct participation. As noted by Michael Schmitt, this

> is popularly symbolized by the farmer who works his fields by day, but becomes a rebel fighter at night. According to the [ICRC's] Interpretive Guidance [on the Notion of Direct Participation in Hostilities], individualso who participate in hostilities on a recurrent basis regain protection from attack every time they return home and lose it again only upon

launching the next attack; hence the revolving door as the farmer passes into and out of the shield of protection from attack.[53]

The revolving door approach conceptualises armed conflict as something that individuals (who are not members of state forces) can drop into and out of multiple times per day, let alone in a day/night cycle. Schmitt argues that:

> the reason civilians lose protection while directly participating in hostilities is because they have chosen to be part of the conflict; it is not because they represent a threat. Indeed, particular acts of direct participation may not pose an immediate threat at all, for even by the restrictive ICRC approach, acts integral to a hostile operation need not be necessary to its execution.

Here, the difference between the idea of direct participation as a choice to participate and the actual activity of participating is important. Returning to the notion of inference, such choices can in theory be inferred from a wide variety of information and intelligence. Schmitt further argues that the revolving door protection 'makes no sense from a military perspective' since states would be prevented from targeting insurgent hideouts until they began preparing to attack.[54]

Who can be killed is determined by the interpretations of international treaty and customary practice, and there appears to be little hope of a unified standard interpretation of these concepts in the near future. The point here is not to determine which side of this debate is 'right'—if that is even possible given the significant disagreements and the nature of customary international law—but to emphasise that the way the United States identifies legal targets draws upon a wider variety of information than the strict functional concept of a continuous combat function as defined by the ICRC. Because of this, it is possible to see why the wide variety of intelligence resources possessed by the US intelligence community are invaluable, since they provide the United States with multiple intelligence sources that can be used to identify members of armed groups and therefore classify them as permissible targets by way of membership.

Identification and intelligence

The law and ethics of war legitimates violence against persons so long as they are identified as a legitimate target, but has little to say on the standards of such identification or the processes involved. Understanding these processes is important in this context because it is the primary restraint on the use of violence in armed conflicts. The kind of decision-making that results in a person being classed as a permissible target for a targeted killing is disaggregated, social and hierarchical. Decision-making in bureaucratic militaries is quite different in character from the kind of decisions made on the battlefield by autonomous personnel or commanders, even if the same set of rules apply to both decisions.

The legal construction of permissible targets reflects the considerable role that military lawyers play in both the design of operations and decisions taking during them.[55] Whereas drafted US soldiers sent to Vietnam had a relatively poor understanding of their obligations under the Geneva Conventions, the Department of Defense's 'Law of War Program', launched in 1974, has inculcated knowledge of these standards and respect for them in all military personnel, including the US Air Force pilots that fly the drones used for targeted killings.[56] Authority over decisions to use force on the ground in Vietnam (and in land warfare in general) was necessarily given to individual soldiers and their immediate commanding officers. In contemporary aerial warfare, decisions to use force are sometimes taken days in advance as part of a heavily standardised targeting process.[57] Understanding the wider context of these decision-making processes is necessary in order to comprehend why the US developed bureaucratic processes like the Disposition Matrix. War-fighting requires procedures, hence NATO's use of a 'Joint Prioritised Effects List' to share targeting information and priorities between coalition partners in Afghanistan. These methods of standardising the action of states (and coalitions of states) also enable them to integrate legal restrictions and lawyers into targeting processes. They also allow the commander-in-chief to be routinely involved in decisions that appear to be tactical in nature.[58] The targeting process ultimately allows for high-level management of decisions that previously would have had to be delegated to lower-level commanders.

The difference in the character of status-decisions is important because it places an emphasis on the structures of compliance with the law of armed conflict, as well as the social nature of the just war tradition. This includes standard protocols and doctrine that restrict the autonomy of decision-making within the military command structure as well as secret generic standards and procedures (like rules of engagement) that are designed to provide a unified basis for decision-making.[59]

In this context, the much-maligned popular characterisation of the drone pilot is a distraction from far more important issues of organisational decision-making. Much is made of the relative inability of drone pilots to identify people on the ground, even though the analysts assigned to drones are able to study video feeds to a far greater degree than pilots in traditional military aircrafts.[60] Targets are sometimes observed with drones for months before a decision is taken on whether or not to strike.[61] In addition to this surveillance, other forms of intelligence collection, analysis and distribution are used to identify individuals as lawful targets. The people who make lethal decisions in contemporary operations are situated in this process. They do not deduce all information relevant to their decisions by themselves, rather they take advantage of the constant accretion of information by military and intelligence organisations. Since these decisions are corporate in nature, the situation of individuals within the military hierarchy matters. Pilots are told where to fly, are given the authority to fire weapons by their commanding officers, and are sometimes guided to a target by other personnel and so on.

To understand this better, it is worth considering the aptly named 'kill box' in contemporary military operations.[62] Kill boxes are a means of restraining the use of force as well as making the use of force more efficient, according to US military doctrine:

> The goal is to reduce the coordination required to fulfill support requirements with maximum flexibility (permissive attributes), while preventing friendly fire incidents (restrictive attributes). Fires executed in a kill box must comply with ROE [rules of engagement] and law-of-war targeting constraints; designation of a kill box is not authorization to fire indiscriminately into the area.[63]

Militaries use grid coordinates to communicate directions and locations in an efficient manner so as to coordinate air-, land- and sea-based forces in a unified manner. A kill box is essentially a cube, defined by these grids from the surface of the earth to a set height, where the use of force is subject to a series of constraints. Often this is done to help mitigate the risk of friendly fire incidents by prohibiting the entry of ground forces into a given space. Not only do kill boxes communicate to all interested personnel the relevant authority required in order to fire into them but they often communicate information about targets within these areas. For example, by communicating a complete lack of friendly troops, and authorising friendly forces to fire into them, a kill box communicates to a nearby pilot that the tank they can see within this zone belongs (in all likelihood) to the enemy force.

With such processes and operational rules in mind, it is clear that judgements of status are not made by a single autonomous individual, but are instead bureaucratic ones. Even commanding officers make status judgements in negotiation with their legal advisers. Pilots, including those of drones, make these kinds of judgements in compliance with rules of engagement, based upon information derived from the current operating environment, and from intelligence analysis provided to them by dedicated analysts. It is for this reason that the lack of clarity about the decision-making processes of the CIA matters, not least because their actions 'fall into a convenient legal grey hole'.[64] After all, the CIA is different in nature from the military, and has separate legal authorities. Why, then, should we care about military forms of thinking and classification? The reason for my focus on the law of armed conflict is because this is how the American state is outwardly justifying its actions. While I am conscious that we cannot know how decisions are made within the CIA, it is unlikely that they depart from the same kinds of processes I am describing. They do, after all, have to perform the same kind of activity as the military, targeting the same kind of people. The principal objection to the CIA's involvement is not that they are ignoring all the standards of law abidance detailed so far, but they are by design far less transparent than the military. As Micah Zenko notes, due to the authorisation structure of covert activity, 'the government cannot legally provide any information about how the CIA conducts targeted killings'.[65] This, he argues, means that their role in the use of targeted killings creates needless problems for the US government due to the fact that it is more difficult to demonstrate public oversight of the CIA than the military. The institutional norms and procedures for the CIA's targeted killings will almost certainly differ from those of the military, but both organisations are still attempting to achieve the same end: identifying individuals as members of al-Qaeda. The American construction of direct participation is so wide that it would be difficult to construct a standard to adhere to it that the CIA would fail while the military would not. At any rate, my argument is not about what the standard exactly is, or should be, but how these concepts can help us think about the role of law in the process of targeted killing. Key to this is the overarching role of the White House in giving authority to both the CIA and JSOC to kill people via targeted killings.

The use of terms such as 'personality strike' and 'signature strike' reflects two different ways of thinking about how such identification can be made. The United States argues that it is in an armed conflict with al-Qaeda, and in defending both types of targeting it argues that both are lawful ways of identifying lawful targets in the context of this armed conflict. At the same time, signature strikes appear to be different from the carefully assembled databases of information that build up pictures of potential targets in places like Afghanistan and Pakistan. The so-called 'terror Tuesdays' of the Obama administration—where a conference of senior decision-makers drawn from the executive, intelligence and military communities debate with lawyers about the possibility of attacking a target—often involve extensive discussions about individual identity and a person's role in militant networks that America considers legitimate targets of attack.[66] From reports, signature strikes appear to be less about a person's identity than inferring their participation from a range of intelligence sources, although 'the distinction between the evidential/inferential apparatus used for a "personality strike" and for a "signature strike" is by no means clear-cut'.[67] Yet both types of strike—if they are to be lawful—require establishing that what is known about a person allows them to be classified as a lawful target of attack.

Personality strikes

The problem with analysing the difference between 'personality strikes' and 'signature strikes' is that military processes are necessarily secret. Nonetheless, there is enough information available for the issue to be approached from a theoretical perspective. The individuation that Issacharoff and Pildes discuss is quite different from the forms of pattern analysis that is depicted in reports of signature strikes. However, both are working towards the same goal: identifying a person as a legitimate target or protected person.

Individuated warfare is about precision—individuating networks and their members as permissible targets from what Michael Flynn refers to as 'civilian clutter'.[68] Doing this on an organisational level requires standardisation and the promulgation of results—hence the creation of large lists of persons that might be a potential target—such as the disposition matrix and NATO's Joint Priority Effects List—which form the basis for analysing further intelligence. New information might confirm a suspicion that a person is directly involved in the running of a terrorist network, or it might relegate them to a position where they lack the organisational connection necessary for fulfilling a 'continuous combatant function' as defined by the ICRC, or the wider membership criteria used by the United States. This is still a militarised process—although dealing in intelligence fragments and suspicion, it is fundamentally about identifying people as permissible targets of attack, not as criminal suspects for prosecution.

Lawyers are a fundamental part of this process. Daniel Klaidman cites the role of lawyers in transforming intelligence assessments into judgements of legitimacy.[69] In other words, the information collected about an individual has to go through rounds of assessment in order to meet this kind of judgement. This is the AUMF process—identifying whether the AUMF gives authority to kill someone, which in turn requires legal decisions and classifications.[70] The procedural dimension to this process of analysis is important. This sharing of responsibility—including practitioners, lawyers and significant political figures from the executive branch—is quite different from the way in which law is used in court cases. While the legal analysis of a given case involves the same skills on the part of the lawyer, the function of analysis integral to the AUMF process is quite different to similar analysis that might appear in a law journal. It is worth noting that much of the literature of the just war tradition is similarly process-blind. The problem is that both approaches often frame analysis and judgement as a neutral activity, which is hard to sustain given its integral role in targeting processes. The individuation of warfare down to the personal level is mirrored by the vast increase in intelligence collection and deliberation about individuals. This also gives lawyers a greater degree of influence on decision-making. Klaidman recounts how Jeh Johnson, then general counsel for the Department of Defense, refused to approve the targeting of al-Shabab in Somalia (with exceptions for senior figures who were also members of al-Qaeda), thereby preventing the military from using force against them and earning the ire of the military in the process.[71]

Personality strikes seem to be more intuitive: governments acquire enough information about a person, lawyers classify them as lawful targets due to their connection to a belligerent group and the military or CIA then kills them. The important consideration is that this is fundamentally an attempt to define individuals in relation to the law of armed conflict, despite the relatively novel bureaucratic processes involved. While it is impossible to say what the precise criteria are for inclusion on such a list, this is in essence an evolution, not a revolution, of targeting and the role of decision-making in relation to the law of armed conflict. Nonetheless, such decision-making is integral to violence. It permits violence against the person involved, just as exclusion from a targeting list may prohibit targeting of a person. Moreover, the bureaucratic nature of targeting is a feature of contemporary American war fighting, as is the role of the executive in making critical judgements of status.

From an alternative perspective, these lists are a means of framing lives, as Butler writes:

> [a]n ungrievable life is one that cannot be mourned because it has never lived, that is, it has never counted as a life at all. We can see the division of the globe into grievable and ungrievable lives from the perspective of those who wage war in order to defend the lives of certain communities, and to defend them against the lives of others—even if it means taking those latter lives.[72]

The key issue here is that we need to recognise that we are operating with different bodies of law, different categories of identification and, most importantly, different forms of truth and knowledge. In the words of Michael Hayden, what personality strikes draw attention to is 'the difference between judicial and intelligence truth'.[73]

For this reason, personality strikes also give us a way of thinking about the fundamental clashes between co-existent legal identities and their relevant identification standards and processes. In the case of US citizens, this is most evident in the important point raised by lawsuits such as the one taken by Anwar al-Awlaki's father before al-Awlaki's death: By what right does the US government have to create and maintain these lists, particularly when they include US citizens?[74] As an

American citizen, al-Awlaki was meant to be protected from unlawful uses of force by the US Constitution, but the Obama administration determined that these protections did not apply. As Steve Coll explains:

> The due-process clause of the Fifth Amendment prohibits 'any person' from being deprived of 'life, liberty, or property without due process of law.' Obama authorized the termination of Awlaki's life after he concluded that the boastful, mass-murder-plotting cleric had, in effect, forfeited constitutional protection by waging war against the United States and actively planning to kill Americans. Obama also believed that the Administration's secret process establishing Awlaki's guilt provided adequate safeguards against mistake or abuse—all in all, enough 'due process of law' to take his life.[75]

The American Civil Liberties Union and the Center for Constitutional Reform 'charged that the authority contemplated by the Obama administration is far broader than what the Constitution and international law allow'.[76] The problem is that the president—as commander-in-chief—has to make these kind of judgments in the context of military activity. As William Boothby writes, '[w]hen applied to the military context, targeting is a broad process encompassing planning and execution, including the consideration of prospective targets of attack, the accumulation of information to determine whether the attack of a particular object, person, or group of persons will meet military, legal, and other requirements' as well as functional matters such as choosing weapons and carrying out attacks.[77] What personality strikes against US citizens demonstrate is that decisions made about whether or not a US citizen should be treated as a military target also involves selecting and privileging the law of armed conflict over domestic law, or vice versa. Is it unconstitutional for the president to define a US citizen as a military target in this way?

There are four ways of thinking about the power being exercised by the US president. The first is that Obama is acting arbitrarily—ignoring the rule of law in favour of rule by decree, becoming 'he who decides on the exception' and exercising sovereignty in the same way as dictators past and present.[78] The second is that the rule of law is abolished by the existence of war. In the words of Carl Schmitt:

> [a]ll the measures taken at the scene of war are governed by martial law. Hence, in a conception of the law where the separation of powers is on the

whole identical with law and order, martial law means abolition of the separation of powers and its substitution by the brutal command of the military chief.[79]

A third is offered by Italian philosopher Giorgio Agamben, that the President is exercising sovereign authority to define exceptions to the rule of law in a form of legal abandonment.[80] This abandonment reflects a power imbalance—the abandoned are separated from the protections of law, yet remain at the mercy of the system that abandoned them. My interpretation is that the president is exercising the authority to define people in relation to two simultaneously applicable bodies of law—yet in the American example, this isn't a straightforward case of exclusion from a system. Given that there are two bodies of applicable law that can apply at the same time, the authority to define people in relation to a body of law is as important as subsequent exercises of authority within its given framework. In this case Presidential authority is exercised by defining which body of law applies, rather than excluding them from the legal system entirely.[81]

The importance here is that the very act of defining that the law of armed conflict applies to actions against a person places them within this same legal framework. Although we can also see defining people in this way as a form of legal abandonment, it's the authority to make such a definition that is claimed by the legal arguments of the Obama administration. The crux of the *al-Aulaqi v. Obama* case and most discussion regarding al-Awlaki both before and after his death was whether the executive branch of the US government had the authority to define al-Awlaki as a target of attack. In other words, whether it could define him as a member of AQAP, define his status based on intelligence and take lethal action pursuant to that definition.

Agamben frames this kind of decision-making as a form of legal abandonment, removing the general protection of law from a person, which leaves them not 'set outside the law and made indifferent to it but rather abandoned by it, that is, exposed and threatened'.[82] It is the indistinguishability between the conditions of being placed beyond the law and included within it that characterises this condition.[83] This exercise of authority leaves persons 'the object of a pure de facto rule',[84] which allows the president to execute them without the protections of law in a formalised way. However, there are a number of problems with this image of the president as exercising sovereign authority to strip legal protection from, or 'abandon', US citizens.

One is that Agamben's view relies on a universal picture of the rule of law, when, as we have seen, international law is itself a patchwork, and its interaction with national law differs from state to state. The second is that although the authority rests with the president in theory, the reality of this form of defining people is that it is bureaucratic in nature, and subject to multiple checks from within the executive branch. The legal procedures and argumentation that, according to Jack Goldsmith, shape and constrain executive action from the battalion level to the president is quite different in kind and nature from the legal process that takes place in American courts, both state and federal, but it also different from a unilateral decision making sovereign.[85] Since these decisions derive most of their authority from law passed by Congress, the president's political authority is not self-derived. The authority claimed by the president is the authority to define people as lawful targets, backed by considerable legal analysis. In this sense, even if the precise limits on this authority are debatable, the stated intention is to stay within the limits of the law, although doing so demonstrates its ultimate elasticity.

Personality strikes highlight the most important problem with Agamben's argument: characterising those held at Guantanamo or identified as legitimate targets for drone strikes as being placed beyond the law ignores the fact that they are being defined in relation to a parallel body of law—the law of armed conflict. In other words, they are not being stripped of their legal standing but are instead being defined as belonging to a second legal regime that supersedes their constitutional rights and protections.

Waging war in this way means extending the view of militaries beyond war zones and certainly transgresses many of the binaries by which people usually bracket political violence. This should not unduly surprise us—militaries plan for war in times of peace and do so in relation to many geographic regions, scanning for potential enemies. The personalised nature of this kind of targeting still causes discomfort on an instinctive level. As individuals, we might readily accept that a foreign military was thinking about our own country and government as a potential enemy, but on a gut level, the idea that a military force might be assessing us on an individual basis is both new and difficult to comprehend. This is especially true since it is clear that governments make mistakes. As Steve Coll notes, the key problem in al-Awlaki's case was that the government could not be sure that its assessment was correct, and the 'risk of error where the executive acts as prosecutor, judge, jury, and executioner, in secret, could hardly be greater'.[86] Instead of a trial, intended to prevent or reduce errors, the executive branch of the US government sifted through intelligence reports, defined him as a lawful target and killed him.

Signature Strikes

America's use of so-called signature strikes has raised a number of questions. Jeremy Scahill argues that:

> [i]n essence, the kill list became a form of 'pre-crime' justice in which individuals were considered fair game if they met certain life patterns of suspected terrorists. Utilizing signature strikes, it was no longer necessary for targets to have been involved with specific plots or actions against the United States. Their potential to commit future acts could be a justification for killing them.[87]

At first glance, the two types of targeting could not be further apart from one another: one relying upon knowledge of a person's identity, with the lack of such knowledge being a defining feature of the other. Analysed side by side, as they often are, signature strikes appear to be a problem. However, if we compare signature strikes to the general activity of military targeting, then the lack of knowledge about a target's identity implicit in the difference between signature strikes and personality strikes appears less outrageous. After all, the only reason identity is a necessary component of targeting is that it is one way of identifying people as members of a belligerent group. Throughout history, the killing of known individuals in war is anomalous compared to the vast numbers of people that have been killed by belligerents with no knowledge of their opponent's identity beyond their connection to a hostile group. Knowledge of personal identity is one way to make such a connection in the contemporary world, but what about 'patterns of life'?

There are many uncharitable interpretations of America's actions. Glenn Greenwald, a trenchant critic of the US government, claims that

'There are many evils in the world, but extinguishing people's lives with targeted, extra-judicial killings, when you don't even know their names, based on "patterns" of behavior judged from thousands of miles away, definitely ranks high on the list.'[88] Accusations that the American state kills people on a balance of probabilities have often emerged in the reporting of drone strikes. Writing in the *New York Times*, for instance, Shane Scott argued that 'it has become clear that when operators in Nevada fire missiles into remote tribal territories on the other side of the world, they often do not know who they are killing, but are making an imperfect best guess'.[89] As per the discussion above, signature strikes appear to rest upon the premise that observations of a person's behaviour are sufficient in order to identify them as belonging to a hostile group, and therefore as a lawful target. Is this plausible?

The problem of signature strikes is one of inference: to what degree can observations, or information, be used to infer a person's identity? The title and epigraph of this chapter are drawn from Philip K. Dick's *A Scanner Darkly*, which is threaded through with questions related to identity and identification. The plot of the book (and the film version starring Keanu Reeves) relies upon the fact that few of the protagonists know the true identity of one another, and in some cases use technological shields in order to mask their identities. The book's epilogue builds upon this theme, as it reveals that the characters are based upon people that Dick knew in real life, thereby making the reader aware of the 'true' identity of those involved.

Here we again encounter the difference between 'identity' as an objective truth and the process of identification. The requirement for militaries to establish positive identification of a target derives from the underlying norms of the law of armed conflict and the just war tradition, but this is not the same as establishing a person (or object's) identity. It is a process of accruing enough information to make an informed judgement about a person or object, but the standard of identification, which is perfect in theory, is rarely perfect in practice. For this reason, '[t]he target identification and selection process is never easy; uncertainty is an element of any armed conflict'.[90] This uncertainty constitutes the fog of war that is an integral feature of all but the most ritualised forms of warfare. The lack of perfect information not only means that any act of identification is prone to error but that the possibility of error is an integral feature to identification itself. Therefore, any attempt to establish the identity of targets is likely to be imperfect as it is always a judgement of intent derived from observations of actions or communicated information.

Returning to the difference between US standards for assessing participation in an armed conflict and the ICRC's interpretive guidance, one can see that the different concepts rely on substantially different sets of information. The ICRC's reliance upon functional criteria restricts the required information to the observation of behaviours and patterns of behaviour that are commonly associated with tactical military activity. The functional criteria are closely tied with 'obvious' warfare (as opposed to Martin Libicki's concept of 'non-obvious' warfare) and the level of inference required to identify this activity as hostile is very low. In contrast, the US interpretation, which allows for identifying formal membership of irregular armed groups, as well as a wider set of functional behaviours that could constitute membership, involves a far wider set of information and activities. Therefore, an alternative way of contrasting the two is in the role of inference in targeting decisions.

Some argue that a pattern of life cannot be enough to identify a person as a belligerent. Yet all 'traditional' military activity is in a sense a pattern of life. We rely upon readily identifiable symbols or symbolic actions in order to differentiate military activity from civilian activity, and these shared interpretations constitute 'obvious' warfare. The problem is that the conduct of contemporary warfare tends to lack such symbolic activity, at least on the part of non-state actors. Any individual pattern of activity therefore requires a comparable pattern derived from observation of a hostile organisation in order to ascertain whether the individual pattern is in itself indicative of membership of that organisation. Accordingly, there are two sets of subjective judgements involved in assessing membership of informal organisations—the theory or concept of the group itself (most likely a subjective judgement derived from intelligence and contact with the group) and assessments of activity or information to determine whether such activity or information matches the pattern of group members.

American pattern-of-life analysis derives from its own interpretations of the applicable rules of war. At the same time, America is driving innovation in the intelligence processes that can identify non-state groups. Of particular relevance here is the concept of 'Activity Based Intelligence' (ABI). It is worth considering activity-based intelligence in the words of practitioners:

> The purpose of ABI has been expressed in numerous forums and can be summarized in the following five elements:
>
> • Collect, characterize and locate activities and transactions
> • Identify and locate actors and entities conducting the activities and transactions
> • Identify and locate networks of actors
> • Understand the relationships between networks
> • Develop patterns of life.
> • unlike many analytic efforts, the intention of ABI is to develop the patterns of life, to determine which activities and transactions are abnormal, and to seek to understand those patterns to develop courses of action. It is focused on understanding relationships between various entities and their activities and transactions. These activities and transactions are not necessarily just tied to geo-spatial actions, but also apply across the cyber, social, financial and commercial domains, to name a few.[91]

The emphasis of activity-based intelligence is on identifying patterns of activity and relationships by examining both activities and transactions. In order to do this, activity-based intelligence (as a methodology) requires a diverse—and large—set of data. It is, in effect, the application of data analytics methods often associated with 'big data'—analysis of datasets beyond human comprehension.

For the US intelligence community, data at scale has much promise. Big data, and forms of data collection and analysis of large-scale datasets, could enable militaries (and other branches of the government) to identify members of irregular forces operating within civilian populations. The analysis of large volumes of data has direct application in a wide range of fields, both military and non-military. IBM's Watson platform, for example, can now analyse medical scans to detect signs of cancer in patients to a greater degree of accuracy than human beings.[92] At heart, the military use of these techniques is an attempt to try and ensure compliance with the law of armed conflict—to distinguish legitimate targets from non-legitimate ones. Even so, such aggregations are by nature probabilistic and prone to error.

If the pattern of life constructed by acquired and shared data is enough to satisfy rules of engagement, then a signature strike is no different from any other use of lethal force. The source of this data might seem quite troubling, but the problem of signature strikes is that they draw attention to the uncertain nature of identification and the role of intelligence in the secret judgements that render people vulnerable to death in warfare. The real issue with signature strikes is that they rely so heavily on aggregations of information drawn from a large number of sources (taking into account the construction of a 'group' signature alongside an 'individual' signature). Where responsibility lies when such strikes go wrong is an important issue, as is the transfer of information that might construct these patterns to and from allied countries. I will cover both of these questions in Chapter 9. But before doing so, I want to draw attention to the intangible harms that arise from America's use of targeted killings.

Conclusions

The rules of war are intimately connected to its character and conduct. The structures that America creates in order to comply with the law of armed conflict ultimately rely upon secret intelligence and the American interpretations of the law. This chapter argued that the American interpretation of what constitutes direct participation in hostilities is central to this. This makes sense on an intuitive level in that it creates parity in terms of associational targeting between the professional militaries of states and non-state actors that seek to attack them. At the same time, this parity occurs in the context of a large disparity in capability between the two.

Data-driven warfare brings with it its own hazards. The use of intelligence in this way means that all those feeding information into the databases and systems used to identify members of a network are also to a certain extent responsible for the consequences. The literature on drone strikes tends to focus upon the two pilot teams controlling individual UAVs as they circle areas of Pakistan and Yemen. But this places far too much emphasis on these pilots as the ultimate arbitrators of life and death. Although those pilots are responsible for the final step of the targeting process, the responsibility for killing is shared with the intelligence analysts and the commanders and lawyers who make these lethal decisions. Although there is little doubt that all involved are trained in their responsibilities under the law of armed conflict, this does not change the fact that our way of thinking about agency and decision-making in war pays little attention to the increased distribution of intelligence collection and analysis. Processes of compliance with the law of armed conflict, and moral questions found in the just war tradition, may need to be reassessed in light of the group dynamics at work.

The rule of law also serves to obscure in this context. Adherence to it means that explanations of these rules may be illegal in American law. We should also note that most, if not all, of this decision-making takes place in facilities far removed from the actual violence. This remoteness is often cited as a problem, but it is the visibility of these decisions (or lack thereof) to which this book now turns.

8

THE BODY AS THE BATTLEFIELD

'Above, where seated in his tower,
I saw Conquest depicted in his power
There was a sharpened sword above his head
That hung there by the thinnest simple thread.'

Chaucer, *The Knight's Tale*[1]

Introduction

From the ground up, the consequences of America's transnational war appear to be everywhere and nowhere at once. The global reach of America's war has resulted in lethal American operations from the horn of Africa to Afghanistan.[2] At the same time, the scale of destruction inflicted by American targeted killings is tiny relative to the countries in which these operations take place. Given that most American operations take place in sparsely populated rural areas, the average citizen of the countries in which they take place is unlikely to witness one, let alone be directly harmed. Nonetheless, given that America's war places civilians at risk of a violent death, we should consider how civilians are protected from harm in the context of armed conflict.

The formal and informal constraints on warfare serve to protect civilians from the effects of war by limiting their exposure to violence. The practicalities of organised force matter—any armed actor needs to organise and equip their forces in order to conduct military operations that result in violence. Politics, practicalities and law therefore typically constrain the reach and effects of particular wars. Sovereignty and neutrality—strong elements of the international system—also tend to prevent the spread of fighting in internal conflicts beyond border regions, although states are prone to support rebels to undermine their rivals.[3] America's war is at once very limited in scope—reserved to the people America identifies as legitimate targets and their surroundings—but also expansive—it follows the network, not the territory. America's transnational war is a particular problem for civilians who are incorrectly identified as a legitimate target, or who happen to be located close to someone that either the CIA or JSOC considers a legitimate target of attack. Where, then, can people go to protect themselves from this conflict?

War that transgresses formal borders is relatively common, but transnational warfare reduces the geographical space for using force—and its consequences—while simultaneously universalising it. The capricious appearance of geographically unrestricted violence is seen as a problem by critics and one that could be interpreted as transgressing the foundations of the laws of war since, as Noam Lubell and Nathan Derejko point out, '[t]he inviolability of state borders is at the heart of the rules on the *ius ad bellum*'.[4] This is linked to O'Connell's criticism of America for conducting violence 'far from battlefields', where the UN Charter and the 1949 Geneva Conventions 'provide little or no right to use military force against individuals'.[5] If neither borders nor battlefields restrict violence, shouldn't we all be afraid?

The argument I want to make in this chapter is that the focus upon precision and accuracy—reducing the conduct of war to discrete individual acts of violence—should also make us consider the intangible harms to which this form of warfare gives rise. Non-governmental organisations have alleged that the persistent use of drones to kill people puts local populations in permanent fear of their lives.[6] This points to a wider interpretation of the meaning of harm to civilians than that which the US government considers to be regulated by the rules of war. Even if these people are not targets, and never will be targets, the constant use of drones in their local areas causes local civilians to fear for their lives.

The US government seeks to justify its way of killing almost entirely in terms of tangible violence—the focus upon reducing or eliminating collateral damage. However, we should also consider the forms of intangible harm that this form of warfare, in its transnational context, gives rise to. In particular, my focus here is on the ability of third parties to an armed conflict to identify or guess where and when it is likely to result in violence. Greatly reducing the ability of civilian populations to assess armed conflicts that are likely to injure or kill them is a form of harming them. This arises from a paradox—the consequence of the changing character of war is that civilians are protected to a greater extent from direct violence, while simultaneously deprived of the ability to discern for themselves if they are in danger. This is also an integral aspect of what Martin Libicki calls 'non-obvious warfare', since if 'the very fact of warfare' is ambiguous to participants, then it is likely to be harder for non-participants to discern.[7]

Working through this concept, it is possible to see that even when America hews to the side of caution in adhering to the law of armed conflict, the way in which it wages war has wider consequences that are not contained within this same body of law. The problem, therefore, is not that America's war lacks geographical restrictions. Far from it, the personal form of targeting reduces the scope of war—in terms of violence—to a significant degree. The problem is that when states adhere to the law of armed conflict by adopting means of warfare that are hard for civilians to discern, they reduce the ability of civilians to avoid personal harm. Moreover, stricter and stricter adherence would militate for greater use of this form of warfare, while the consequential harm that I am concerned with exists in law by way of analogy, if at all.

New wars, new harms?

The concept of precision lies at the heart of the claims America makes about its war with al-Qaeda. John Brennan emphasised that 'there is absolutely nothing casual about the extraordinary care we take in making the decision to pursue an al-Qaida terrorist, and the lengths to which we go to ensure precision and avoid the loss of innocent life'.[8] This statement contains two claims: that the actual harm caused by the armed conflict is limited, and that the scope of possible harm is limited. Counter to this, critics argue that America's transnational armed conflict is borderless and relatively unbounded. Philip Alston asks

> what are the parameters of the right to self-defense that has been claimed? If Russia or China are attacked by external non-state actors, can they too claim a right to self-defense which is not limited in time or in territorial scope, and thus undertake attacks on their enemies around the world?[9]

In this mode of thought, technology and law combine to enable the United States to wage war without reference to battlefields, borders or local populations. Transnational war deletes all traditional forms of protection for civilians, leaving them at the mercy of drones that circle overhead.

Moreover, this violence is held to lack the restraints that we associate with warfare: the cost of long-term military activity usually militates against extended operations, except where they become self-sustaining through profit from captured resources.[10] War that is fought up close and personal allows for human empathy, and the conscience of soldiers impedes unrestricted killing, as they can recognise members of an opposing force as fellow humans, even if this recognition is only temporary.[11]

From this perspective, America's war lacks all the forms of restraint that are normally associated with war itself. This is particularly pertinent because if we consider armed conflict as existing beyond 'hot' battlefields, and the law contains no specific territorial limitations, then the scope of armed conflict lacks any geographical limitation. The quest for decisive battle aside, war requires warfare, and warfare has until recently required combat that puts participants at risk of harm and bodily injury. This risk is an unspoken constraint on the use of force in war, but similar unspoken constraints of warfare operate in a variety of ways. One inherent restraint to the use of force is that participants refuse to commit or order acts of violence that they feel are immoral or illegal, such as Erwin Rommel's refusal to implement Hitler's orders to execute commandos in the Second World War.[12] Conversely, soldiers fearful for their lives may desert, rather than go into battle where they may be killed. Contemporary professionalised militaries go to great lengths to inculcate unit cohesion and combat motivation into their troops as doing so means that they are more likely to place themselves at risk in service of military objectives, without regard for bodily injury.[13]

Another constraint on the use of force is that killing is an act that most humans are usually conditioned by society to avoid committing. In the stress of combat, some soldiers and personnel, faced with a personal choice to kill, refuse to do so, although evidence shows that a limited number of soldiers may even enjoy the act of killing.[14] Remote warfare removes many of these implicit restraints. This is not so much the 'PlayStation mentality'[15] that some critics allege exists in drone pilots or 'cubicle warriors'.[16] Here, critics argue that removing pilots from the immediate vicinity of violence reduces war to a 'video game' and therefore makes pilots more likely to commit acts of violence. However, based on first-hand testimony and interviews, journalist Chris Woods states that this is not the case. Rather, pilots and their officers consider themselves as having 'a war-fighting mentality'; hence '[p]hysical absence from the battlefield … was not the same as emotional remoteness'.[17] The organisational dynamics at work make individual reticence far less of a constraint than physical warfare involving close-combat. In particular, should an individual refuse to fire in this situation, the control of these systems can be passed to another person without significant disruption of the operation as a whole.

A second way of thinking about targeted killings is that America's form of warfare is actually quite limited. When the target of violence is defined as a network of human beings, then the targets of violence tends to be those human beings.

Military campaigns waged against states often involve large-scale attacks on infrastructure to disrupt the ability of the state's military to function and resist. In the second phase of NATO's 1999 aerial campaign in Kosovo, the alliance turned its focus to 'the four pillars of Milosevic's power—the political machine, the media, the security forces and the economic system', which entailed escalating the use of force to target 'national oil refineries, petroleum depots, road and rail bridges over the Danube, railway lines, military communications sites, and factories capable of producing weapons and spare parts'.[18] Similarly, Israel's relatively short war in Lebanon in 2006 caused huge damage to the wider infrastructure of Lebanon itself. Israeli attacks targeted Lebanon's airports, ports, bridges and road networks.[19] In contrast, the damage caused by American attacks that are justified in this way is relatively limited—small groups of individuals, with insignificant effects on wider infrastructure. Although unbounded in geographical terms, the scope of armed conflict is reduced to the personal level. This is perhaps the limit of a trend towards perfection and restriction noted by Michael Ignatieff:

> Ever since the moment during the Gulf War in 1991 when reporters saw cruise missiles 'turning left at the traffic lights' to strike the bunkers of the Iraqi regime, the Western public has come to think of war like laser surgery. Displays of this kind of lethal precision at first awakened awe; now they are expected. We routinely demand perfection from the technology that surrounds us—our mobile phones, computers and cars. Why not war?[20]

The copious targeting processes required for this form of warfare are also designed to ensure compliance with the laws of war.[21] What, the defenders of remote warfare might argue, could be more humane than a form of warfare that eliminates a select group of people, leaves the rest of a country intact and even reduces the risks of harm to the pilot?[22] However, to examine the scope of possible harm before the types of harm inflicted would be wrong, since the scope of possible harm is founded upon the type of harm under consideration. Before considering the scope of harm, it is necessary to examine the first idea, that this form of warfare is somehow more humane than prior forms of military activity.

The 'precision warfare' inherent in America's transnational war is justified in terms of efficiency, but also in terms of humanity. As Eric Holder, the US attorney general, stated:

> Under the principle of proportionality, the anticipated collateral damage must not be excessive in relation to the anticipated military advantage. Finally, the principle of humanity requires us to use weapons that will not inflict unnecessary suffering.

> These principles do not forbid the use of stealth or technologically advanced weapons. In fact, the use of advanced weapons may help to ensure that the best intelligence is available for planning and carrying out operations, and that the risk of civilian casualties can be minimized or avoided altogether.[23]

Humanitarian attitudes in warfare attempt to reduce the harms inflicted by war in two general ways. One is that necessary acts of lethal violence are committed so as to avoid excess pain and suffering to those attacked. One early example of this is the 1868 St Petersburg

Declaration that 'fixed the technical limits at which the necessities of war ought to yield to the requirements of humanity' by banning small exploding projectiles and fulminating bullets that could explode inside human beings, as 'the employment of arms which uselessly aggravate the sufferings of disabled men, or render their death inevitable' would 'be contrary to the laws of humanity'.[24]

The second way that humanitarian attitudes constrain warfare is the attempt to keep the consequential or wider harms of warfare to a minimum. This is best expressed in the wording of Common Article 3 to the Geneva Conventions: 'Persons taking no active part in the hostilities … shall in all circumstances be treated humanely, without any adverse distinction founded on race, colour, religion or faith, sex, birth or wealth, or any other similar criteria.' Similarly, basic prohibitions against acts such as 'violence to life and person, in particular murder of all kinds, mutilation, cruel treatment and torture' should serve to protect civilians from the ravages of warfare.[25]

However, there is much disagreement as to how the principle of humanity operates in relation to the law of armed conflict. One of these is the concept of a 'use of force continuum' advanced by Jean Pictet before the 1977 Additional Protocols. Pictet noted that 'human potential, by which we mean individuals directly contributing to the war effort, may be reduced in three ways: death, wound or capture' and that these three were roughly equal in efficiency.[26] Pictet argued that 'Humanitarian reasoning is different. Humanity demands capture rather than wounds, and wounds rather than death; that non-combatants shall be spared as much as possible; that wounds shall be inflicted as lightly as circumstances permit.'[27] Pictet wanted states, and military commanders, to be legally bound to use the minimum force necessary against a person. States disagreed, and America (among others) does not consider itself bound by this concept.[28]

As a result of this rejection by states, while the use of legally prohibited means to kill a person is banned, there is little meaningful legal difference between firing a bullet at a person and killing them with a cruise missile, except with reference to the consequences or collateral effects of such a strike; nor are states required to capture instead of kill under the law of armed conflict. While civilian populations are (in theory) protected from the direct effects of war, indirect harms, such as psychological damage wrought by presence in a conflict zone, are not explicitly regulated in the law of armed conflict, although psychological trauma is integral to war crimes such as sexual assault.[29] The overriding American defence of its use of targeted killings is that they are precise relative to previous military campaigns: '[w]ith the unprecedented ability of remotely piloted aircraft to precisely target a military objective while minimizing collateral damage, one could argue that never before has there been a weapon that allows us to distinguish more effectively between an al-Qaida terrorist and innocent civilians'.[30]

This requirement of precision derives from the previously explained requirement to adhere to the rules of war as closely as possible (albeit America's interpretation of what these rules permit). At the same time, this is an examination of harm that is limited to the types of harm that are explicitly considered within the law of armed conflict and typically discussed by theorists of just war.

Precision is an entirely relative claim. Although there is no objective standard for judging precision, '[p]recision warfare intersects (or has the potential to interact) with international humanitarian law in four key areas: the prohibition of indiscriminate attacks; the principle of proportionality; the requirement to take precautions in attack; and perfidy and other misuses of protected status'.[31] That said, the principal defence of American actions is that they are aimed at lawful targets, and that the consequential harm is reduced, both by better targeting processes as well as the use of weapons that minimise wider damage.

Given that these concepts are open to interpretation, it's easy to see why some accept America's position, and others do not. Still, there are also hard facts that limit the range of plausible interpretations and defences. Early public defences of American targeted killings that emphasised few, if any, civilian casualties have been shown to be incorrect.[32] Responses to America's claims of precision have therefore ranged from acceptance to the incredulity of the ACLU: 'Zero civilian casualties—during a period when there were more than 100 CIA drone strikes—sounded almost too good to be true. As it turns out, it was.'[33] The concept of collateral damage is tied to any claim of precision in warfare. Claims of low (or non-existent) collateral damage imply greater precision in the use of force, reducing the consequential effects of armed conflict. Collateral damage refers to both the foreseen or predicted consequences of an attack, as well as the actual consequences. Most military professionals appear to accept that collateral damage is inherent in warfare—that somewhere in the course of hostilities their forces will have to balance the consequences of an attack that will harm civilians, or that mistakes in targeting will harm civilians. Even those who argue for the 'humanisation' of the laws of war such as Theodor Meron recognise that such humanisation 'cannot give complete protection to civilians and outlaw collateral damage that does not violate the rules of proportionality'.[34] Collateral damage is considered legal only insofar as it is necessary, since military necessity 'permits the destruction of life of armed enemies and other persons whose destruction is incidentally unavoidable by the armed conflicts of the war'.[35] Conversely, and quite understandably, most NGOs have a lower threshold for tolerating this kind of damage. It is this difference in acceptance of harm to civilians that results in vociferous debates over the consequential harm to civilians between governments and NGOs. Despite this difference, a central element of American claims of precision is that its methods reduce the scope of harm to the minimum necessary to achieve the task of killing.

Civilian casualties grab attention for the reason that even permissive interpretations of the rules of war do not justify killing innocents, but instead accept civilian deaths as a consequence of war and warfare. Regardless of conflict, when the rhetoric that attends war turns to a positive acceptance of killing civilians, we know that the conflict has transgressed the boundaries that separate war from mass murder. Public debates regarding civilian casualties will never be settled in democratic societies because the standards of acceptability are subjectively defined by a range of political actors in society. NGOs seeking to limit the harm of conflict to civilian populations will always press states to reduce civilian deaths to the minimum possible, irrespective of military necessity or the practicalities of conflict. To expect otherwise would be absurd. This chapter has so far argued that the diverging interpretations of civilian casualties, as reflected in arguments over the number of civilians killed by American targeted killings, are non-reconcilable, and therefore the differences expressed are non-resolvable. Important differences exist, for instance as to whether America is required, by international law, to reduce the effects of armed conflict on the civilian population as much as is feasible.[36]

Strict interpretations of precaution rely upon Additional Protocol I; although the United States is not a party to this protocol, the recent Department of Defense Law of War Manual 'emphasizes the obligation to consider feasible precautions during target selection and engagement, essentially echoing the obligation established by Article 57 of the 1977 Additional Protocol I to the Geneva Conventions of 1949 (the primary source of treaty based regulation of the targeting process)'.[37] The statements of the Obama administration predicate the legitimacy of its use of force on a similar reduction in the scope of harm that the conflict entails with constant reference to the 'extraordinary precautions we take', to quote John Brennan.[38]

The US government argues that by reducing the scope of direct harm to the minimum possible, the use of targeted killings and precision weapons reduces the overall possibility of direct death and injury to a relatively small number of people. America's transnational war has, however, brought attention to the alternative concepts of harm that are enmeshed in these differences. Harm, it must be said, is invariably attached to responsibility. One key example of this is the assertion that America bears responsibility for the psychological impact of long-term drone operations, that, according to Kat Craig, legal director for the UK NGO Reprieve, 'In places like Yemen, the US drone programme is terrorising entire civilian populations, nearly half of which are children.'[39] This is raised as a counterpoint to American claims of precision—that even if individual acts of American violence are precise, the operations as a whole are not: they have significant consequences for the civilian population.[40] But should these physical and psychological traumas be the only way we consider harm in armed conflict?

An alternative way of thinking about harm, and the responsibility states have for the means of violence that they employ, is the way in which they disempower civilians. We tend to consider the rights of civilians in war 'in situ'—to the extent that they exist in parallel to armed conflict, but that parties to conflict are required to separate them from its effects if at all possible. At the same time, the ability of civilians to react to the onset and conduct of armed conflict is an important element of civilian protection. Even if they are unable to preserve their way of life, civilians have some degree of agency to protect themselves from direct harm when they are given the latitude to flee from a conflict. There is no obligation for citizens to avoid areas of hostilities, or to flee, although military operations intended to drive civilians from their homes, as utilised to strategic effect in the breakup of the former Yugoslavia, are illegal.[41] The agency of civilians is an important aspect of their protection, and one that is challenged by remote and aerial warfare. Civilians can flee from approaching armies, but they can hardly escape a missile that they will never hear coming. This is an intangible harm of the American way of attacking al-Qaeda: the removal of agency from affected civilian populations by the extensive use of remote weapons. That is not to say that this is illegal, nor immoral (at least in terms of the just war tradition), but it is important to consider because this kind of harm lies outside the scope of both the just war tradition and international law.

The ability of civilians to identify the existence of war and armed conflict permits them to make decisions that could save their lives. Does the removal of this ability constitute harm? From the ground up, warfare is capricious—its effects are neither uniformly distributed, nor fair in any sense of the word. Even if American targeting is finely calibrated, directed and analysed, for the unfortunate civilians caught in blasts these strikes are unpredictable and lethal.

War is a violent political relationship. Although hostility and enmity define armed conflict, the way states make war defines their relationship with other political communities. The rules of war ultimately embody the notion of separating the threatening and non-threatening elements of a hostile political community. Transnational armed conflict challenges this because it ultimately involves many political communities that have no relationship to the armed conflict except that they get caught between belligerent parties. The kind of relationship with these communities embodied by American ways of warfare is that while America cares about a specific set of direct violent harms, it does not consider itself responsible for other forms of harm. Although this is entirely defensible from within the framework of international law and the just war tradition, it is hardly good for America's public image, as will be examined in the following chapter.

The scope of harm is an important consideration in warfare, and the legitimate scope of harm is usually conceptualised as the battlefield. However, military practice defines the scope of military activity in a far broader sense, as a 'battlespace' that is usually constrained by territorial borders of sovereign states due to inter-state politics, as well as the practical limits on warfare. The practical effects of armed conflict are neither uniform, nor easily constrained. The American claim of precision is that it reduces the effects of warfare, and the damage it causes, to the minimum possible. In this sense, the claim of precision is not only that it is targeting the correct people but also that it is reducing the scope of warfare to a considerable extent. The next section will further explain the difference between thinking of the scope of war in territorial terms and this more limited scope, by explaining the role of concepts associated with the battlefield as a limit on violence in each.

Battlefields and warfare

A common image of the scope of permissible harm is that which occurs on a battlefield. However, this raises the question of where, if anywhere, the battlefield is in the War on Terror.[42] Some argue that the kind of killing America's war involves is qualitatively different from normal forms of military violence:

> Unlike ordinary battlefield strikes, the fact that the targeting forces have control over the time, means, and methods of strike mandates that a heightened degree of care should be exercised to choose an occasion and means that will minimize collateral harm to uninvolved individuals, especially where the operations are carried out outside an immediate conflict zone.[43]

As targeted killings do not 'look' like traditional forms of warfare, they also challenge the application of concepts associated with war. One conceptual challenge associated with targeted killings is the unclear spatial constraints on the use of force. Armed conflict describes a political and legal relationship; however, individual acts of violence are physical in nature. These acts are normally analysed in the context of battlefields and battlespaces, which are ways of categorising physical space and contribute to the 'geographical scope' of armed conflict.[44] This concept of a spatial constraint on the use of violence is what leads O'Connell to argue that killing terrorist suspects 'far from any battlefield' is illegal.[45]

One function of the battlefield is that it divides physical territory into areas where violence occurs and areas where it does not.

Traditional battlefields do not 'move' with participants, which made it possible for soldiers in the era of mass warfare to disengage. Noam Lubell argues that 'Individuals do not carry the battlefield away with them whenever they relocate to a different territory, otherwise there would be no possibility to disengage from an armed conflict.' But he also qualifies the idea of the battlefield by pointing out that 'only if the individual or group are continuing to engage in the armed conflict from their new location [can] operations taken against them ... be considered to be part of the armed conflict'.[46] Yet drone strikes kill people far from any battlefield, and that violence does not have any spatial limits within a given territory. Another way of interpreting this is that persons are targeted without regard to territory. In effect, as journalist Jeremy Scahill subtitles his book on America's actions since 9/11, 'the world is a battlefield'.[47]

As Chapters 3 and 4 argued, the rules of war do construct a permissive space for the use of force. However, the argument of critics is that this space should be constricted to battlefields. At the same time, the notion of a battlefield is often construed in a relatively simple way by the same critics. The term 'battlefield' is itself deprecated by many professional militaries on the grounds that, while land forces may clash, most conflicts involving advanced opponents take place in the context of aerial operations, 'information operations' and other forms of military activity that can determine the course of a physical clash of arms far from the actual site of violence. Any violence that goes beyond the range of infantry directly firing at one another would likely be unrecognisable as a battlefield to soldiers in previous eras, given that the practice of using lethal force beyond visual range in an effective manner is less than two centuries old, as Jonathan Bailey explains: 'Indirect fire was the most important innovation in artillery practice for 300 years. Experiments with indirect fire were made by the Russians using howitzers as early as the 1750s, but major technical development was not undertaken until the last decades of the 19th century.'[48] The phenomenon of the 'vanishing battlefield' that occurred with the increasing lethality and range of nineteenth-century weapons predates the drone by a century. As breech-loading rifles and rifled artillery were introduced in this period, '[i]t was generally recognised that the introduction of these new arms would transform the conduct of armies in the field'.[49] The nebulous geographical constraints on the use of force are therefore a direct result of military capabilities, and said constraints are always linked to military technology and organisation. The battlefield is both a ritual and relational concept, and the lack of an identifiable and definable battlefield is associated with almost all forms of aerial warfare.

The concept of battlefields derives from the era of pitched battle and massed conventional forces, often in an idealised form. In this sense, the concept of the battlefield as it is used to criticise America's use of targeted killings does not reflect the messy variance of this concept in military history. Furthermore, as Rupert Smith notes, the era of tank-centric battle is over: the last one took place in the 1973 Arab–Israeli War.[50] Tanks were still used in the 2003 invasion of Iraq, but this time in support of artillery and airpower, or deployed 'piecemeal ... to provide heavily protected infantry support vehicles in urban operations'.[51] The age of two armies manoeuvring to fight on a battlefield has given way to the age of battlespace, where operational areas are defined in three physical dimensions, as well as non-visible dimensions such as time, information and electromagnetics.[52]

A fair reading of O'Connell would be that America's potential area of operations, where it may employ military force, is unclear. Given the reach of modern technology, this is an important concern. As Noam Lubell and Nathan Derejko point out, 'The concept of the battlefield is as unpredictable as it is provisional, and defies static geographical delineation.'[53] This geographical delineation is usually identified via the presence of visible military operations, but the law of armed conflict does not prescribe conducting armed conflict solely by physical confrontation, even though physical confrontation has played a role in almost every armed conflict to date.

It is worth considering that killing with cruise missiles is as confrontation-free as killing via drone-launched missile. Nevertheless, a recent Stanford/NYU report into the use of drones noted that interviewees, who resided in the Pakistani areas of operation, 'described the experience of living under constant surveillance as harrowing' due to the constant fear of an attack.[54] The terror felt in civilian areas was surely no less intense during the Second World War even though the rockets Nazi Germany fired at Britain were unguided. Despite the differences in technology, the paranoia and fear caused by rockets from the sky appears similar, and in the case of Pakistan, remains imminent so long as drones fly over civilian areas. The fear of the unknown is justified. However, law constrains, regulates and constitutes American targeted killings as a way of warfare, and in a manner that makes it possible to define physical areas where violence is likely to occur.

There is clearly a tension between the image of war fought on defined battlefields and war as it tends to be conducted in the present day. But critics of targeted killings point out that battlefields served a key purpose: restricting violence. Framed in this way, permitting violence 'beyond the battlefield' empowers states to use force wherever they want. To an extent, this much is true, but this issue needs to be considered in the context of the changing character of war. After all, the disappearance of defined battlefields is part of a longer-term trend of war fighting that increases both the potential distances at which physical violence occurs in armed conflict, as well as the ongoing permeation of areas disconnected from soldiers and warriors with military activity. Strictly speaking, war has always involved non-physical elements—its psychological dimension is integral to what Clausewitz called the 'diverse nature of war'.[55] Until perhaps the last hundred years, wars tended to be decided by the massing of physical armies that would contest physical space and terrain and sometimes destroy one another (and lay waste to their surroundings in the process). Without weapons capable of destroying an opponent beyond the physical line of sight, or weapons so destructive that they could destroy massed physical formations with ease, battles (or their avoidance) remained central elements to the conduct of war. As Mikkel Vedby Rasmussen writes:

> During the First World War, technology did not allow attrition to take place without large-scale slaughter: 300,000 French soldiers died in the battle of Verdun, this being the price that France had to pay to show Germany that it was not possible for her to mount an offensive that could end the war on terms favourable to her.[56]

The social organisation of an army and the technology required to sustain it in the field were important elements in this process. Armies that required sustained lines of communication could be induced to battle, whereas armies or groups that lived off their surroundings were less susceptible.

Battles no longer decide wars, even if the wish for decisive battle and what Brian Bond termed 'the pursuit of victory' linger in the minds of military leaders and politicians.[57] Long before this turn, battles themselves stretched from one day affairs into multiple-day engagements, to the grinding month or year-long campaigns of the First and Second World Wars. The notion that warfare can be constrained to battlefields is seductive, but one that is ahistorical. Warfare beyond battlefields has long been necessary, so long as opponents employed raiders or modern-day commandos. For civilians, the presence of marauding armies 'living off the land' could bring greater hardship than a nearby military engagement. Above all, restricting violence to a defined battlefield requires an opponent willing to engage in those terms. Since battlefields are a product of antagonists, which is to say that they can be mutually agreed upon, a refusal by one party to fight a pitched battle requires the other to either impose battle upon them, or goad them into fighting (by forcing them to defend a vital asset of some description).

In this sense, the key element of remote warfare is the ability to impose violence upon an opponent. There is more continuity to remote warfare than actual change, but this indicates a marked alteration in the power relationships between opponents in that neither can escape violence. Far from making war 'remote', drones and guided missiles bind political opponents together with violence. What is lost is the ability of third parties to discern that conflict is occurring.

Rather than thinking of battlefields as an innate constraint on warfare, it is better to recognise that they are the product of rules, technology and opponents. Although battlefields typically constrained mass slaughter to a particular location, they did not necessarily protect civilians 'beyond the battlefield'. Nor did battlefields serve to constrain opponents—the need to fight decisive battles resulted in battles on attendant patches of physical terrain, but this was the choice of military commanders. The history of warfare is replete with wars that were far more lethal for civilians than combatants because commanders avoided pitched battles and instead manoeuvred their assembled hosts, draining the resources of the countryside as they went. For example, according to modern estimates of military casualties in the Thirty Years War, only 450,000 of the eight million killed by the conflict were military deaths. Military history tends to focus upon these commanders and armies, and the dance between opposing forces that leads to some form of violent resolution, but this operational artistry was devastating for the peasants and farmers that faced starvation or worse as a result of passing armies.

The body as the battlefield

In order to identify the scope of possible harm in America's transnational war, it is necessary to refer to the way in which America constructs spaces of permissible violence. International politics and American interpretations of law are the primary constraints on America's use of targeted killings. American conduct matters, as Laurie Blank points out:

> in declaring that it is 'at war with terrorists,' a state may envision the whole world as a battlefield. But the state's actual conduct in response to the threat posed offers a more accurate lens through which to view the battlefield. Areas where the state uses military force, particularly multiple facets of military power, on a regular or recurring basis, should fall within the zone of combat. In contrast, those areas where the state chooses diplomatic or law enforcement measures, or relies on such efforts by another state, do not demonstrate the characteristics of the battlefield.[58]

Yet it is the law of armed conflict that defines who can and cannot be targeted with lethal force, as discussed in Chapter 5. Given that al-Qaeda functions as a networked group, the only legitimate targets are the persons or objects connected to that group—network members and facilities—and its members are the primary targets of attack, even when removed from the 'battlefield' or directly engaged in violent acts by virtue of their leadership or organisational function.[59] The importance of this intersection of warfare and armed conflict is that it inverts our thinking on the geographic or physical boundaries of violence in armed conflict. To misquote Barbara Kruger, instead of battlefields constraining the use of violence to humans within their boundaries, the body becomes the battlefield.

Violence is therefore limited to those persons that the United States identifies as fulfilling a continuous combatant function. Although the Obama administration has made certain details of this process known via leaks to the news media—notably 'terror Tuesday' meetings where these matters are discussed—who gets added to the 'disposition matrix' of possible targets, and why, remains secret.[60] Due to the organisation of al-Qaeda, and associated groups, the battlefield is collocated with themselves. This has an important consequence for civilians, since they may not know who America has defined as a permissible target, and thus may be completely unaware of the danger to themselves.

The 'personal battlefield' is important because it allows America to consider its actions as precise—because in these terms they are—even while launching attacks over large physical distances at persons ranging from 'high-value targets' to those identified as permissible targets of attack based on a pattern of life. This precision has consequences in that the wider harms discussed above are likely to affect civilians and populations drawn into the scope of the conflict by the physical presence of permissible targets. That said, assessing these wider harms, and weighing them against the more traditional forms of harm regulated by the rules of war, is difficult, if not impossible. One point should be made, however, that as precise as warfare may get, in terms of the traditional harm of physical injury and destruction regulated by the rules of war, this is unlikely to serve as an effective defence against the ultimate responsibility for the wider harms caused by these methods of warfare, as nebulous as they may be when compared with the traditional harms of war.

One explicit problem raised by scholars is the removal of agency from participants to an armed conflict. Michael Lewis points out that drones cannot be used in situations governed by human rights because they offer no chance of surrender—a person is deprived of agency and therefore has no ability to surrender themselves to authorities.[61] With reference to the concept of the personal battlefield, how can participants remove themselves from an armed conflict? Noam Lubell and Nathan Derejko argue that:

> Neither the battlefield nor the hostilities relocate together with any individual who was on it or previously participating in it; if that were the case, it would be impossible to disengage from an armed conflict. Equally, however, by walking away from the primary combat zone, individuals cannot become immune from attack regardless of their status or the activity in which they engage.[62]

In this way of thinking, no geographic mode of escape exists (except to move to a territory or jurisdiction where America is unwilling to use force, such as the United States itself), but there is a functional one: cease participation. The armed forces of states are liable to be attacked anytime, anywhere for the duration of an armed conflict. Gary Solis writes that even in the 'unrealistic' situation that

> a combatant is home on leave and in uniform, far from the combat zone, and is somehow targeted by an opposing combatant, she remains a legitimate target and may be killed—just as the opposing combatant, if discovered outside the combat zone, may be killed by *his* enemy. That illustrates the downside of combatancy: A lawful combatant enjoys the combatant's privilege, but also is a continuing lawful target.[63]

However, members of the armed forces who are injured and unable to fight (rendered *hors de combat*) cannot be targeted, and the law of armed conflict requires that if they surrender, that this surrender be accepted, save in instances where it is thought to be a perfidious attempt to abuse the protective aspect of the law of armed conflict.[64] Furthermore, once a member of the armed forces of a state ceases to be a member of the armed forces, they are no longer liable to attack.

The formal and explicit nature of membership in state armed forces is, however, at odds with membership of a non-state armed group or terrorist network. There are a multitude of methods of attack where surrender is impossible (at least until someone figures out how to surrender to an airstrike from a B-2 bomber, or ballistic missile). The problem with irregular armed groups and terrorists is that, unlike state armed forces, there are no formal criteria for ceasing participation. A transnational armed conflict without exit consequently leads to the question: How could members of al-Qaeda remove themselves from this conflict? In legal debates related to the concept of direct participation in hostilities, this is a central challenge—the so-called 'revolving door' theory associated with the loss and regaining of civilian status.[65] This problem is likely solved by people distancing themselves from the networks that America is at war with. In the case of transnational armed conflict, this is a pertinent issue but not as important as the similar problem that civilians face: the impossibility of disengaging from an armed conflict that they are not directly involved in.

The personal battlefield, although justifiable in terms of the rules of war and military practice, denies agency to civilians as well as participants in an armed conflict. Ultimately, the most protective element of battles and battlefields is the signal that they send to civilians to run. It is difficult to arrange a large-scale battle without giving civilians clues that something bad is coming. The loss of the battlefield, as a defined physical space, deprives civilians of forewarning that physical violence is about to occur. This element of the battlefield is not, however, contained in the rules of war. Whereas these rules require militaries to take precautions before using violence, they do not require these militaries to give forewarning to civilians. Although many militaries do this as a matter of practice, '[s]tate practice considers that a warning is not required when circumstances do not permit, such as in cases where the element of surprise is essential to the success of an operation or to the security of the attacking forces or that of friendly forces'.[66] This is the principal problem of Libicki's 'non-obvious warfare'. Whereas Libicki was concerned with the inability of opponents to identify hostile acts, the consequences for civilians are just as severe. What happens when war is waged in a manner that civilians cannot identify as war? Such an understanding falls outside the way in which we tend to think about the protection of civilians in war: war's visibility is not part of the rules. It is this intangible harm that we must now consider.

Caring and killing

The consequence of war without combat is that civilians are unable to discern the risk of physical violence. The rules of war serve to enable warfare, as well as to limit (where possible) its deleterious consequences. The rules are not the only limit on violence in warfare. One of the consequences of America's war is that it draws attention to the changing way in which professional militaries like America's use force and violence, and the gap between contemporary military practice and commonly held beliefs about the nature of war itself. In the first instance, critics draw attention to the lack of ongoing violence that appears indicative of war.

The lack of battlefields and easily discerned combat is a problem for civilians. Drones may be visible, audible and closely regulated, but their use demonstrates that these characteristics do not make it any easier for third parties to reduce their risk of being accidentally killed. Civilians in Pakistan or Yemen have no way of determining who America considers a legal target of attack, and are therefore unable to separate themselves from those persons and the violence that may be directed at them. Civilians watching a soldier or tank roll down the street can walk in the opposite direction, but civilians in the presence of constant drone flights have no idea who or what their missiles will target. Waging war with non-obvious means, though not illegal, reduces or removes the ability of civilians to escape violence.

The idea of the personal battlefield highlights the role of visible ('obvious') means of warfare as a source of knowledge that civilians use to reduce their chances of being hurt during an armed conflict. This can be contrasted with the non-obvious means that America uses, which make it impossible for bystanders and civilians to extricate themselves from the armed conflict. Refugees are symbolic of a simple and traditional way in which civilians have attempted to avoid direct death resulting from armed conflicts. The relative lack of refugees from America's armed conflict with al-Qaeda points to a problem that the law regulating warfare does not address. How can the civilians who America is not attempting to kill place themselves in a position of relative safety vis-à-vis the conflict in general? Whereas al-Qaeda attacks civilian targets on purpose, the United States purports to act lawfully, which includes protecting civilians. The way in which those civilians can protect themselves from becoming 'collateral damage' is therefore an important issue. By fighting in a 'non-obvious' manner, America deprives those civilians of the ability to extricate themselves from the armed conflict. Since the identity of belligerents is not publicly known, civilians are unable to distance themselves in the manner that they might otherwise do in 'obvious' warfare. One practical example of this is the attack that killed Abdulrahman al-Awlaki, a US citizen.

Abdulrahman was the son of Anwar al-Awlaki, the previously discussed American member of al-Qaeda in the Arabian Peninsula (AQAP) killed in a targeted killing in 2011. Although the strike that killed Abdulrahman highlights some of the same Constitutional issues as the one that killed his father, Abdulrahman wasn't a member of AQAP, and was apparently killed by mistake. The sixteen-year-old perished in a strike that was purportedly meant to kill Ibrahim al-Banna, an AQAP member.[67] Even if Abdulrahman's death was a mistake, as numerous government and military sources allege[68]—and they are taken at their word—this still leads to a disturbing consequence: How could he have known he was at immediate risk of death? Yemen was not peaceful at the time, and Abdulrahman had travelled there to search for his father, Anwar al-Awlaki.

Abdulrahman was killed when '[h]e and his cousins had joined a group of friends outdoors to barbecue' while mourning his father's recent death.[69] It is quite probable that Abdulrahman had no idea he was close to a potential military target and thus liable to be killed as 'collateral damage'. While the same could occur in 'obvious' warfare, these considerations highlight the interaction between the means of armed conflict and the law that constitutes and regulates it. For example, in an 'obvious' armed conflict, civilians might be at a relatively high risk of death or injury, but the means of war allow them to make conscious decisions to limit their exposure to violence (such as leaving a region before an invading army contests its control). In a non-obvious armed conflict, civilians may in fact be at a far lower risk of death or injury, but the lack of knowledge makes it impossible for them to take even basic measures to protect themselves from violence. Since target sets are not generally known, or identifiable in the same manner that a tank might be, the pervasive dread of UAVs reported in both Pakistan and Israel indicates that perceptions of threat are not in line with these reduced risks.[70] The law of armed conflict permits collateral damage—including civilian deaths—but this highlights that the way in which the Americans are engaging in an armed conflict, though legal, deprives civilians of the general ability to remove themselves from the location of attack. Though not illegal in itself, this is an inherent feature of this method of warfare.

In the context of missile strikes that kill wedding parties and accusations of widespread psychological damage inflicted on entire populations, classifying the problem of agency-denial to civilians as 'harm' is open to criticism as trivial. The point raised here is not that this harm should be considered on the same level as others discussed in this chapter, but that it is a feature of transnational warfare that is neither covered by the rules of war, nor easily regulated by them. Military practices that aim to protect civilians by alerting them to imminent danger range from the simplistic—such as leaflet drops warning of imminent military operations—to relatively advanced—such as Israel's use of 'roof knocking' where

> the [Israeli Air Force] targets a building with a loud but non-lethal bomb that warns civilians that they are in the vicinity of a weapons cache or other tar-

get. This method is used to allow all residents to leave the area before the [Israeli Defense Forces] targets the site with live ammunition.[71]

Roof knocking is important because it highlights the way in which militaries attempt to reduce the ambiguity of military operations for civilians and give them a chance to protect themselves. The concept was 'developed to deal with cases in which residential buildings are used for military purposes, such as, for instance, ammunition depots'.[72] However, roof knocking is also open to criticism for a number of reasons. Janina Dill, for instance, points out that international law prohibits terrorising civilians and that it is 'deeply plausible that a warning that one's house will be bombed, in the absence of a real possibility to get to safety, does just that: it induces terror. Of course, from the practice alone we cannot infer that terrorising the civilian population is its primary purpose.'[73] A UN report on the 2014 war in Gaza stated that

> In some cases, it appears that concerned persons did not understand that their house had been the subject of a 'roof-knock', such as the in case of the Dheir home, where the family in the house did not understand that the strike was a warning until they were told by a neighbour that they had to flee.[74]

Furthermore, this practice is used to shift the blame for civilian casualties from the attackers to the civilians that are attacked.[75] Roof knocking highlights the ambiguity for civilians that is inherent in killing at a distance. While well intentioned, it appears to be very difficult for militaries to communicate immediate danger to civilians without also terrorising them. The ultimate importance of this is that the ambiguity of remote forms of warfare is a problem for civilians, and one that some militaries are beginning to recognise. States are unlikely to consider this their formal responsibility, but it is at least arguable that states that choose to use ambiguous means of warfare in armed conflict are responsible for the resulting lack of, or reductions of, the agency that civilians require to protect themselves from armed violence.

Conclusion

The idea of a personal battlefield is one that makes sense if we consider many of the constitutive aspects of American national security policy and military practice. A legalistic society possessing advanced military technology is likely to view the idea of reducing the harm of war to the absolute minimum possible while still being able to wage it effectively as a positive development. I used the case of Abdulrahman because of his connection to the American state. No doubt, there are numerous teenagers who have been killed simply because they happened to be nearby to someone that the American state considered to be a lawful target. Abdulrahman's case highlights the general problems civilians face in the context of America's war. However, it demonstrates two further things that are relevant to the discussions in this book.

The first is that we do not necessarily need to take a vehemently hostile attitude to the law of armed conflict in order to identify some very serious problems that are inherent to it. After all, this body of law, and America's interpretation, has produced a military that is able to selectively kill with minimum casualties. In the context of the history of war and warfare, this precision is unheard of. At the same time, many problems that we can and should take seriously, such as the psychological effects of warfare on civilian populations, require translation into this body of law. The upshot is that we need to be extremely conscious of novel types of harm.

This goes far beyond the present example. Take, for instance, the law of military occupation.[76] Does this law provide an appropriate framework for thinking about privacy rights? The reason I raise this point is that we have transitioned to a digital age. The modern law of occupation has its origins in the eighteenth-century writings of Edmund Vattel, but has now developed into a distinct and important branch of the law of armed conflict. The use of novel technology in the context of military occupation poses new questions to which the existing law has no clear answer. The collection of biometric data is emerging as an important dimension of counter insurgency operations. The existing law of armed conflict is silent on this cutting-edge element of military operations. Therefore America's extensive collection of biometric data from the Iraqi population during its occupation of Iraq doesn't appear to have been unlawful. But what happens next? In the Iraq example, the US government refused to return the data to the Iraqi government.[77] In a domestic context, the refusal to delete this kind of information is easily framed as a privacy violation. The law of occupation is essentially framed to reduce the impact of military occupations on a civilian population while enabling an orderly military occupation. But what happens when that occupation results in the permanent (and ongoing) violation of the privacy of many or all individuals in the territory? This kind of question is beyond this book, but there is a clear parallel here in the idea of harms that are not explicit in the law of armed conflict and require translation to make sense within this framework.

The second issue that Abdulrahman's case raises is the visibility of armed conflict. The idea that a citizen could be killed by accident, or as collateral damage, by their own government, many thousands of miles from their own country, in a semi-secret operation in a half-avowed war is extremely troubling. Moreover, Abdulrahman's condition is a general one: when wars are constituted by legal interpretations and memoranda, then they become less visible by default. While the Obama administration has taken substantial steps to communicate its policy on targeted killings, this doesn't change the underlying fact that it is waging a covert war that lacks clear territorial limits. The operational secrecy required to ensure the survival of military personnel is important, but when one-off operations stretch into months, years, and decades, a democracy should admit where it is using violence.

9

GYGES' KNIFE

'We see war as a surgical scalpel and not a bloodstained sword. In so doing we mis-describe ourselves as we mis-describe the instruments of death.'

Michael Ignatieff, *Virtual War*[1]

Introduction

On 21 August 2015, a Hellfire missile hit a vehicle containing Reyaad Khan, killing him and two other people in the car.[2] The missile, fired from an MQ-9 Reaper, was the same type of missile used to kill al-Harithi and Anwar al-Awlaki. The Reaper was no different from the one used to conduct numerous other targeted killings. Yet there were three substantial differences between targeted killing of Reyaad Khan and those that this book has covered so far.

Reyaad Khan was not a member of al-Qaeda. Instead, he was a member of Islamic State of Iraq and Sham (ISIS), a group that rose from the remnants of AQI to capture and control significant swathes of Iraq and Syria in 2014.[3] Secondly, Reyaad Khan was a British citizen, which matters because of the third important difference: the targeted killing was carried out by British armed forces on behalf of the British state. Of the two people killed alongside him, defined as 'ISIL fighters' by David Cameron, the UK's prime minister at the time, one was Rahul Amin, also a British citizen.[4]

From the outset, this book has examined the specific issues associated with transnational war against al-Qaeda—more or less precluding detailed examination of the running internal conflicts in Afghanistan, Iraq, Pakistan, Somalia and Yemen. In each of these conflicts, it is possible to see the intersection of the concept of a transnational war waged against a transnational opponent with localised conflicts and struggles. While I have tried to describe the concept of a transnational war in general terms, it is clear that particularities matter. Central to this is the claimed authority arising from the 2001 AUMF. In 2009, Kenneth Anderson wrote that:

> Islamist terror appears to be fragmenting into loose networks of shared ideology and aspiration rather than tightly vertical organizations linked by command and control. It will take successive feats of intellectual jujitsu to cast all of the targets such developments will reasonably put in the cross hairs as, legally speaking, combatants.[5]

Seven years later, it appears that the Obama administration's skills are well honed and working well. The rise of ISIS highlighted the amorphous and open-ended nature of the 2001 AUMF once again. Barack Obama used the pre-existing authority provided by the AUMF to strike ISIS in Syria.[6] This once again drew attention to its wide-ranging authority, and ongoing calls to reign in or reform the 2001 AUMF from experts on both sides of America's sometimes partisan debates on national security law and policy.[7] Other reforms offered by the Obama administration—transferring control of targeted killings to the US military and publishing its policy on the use of targeted killings[8]— appear quaint in comparison to the ability of the executive branch to interpret the AUMF as it sees fit.

In this final chapter, I am going to explore the rise of ISIS in order to connect some of the issues in this book to a wider context. There are clear differences between the idea of a war on ISIS and a war on al-Qaeda. The most prominent difference is that the military campaign against ISIS is conducted as part of an openly constituted military coalition, waging a far more intensive air war. The second difference is the structural and organisational difference between ISIS and al-Qaeda. Are ISIS terrorists or insurgents, or is it a social movement or proto-state? Given Islamic State's capabilities, expertise and de facto territorial control, Jessica Stern and J.M. Berger point out that it is at 'the very edge of the definition' of a non-state actor.[9] Whatever the definition, ISIS controls territory—its declaration of a Caliphate on 29 June 2014 underlines the degree to which territorial control is integral to the group's ideology, structure and purpose, as ISIS 'requires territory to remain legitimate, and a top-down structure to rule it'.[10] However, it still displays many of the elements of a transnational network, highlighting the relevance of the discussions in this book to future organisations.

The inter-state dimension of wars waged on groups like al-Qaeda and ISIS is significant, and allows us to consider the implications of information sharing and shared responsibility for acts of violence. The legal constitution of conflict detailed in this book is distinctly American, but the coalition arrayed against ISIS contains sixty-six states 'contributing to the coalition in a manner commensurate with [their] national interests and comparative advantage' who are acting on the basis of their own interpretations of international law.[11]

The ISIS example allows us to consider the future of many of the concepts that America has advanced in the previous fifteen years, notably the idea that states may intervene on the territory of states that are 'unwilling or unable' to deal with threats on their own turf. It also allows us to consider the comparative constitutional contexts in which decisions to use force are made, and how this either allows for, or limits, the spread of American interpretations of law.

Islamic State

ISIS highlights the fundamental limit of America's transnational war: the United States can kill terrorists, but it is near-impossible to kill ideas. Given that this entire book is essentially about the power of ideas to shape, constrain and enable human action, this is a problem. To fully explain the rise of ISIS would require a book-length treatment, paying particular attention to the divergence of ISIS's ideology from al Qaeda's.[12] Two important causal factors in the rise of ISIS are the onset of the Syrian Civil War, and Iraq's sectarian politics during and after the exit of US forces in 2011.[13]

Syria's descent into civil war in 2011 allowed jihadist groups to flourish in the country and it also weakened the Syrian government's authority in large areas of the country, notably in eastern regions that border Iraq. Across the border, Islamic State in Iraq (ISI) faced setback after setback, until it acquired a new leader, Abu Bakr al-Baghdadi, and formed an alliance with Baathists.[14] ISI first helped to establish Jabhat al-Nusra in Syria, which became one of the most important militant groups in the country, and then in 2013 unilaterally declared a merger between itself and al-Nusra: the creation of the Islamic State of Iraq and the Levant (ISIS). This angered the core al-Qaeda group under al Zawahiri, who had not approved the merger, as well as al-Nusra, which pledged allegiance to al-Qaeda, not ISIS.[15] In the face of al-Nusra's hostility, ISIS expanded into Syria. The importance of this is the outcome: ISIS won, and it broke from al-Qaeda in the process. Moreover, ISIS then managed to capture and hold huge swathes of territory, from Raqqa in Syria, to Fallujah and Mosul in Iraq. By routing the Iraqi army during its 2014 capture of Mosul, ISIS also captured hundreds of millions of dollars' worth of American military hardware.[16] ISIS had money, territory and a hardened fighting force. But it did not have recognition as a state. Far from it: ISIS's successes spurred America into forming an inter-state coalition to wipe it off the map.

Though originating in a local al-Qaeda franchise, there is a strong transnational element to ISIS, both in terms of ideology and personnel. In 2015, James Clapper, the American director of national intelligence, noted that there were 3,400 citizens of Western states fighting for ISIS,[17] and in May of that year a UN Security Council Committee reported that there were more than 25,000 foreign fighters who were involved with al-Qaeda and splinter groups such as ISIS, coming from over 100 different states.[18] The group's willingness to use social media and other digital platforms gives their message a reach that no democratic national censorship regime can counter. Yet ISIS's self-definition as a caliphate is fundamentally tied to physical territory.[19] Like al-Qaeda, territorially dispersed groups now swear allegiance to ISIS, from the Caucasus to Libya.[20]

One of the clearest differences between ISIS and al-Qaeda is in the scale and type of violence that it uses. In particular, the pressure on al-Qaeda's core group, now led by Ayman al-Zawahiri, has prevented them from conducting or organising attacks on the scale of 9/11. Zawahiri, according to a quoted official, is now 'a marginalized figure fighting for relevance as head of a decrepit institution'[21] although regional groups affiliated with al-Qaeda are still active. In contrast, individuals inspired by ISIS have committed medium-scale violent attacks beyond the Middle East. This is the main way that ISIS 'attacks' targets beyond its territory.[22] In Iraq and Syria, ISIS's military forces have murdered captives, enslaved populations and committed brutal acts of butchery on film in order to communicate this to the world.[23] ISIS and its affiliates have struck at the populations of foreign states irrespective of religion or location.

Some of these attacks display the confused and overlapping transnational ties inherent in these organisations. The 7 January 2015 attacks on the offices of *Charlie Hebdo*, a French magazine in Paris, was committed by two brothers with links to both AQI and AQAP, whereas a gunman who killed four people in a Parisian grocery shop on the same day (who also claimed the attacks were coordinated), proclaimed allegiance to ISIS.[24] Others display the sectarian origins of ISIS's ideology, such as the March 2015 suicide bombing of Shiite mosques in Yemen.[25] Attacks blamed on ISIS in 2015 represent a heterogeneous litany of bloodshed, from tourists (including many British citizens) murdered on a Tunisian beach,[26] to the November 2015 attacks in Paris that killed at least 129 people.[27]

The response of Western democracies has been piecemeal, but reflective of their individual political cultures. The United State began targeting IS as part of its ongoing war, launching airstrikes in both Iraq and Syria.[28] This was part of a global coalition to 'to degrade and ultimately destroy the terrorist group known as ISIL'.[29] Despite the involvement of dozens of states, the vast majority of the strikes have been carried out by America. By May 2016, the journalism and conflict monitoring organisation Airwars reported that 3,751 out of 3,988 coalition strikes in Syria were American, as were 5,789 out of the 8,631 strikes in Iraq.[30] Britain's response was defined by politics—parliament had rejected the UK government's 2013 request for authorisation to intervene in Syria, before ISIS's rise.[31] This decision was then reversed in a parliamentary vote in December 2015, when MPs voted by a majority of 174 to support a motion that 'this House notes that ISIL poses a direct threat to the United Kingdom … and accordingly supports Her Majesty's Government in taking military action, specifically airstrikes, exclusively against ISIL in Syria'.[32]

We should note that between these two votes, the government had been conducting airstrikes in Iraq as part of the coalition, but the killing of Reeyad Khan, despite the justification of self-defence, raised serious questions regarding the ability of the UK's government to use force against the expressed will of parliament.[33] At the time of writing, the results of coalition operations are inconclusive, but ISIS appears to be on the back foot. Iraqi forces have now retaken Fallujah.[34] Given that ISIS bases its identity as a caliphate on territorial control, such challenges matter.

The air war against ISIS gives us an immediate comparison to America's transnational war in that it is much larger in scale. Airwars tracks the daily reports given by coalition members, and it is clear that the way the targets are described is more in terms of conventional warfare than a war against a network.[35] This war should also give us reason to pause and consider some of the fundamental limitations inherent in the kind of war that America claims to be waging against al-Qaeda.

The early criticism directed at the notion of a 'war on terror' is that 'terror' is not something that can be attacked with physical means. As we have seen, the inherent idea of a transnational war, or transnational armed conflict, is that the American state is instead at war with a network that is in part constituted by a transnational idea. ISIS demonstrates the limits to this kind of war and warfare. After all, it emanates from a supposed victory—the destruction and marginalisation of AQI—yet now commits unhindered carnage. The AQI–ISIS example raises a simple question: What happens after you defeat a network? Given AQI's resurrection and transformation, if the US did manage to hunt down the core of al-Qaeda, what's to say that it, too, would not rise again in another form?

This returns us to the problem of 'foreign fighters'—participants in civil conflicts driven by transnational identity. This problem goes beyond ISIS: up to December 2015, an estimated 27,000 to 31,000 foreigners travelled to Syria to join fighting groups, from eighty-six different countries.[36] These 'transnational insurgents', as David Malet refers to them, are not restricted to the present day. Indeed, there is a long history of non-citizens mobilising to participate in other people's civil wars and insurgencies. Malet argues that they have been present in one in five civil conflicts in the past 200 years.[37] The same cluster of transnational identities that draw participants to AQ and ISIS (mindful that they differ in important respects) are not restricted to these groups, nor will they be eliminated if, or when, these groups fall apart under military pressure. Since many of these networks are created by alliances, pledges of allegiance and so on, the same malleability that allows these networks to flourish also allows them to split, reshape and reform. When networks decay, or are pulled apart by military pressure, the remnants might give up the struggle, but many will remain motivated to join or ally themselves to another and continue the fight.

With this in mind, we should remember Jeh Johnson's comments regarding the end of al-Qaeda: While America might eradicate the entirety of the group that was responsible for 9/11, what comes next?[38] Although it is possible to make a conceptual jump to a war against a network instead of an organised group, the law of armed conflict has always required clear belligerents. This brings to mind efforts to ban synthetic drugs by referring to their chemical composition in law, since able chemists can effortlessly tweak chemical samples to sidestep such bans.[39] If individuated warfare is a way of thinking about waging war on networks, then the wider problem is the transnational pool of adherents. At this point, the concept of transnational war reaches its limit: the language or concept of war can apply to wars waged against loosely structured networks, but it can't properly admit the idea of war waged against disaffected people solely linked by shared grievances. Just to be clear: I don't think that we should stretch the concept of war to apply it in this way.

Foreign fighters also cause considerable problems for states because they can, and do, disengage from conflicts. Yes, some of the foreign fighters in Syria are hardened jihadists, having fought in places like the Caucasus or the Balkans, but many are first-timers. Europe has seen waves of its citizens travel to Syria and return, yet European states have no unified measures to prevent citizens joining IS or in dealing with them once they come back due to differences in national legislation and political culture.[40] This is a problem that war and warfare cannot solve. The practical roots of transnational jihadism in the late 1970s and 1980s have been well documented and explained,[41] but transnational jihadist terrorism also creates a social and political constituency that cannot be 'solved' through violence or direct force. Returning foreign fighters pose a core problem for liberal democracies in that efforts to 'solve' ideology or to eliminate 'extreme' thought essentially impinge upon the freedom of belief and expression that is meant to be the essence of a free society.

A very British killing

The argument I have developed in this book is that we cannot readily understand American targeted killings, or their justification, without reference to America's constitutional system and its interpretation of law. This is also an argument that suggests American targeted killings are to a certain degree unique to that country. The UK, for example, has a different legal framework regulating the use of lethal force.[42] The precise details of the debate over the powers afforded the president of the United States by the 2001 AUMF are, for other countries, near meaningless. The UK does not have a president, and whereas British soldiers fight 'for queen and country', their American counterparts fight for the Constitution and their country. But all liberal democracies face similar questions, and the British use of a targeted killing against one of its own citizens provides an important chance to reflect on contemporary American debates regarding the reform of the 2001 AUMF.

Again, ISIS is the problem. More specifically, the fact that ISIS is not al-Qaeda and publicly broke ranks with al-Qaeda. In the initial phases of striking against ISIS on 8 August 2014, Obama cited his 'constitutional authority to conduct U.S. foreign relations and as Commander in Chief and Chief Executive'—integral to the office of the president—as his authority to use force against ISIS.[43] An important detail here is that the president is required to inform Congress of this under the War Powers Resolution (1973). This allows the president to commit US forces to an armed conflict, but the president must notify Congress, and may only exercise this authority for a total of ninety days. This should not surprise us; after all, one of the purposes of the executive branch is to take decisions in an emergency. The important change came on 23 September 2014. Obama notified Congress twice, regarding Iraq and Syria, regarding military action against ISIS in each country, but this time citing the 2001 AUMF and the 2002 Authorization for Use of Military Force against Iraq Resolution as authority to conduct strikes against ISIS in Iraq, and the 2001 AUMF as authority for the use of force in Syria.[44] These were claims in addition to that of the War Powers Resolution, but this remains the legal authority to use force against ISIS in Iraq and Syria to this day.

The logic of using the 2001 AUMF in Syria is that ISIS is the successor to AQI, and AQI's connection to al-Qaeda therefore brings them within the scope of the 2001 AUMF. Given ISIS's open hostility to al-Qaeda, this seems a stretch, but deadlock in Congress means that, to date, no new authorisation is forthcoming. Although 'the failure to pass a new AUMF would have little operational impact',[45] this takes America from a situation of interpretative definitions to one where the executive branch is waging a war without Congressional approval. The shifting boundaries of America's transnational war are now irrevocably tied to an aerial campaign with no clear end in sight.

The question of executive authority and freedom to use force in an emergency is a central political issue in any democracy. This is no different in the UK. Unlike the United States, with a written constitution separating the functioning of the state, the UK's parliamentary democracy means that the party able to form a majority in the House of Commons forms a government. This government either exercises powers conferred by parliament, or by Royal Prerogative, for powers derived from the Crown. The prime minister and the cabinet have the constitutional right to decide on military action, but the UK has an unwritten constitution, so this is not codified in writing. The important element to consider is parliament, the primary democratic body of the UK's political system. Parliament voted for the use of force in both Iraq in 2003 and Libya in 2011. Parliament's role in authorising action is understood to be a constitutional convention, but the exact role of parliament, and the reliance upon Royal Prerogative for the use of force, has been debated and examined frequently since the 2003 Iraq War.[46] As mentioned, parliament voted against authorising the use of force in Syria in 2013 (then in response to the actions of the Syrian government), thereby confining the use of UK forces to Iraq. National interpretations of law determine the contours of America's transnational war, just as they determined the contours of the UK's use of force against ISIS. This led to the slightly odd situation of British troops being able to kill members of ISIS in Iraq, but not across the border, despite being part of a coalition that was carrying out strikes in both countries. It also meant that on 7 September 2015 David Cameron blindsided both parliament and the UK by announcing what is, in effect, the first British targeted killing of the post-9/11 era.

Part of the shock was that Cameron's speech was expected to refer to the issue of admitting Syrian refugees to the UK and EU-wide policy regarding the distribution of refugees and asylum seekers across the continent. Halfway through, however, he turned to the topic of British members of Islamic State:

> Today I can inform the House that in an act of self-defence and after meticulous planning Reyaad Khan was killed in a precision air strike carried out on 21 August by an RAF remotely piloted aircraft while he was travelling in a vehicle in the area of Raqqah in Syria.
>
> In addition to Reyaad Khan who was the target of the strike, 2 ISIL associates were also killed, 1 of whom—Ruhul Amin, has been identified as a UK national. They were ISIL fighters and I can confirm there were no civilian casualties.[47]

Cameron went on to echo the American idea of an 'unwilling/unable' test:

> Mr Speaker, we took this action because there was no alternative. In this area, there is no government we can work with. We have no military on the ground to detain those preparing plots. And there was nothing to suggest that Reyaad Khan would ever leave Syria or desist from his desire to murder us at home. So we had no way of preventing his planned attacks on our country without taking direct action.[48]

The importance of the UK's justification is threefold. One is that it is evidence of democracies beyond the United States using the same normative outlook as the United States (and of this outlook influencing a state's interpretation of international law). The second reason is that the UK is fundamentally different from the United States in its constitutional arrangements and therefore this normative outlook is open to challenge both in domestic and foreign courts. The third reason that the UK's justification is important is that it also relies upon a different legal basis for action. The United States justifies its use of targeted killings from an overarching position that it is engaged in an armed conflict with al-Qaeda and associated forces. Not so for the UK, according to Cameron's speech: 'We were exercising the UK's inherent right to self-defence. There was clear evidence of the individuals in question planning and directing armed attacks against the UK. These were part of a series of actual and foiled attempts to attack the UK and our allies.'

The UK appears to be maintaining its position that it is not engaged in any form of transnational armed conflict. Rather, if Cameron's reference to 'armed attacks' is a reference to international law, then the UK is adopting the position advanced by the United States that terrorist attacks can constitute armed attacks, and that these merit the resort to force in self-defence. Whether this is meant to be self-defence as regulated by Article 51 of the UN Charter, or the customary right of pre-emptive self-defence[49] is an open question, since the government has refused to publish the opinion of Jeremy Wright, the attorney general, which is an important aspect of the justification since he 'was consulted and was clear there would be a clear legal basis for action in international law'. The UK also offered an international justification for this action. As per Article 51 of the UN Charter, the UK government wrote to the president of the UN Security Council to inform it of the UK's recourse to self-defence.[50] The UNSC letter demonstrates the UK 'speaking as a state' to the international community: 'ISIL is engaged in an ongoing armed attack against Iraq, and therefore action against ISIL in Syria is lawful in the collective self-defence of Iraq.'

Domestic commentators noted the difference between the justifications offered to the UN and parliament.[51] It is clear from the choice of language that Cameron's speech was calibrated to be a similar kind of justification to those offered by the Obama administration in its defence of targeted killings. Cameron went on to argue that: 'in the prevailing circumstances in Syria, the airstrike was the only feasible means of effectively disrupting the attacks planned and directed by this individual. So it was necessary and proportionate for the individual self-defence of the UK.'

Furthermore, Cameron outlined the process, noting that the UK's intelligence agencies had 'identified the direct threat to the UK from this individual [Khan]', and that a decision was taken at 'a meeting of the most senior members of the National Security Council' to direct the military to 'take action' against Khan, which was signed off by the attorney general, and ultimately authorised by the defence secretary.

Perhaps to forestall inevitable criticism, Cameron explained the *in bello* legal rationale: 'The strike was conducted according to specific military rules of engagement which always comply with international law and the principles of proportionality and military necessity. The military assessed the target location and chose the optimum time to minimise the risk of civilian casualties.'

We should note, here, that this is an interesting mix of justifications. Reference to armed conflict by the United States necessarily requires adherence to the law of armed conflict and its precepts of proportionality and military necessity. The question of the law applicable to the use of force in self-defence is less clear. Cameron's speech was directed at a domestic audience, and, for this reason, it contains elements that are specific to the UK. One of them is the claim that 'this strike was not part of coalition military action against ISIL in Syria—it was a targeted strike to deal with a clear, credible and specific terrorist threats to our country at home. The position with regard to the wider conflict with ISIL in Syria has not changed.'

Without reference to the UK's recent politics, this addendum is incredibly curious: Why argue about the lethal threat posed to the UK by members of Islamic State, and then immediately claim that the UK was not engaged in lethal action in concert with the coalition of states currently bombing Islamic State in Syria and Iraq? Given that the UK is currently engaged in lethal operations in Iraq, this makes little intuitive sense. However, we must recall that parliament voted against military action in Syria in 2013. Cameron's speech therefore trod a very fine line: arguing that the defence secretary had the authority to authorise specific lethal operations in self-defence, while simultaneously arguing that this did not run counter to the will of parliament.

One of the central conundrums of targeted killings is how they are defined. The killing of Reeyad Khan demonstrates the importance of comparative constitutional and political considerations in the structure and use of targeted killings. From a constitutional perspective, the Khan strike was a very British killing.

This leads to a political question that has no inherent answer. If one considers that there are circumstances in which the executive branch of a government needs to authorise lethal action abroad, then how should this decision be informed and authorised? What does the principle of the rule of law require in such circumstances? If both the UK and the US approaches to the law produce similar outcomes, then what is the point? Is law then little more than a veneer for political decisions? I don't agree with this idea. If anything, comparing the two constitutional orders highlights the way the American system is structured to ensure compliance with the rule of law (albeit the American interpretation of law). This provides a perspective that is often missing in analyses that focus solely on the American state.

The American system cannot be 'applied' to the UK any more than the UK's decision processes can be transferred across the Atlantic, but we can learn from common problems. The role of national law, and legal authorisation, in targeted killings is a common problem. Specifically, it is about how to make decision processes as transparent as possible, while still retaining the possibility of effective action by the executive for the purposes of national security. If you disagree with this aim, then consider it framed in another way: What is worse for a democratic country? A three to six month 'AUMF process' of authorisation as part of a wider national security bureaucracy that takes the time to pore over fragmentary intelligence in order to identify and classify people as possible threats, decisions on lethal action being taken by the President himself, and mandatory reporting channels to inform the elected Congress of these decisions. Or, a prime minister and at least two more MPs, meeting as a partial meeting of a sub-committee of the Cabinet of a government, with little else known about this process, at some indeterminate point in time, with the decision being formally communicated to Parliament weeks after the event in question? These processes reflect their relative political systems, but in my mind, America's hyper-bureaucratic approach seems far more amenable to challenge, both internally and externally, than the British one. Moreover, the importance of lawyers in the American process, and their integration at nearly every level, means that bad legal opinions (like the torture memos) can quickly be weeded out. For matters of national security that can't be subjected to open courts, the American way of utilising targeted killings appears more likely to reinforce the rule of law.

This account is of course a snapshot, a picture taken of the present day that omits the legal activities of a plethora of NGOs, journalists and others who have dedicated years to bringing different facets of the American use of targeted killings to light. I will say a bit more about these groups at the end of this chapter, but for now, the American system as it stands now appears far better than it was a decade ago. If we think of any targeted killing as reliant upon the following elements:

1. The relevant bodies of law
2. The interpretations of the relevant law
3. The definitions of legal targets according to these interpretations
4. The practical processes and assessments to ensure adherence to the law
5. The standards required to identify someone (or something) as a lawful target
6. The set of information about someone (or something) used to make decisions
7. The relevant political authority
8. The policy decision to use force
9. The structure of decision making deriving from this authority
10. The judgement to categorise someone (or something) as a lawful target
11. The case-by-case decision to use force against a given target
12. The subsequent chain of decisions that lead to the actual use of force

In a democratic state under the rule of law, which of these elements need to remain secret in matters of national security? More importantly, what needs to remain secret for a short time to maintain operational security, and what needs to remain secret in perpetuity? If we look at the United States, then I think we know seven out of these twelve factors (1, 2, 3, 4, 7, 8, 9), or at least there is enough material on the public record that enables informed discussion about the US government's decisions and interpretations of law. In the case of the UK, the government has explained its position or published material on five out of twelve (elements 1, 2, 7, 8, 9). Although I will discuss accountability in the next section, it is clear that some elements on this list are unlikely ever to become public (for example, point 6, which would require the publication of all intelligence about a target). Even if the redacted Awlaki memo released following a freedom of information request does not give us all of the US government's account, it is decidedly more informative than the public description of the legal advice provided to the UK government by the attorney general.

The attorney general has not disclosed the advice given to the UK government, and government lawyers did not give evidence to an inquiry by the Joint Committee on Human Rights, a parliamentary select committee, citing the need to 'protect the principle of Legal Professional Privilege' since '[i]t is important that we [the Government] are able to seek legal advice in confidence, particularly in matters concerning national security'.[52] The secretary of state for defence also took advice from lawyers working for the Ministry of Defence,[53] but as this, too, is private, the interpretations of relevant law (to the standard of formal legal reasoning citing authority and precedent rather than verbal explanation) remain unknown.

The subsequent parliamentary authorisation for the use of force in Syria renders the domestic question of the use of armed force moot. However, the questions posed by the strike that killed Reeyad Khan are core questions regarding the law applicable to the UK's equivalent of war powers. It also highlights the problems inherent in a form of warfare that is so closely tied to intelligence activity. When considering the issues of transparency and accountability in the decision to use force, it is also necessary to consider the essentially intangible nature of many of the key capabilities that enable the use of targeted killings by liberal democracies.

What's a little information between friends?

The American capability to conduct targeted killings relies upon many intangible elements. This is why the focus upon 'drone proliferation' is a distraction from the wider concerns of intelligence and capability sharing. Some commentators have noted that information and infrastructure are integral to America's use of drones, but I think we need to stand the debate on its head.[54] When we consider the spread of targeted killings as a capability in itself (boxed up with the technology, norms, legal interpretations, bureaucracy, etc.), then the spread of drones should be the least of our current worries. After all, drone proliferation is a relatively transparent activity—it's difficult for states to hide the fact that they are developing and procuring these systems—whereas the 'back end' of targeted killings is intangible and difficult to track.

In Chapter 6, I highlighted the role of intelligence production and sharing in targeted killings. One consequence of the US reliance upon intelligence for targeted killings is the awkward position that its allies find themselves in. The United States has extensive intelligence sharing arrangements with the 'five eyes' group (made up of the United States, UK, Canada, Australia and New Zealand) as well as with European states, NATO members and other US allies.[55] While authoritarian governments might not have any qualms about the use of intelligence shared with the United States to kill people, the question arises for European states that are party to the European Convention on Human Rights. At what point does sharing intelligence with a state known to be using this intelligence to kill people constitute participation in, or responsibility for, this killing?

Again, we can turn to the coalition war against ISIS for an example of the problems that this can cause. On 12 November 2015, a pair of US drones killed Mohammed Emwazi, an ISIS propagandist and executioner, in Raqqa, Syria. The issue? A British drone was also present,[56] since according to David Cameron the UK had been working 'hand in glove' with the United States to track and target Emwazi.[57] This was again explained as an act of self-defence. As the development of the Predator in the Balkans demonstrated, drones do not need to be armed in order to contribute to the use of force. This highlights the essential role that drones, and intelligence, surveillance and reconnaissance (ISR) platforms play in contemporary warfare. The question that the Emwazi strike raises is whether there is much difference between providing the laser signal used to target a laser-guided bomb or releasing the weapon yourself. The Emwazi strike lies on a spectrum either side of the laser pointer—maybe the other drone was effectively a bystander, maybe its pilots were integral to the success of the mission. We do not know.

The importance of this point is that European states operate with different understandings of the law of armed conflict, as well as different domestic jurisprudence defining the relationship between the law of armed conflict and human rights law. Moreover, state parties to the European Convention on Human Rights are subject to the jurisdiction of the European Court of Human Rights. We should remember that when framed as human rights violations, targeted killings are what Philip Alston calls 'extrajudicial killings'—and could contravene the fundamental protections for life contained in Article 2 of the European Convention on Human Rights.[58]

The argument of this book has thus far turned on America's internal definition that an armed conflict exists between itself and al-Qaeda. Both domestic and international courts may take a different view on this issue, and if they do, assistance by states raises the question of legal liability for human rights violations. Indeed, there have already been such cases that raise the question of state responsibility. In the UK, Reprieve, a human rights NGO, helped bring a case against William Hague, the former foreign secretary, on behalf of Noor Khan, whose father was killed in a 2011 strike in Pakistan, to force the government to clarify its position on US strikes.[59] A 2012 court case alleged that GCHQ's civilian staff were complicit in 'war crimes' for aiding US targeted killings.[60] It is clear from recent cases in Britain and Germany that intelligence shared with the United States can lead to lethal operations, and that the legal responsibility for consequent deaths is unclear.[61] The flow of data through territories is another issue—the physical requirement to pass information from fibre-optic cables to satellite relays in Europe means that any decision made in America passes through European states. The transmission of data via German territory is one example of this that has led to legal challenges, although the German courts recently rejected an attempt to hold the German government responsible for complicity in a strike in Yemen.[62]

The ethics and law of intelligence sharing lie beyond the scope of this book. Nonetheless, it is a real problem for states allied to America that hold a different position from that of the United States on political or legal grounds. Since the legal rationale for killing in the context of an armed conflict requires identification of a person as a member of a belligerent group, all data that may lead to that conclusion forms a part of this decision, however small, fragmentary or ambiguous. States may refuse to divulge the nature of the information that they pass to America about al-Qaeda and related groups, but we can be sure that such information transfers exist in some form due to existing reporting on intelligence sharing arrangements. States could erect rules of thumb, such as refusing to pass information that would allow America to take immediate lethal action against a person, but whether these limits would absolve the state of responsibility (in a political/moral sense, since state responsibility in international law is an exceedingly murky area) for consequential violence is unclear. In my opinion, states passing information to America about persons whom the American state is likely to try and kill bear some responsibility for the consequences, no matter how many caveats are added to the transfer. This is in addition to other issues arising from the transfer of information to conduct the strikes. The coalition strikes against ISIS are, again, a good example of this. Who bears responsibility for the estimated minimum 1278 civilian casualties that have resulted from discrete attacks?[63] The state that released the individual munition, or the coalition of states working together to attack ISIS? If the UK enables a coalition partner to carry out an attack that causes civilian casualties, should we then apologise on their behalf? At the moment, the answer appears to be no. I don't think that this abnegation of responsibility is sustainable, nor is it wise.

This book has largely ignored the international politics of targeted killings, but there are clear issues that warrant attention. Worries over the proliferation of drone technology are much the same as worries over the proliferation of cars, or any other dual-use technology. Anyone seeking to prevent the development of vehicles that allow remote operation has to contend with the interests of companies ranging from resource extraction to logistics, by way of Silicon Valley. The issue is not the proliferation and transfer of individual platforms, but the ability to lease the entire mechanism developed for exercising power that has been developed by the American state.

A case in point is Colombia, where in 2013 the *Washington Post* reported that the CIA, JSOC and the NSA had enabled the Colombian government to carry out a targeted killing campaign against FARC, the narco-guerrilla organisation that has been a feature of Colombian politics and instability since 1964.[64] The Colombians did not need drones—instead they relied upon American intelligence support, as well as conversion kits that transformed dumb munitions into precision weapons, guided home by the same GPS satellites that enable American Reapers to dispatch to transnational targets. The ability to transfer the killing apparatus that the American state has developed to target al-Qaeda to third-party states demonstrates the wider relevance of the issues discussed herein. That the technology involved is inherently 'leashed' enables the American state to control the use of capabilities it provides to partner states. That it did so in a covert manner to a state with a questionable human rights record with none of the justifications discussed in this book is worrying. Any insurgent squaring off against an American ally has reason to worry.

America's allies, particularly in Europe, should also worry. Remote warfare always requires a path, be it the trajectory of a ballistic missile or the signal connecting a pilot in Nevada to an aerial platform in South Asia. Common practices of warfare are coming under greater scrutiny from the media and democratic audiences mostly due to the role that they play in America's wars. These are general problems, but likely ones that would not cause such unease were there not large question marks hanging over the legality of America's transnational war. It is common for members of NATO militaries to spend periods of time functionally part of an otherwise foreign (allied) military. As Britain recently found out, there is deep public unease when service personnel are involved in lethal operations which the UK is supposedly not involved in. Despite parliament voting against using lethal force in Syria in 2013, in the summer of 2015 Michael Fallon, the Secretary of State for Defence, informed Parliament that:

> Since the international Coalition commenced military operations against ISIL last year, up to 80 UK personnel have been embedded with US, Canadian and French forces. They have undertaken a range of roles including planning, training and flying and supporting combat and surveillance missions. A small number of embedded UK pilots have carried out airstrikes in Syria against ISIL targets: none are currently involved in airstrikes.

> The convention that before troops are committed to military operations the House of Commons should have an opportunity to debate the matter, except in the event of an emergency, applies to the deployment of UK forces. UK personnel embedded within other nations' armed forces operate as members of that military.[65]

The legal responsibility of the UK state is unclear in this regard.[66] But this highlights the less tangible dimensions of warfare writ large, rather than those wholly associated with drones. Drones are a focus of these worries for a reason, but regulating drones, or preventing their proliferation, will in no way make these underlying questions of intangible contributions to the use of force go away.

The difference between America's transnational war and the coalition war against ISIS is that America's allies in Iraq and Syria are free to contribute to the use of force depending upon their given political and legal constraints. America's transnational armed conflict, however, creates problems for America's allies that routinely share intelligence with it. America has a considerable degree of latitude to interpret international law without fear of formal censure, whereas state parties to the European Convention on Human Rights (e.g. a considerable number of America's closest allies) do not.

Transnational witnesses

If targeting groups like ISIS requires methods of warfare and capabilities that give decision-makers considerable reach, conducted in secret, then how can accountability mechanisms function in this context? Most discussions regarding transparency recognise the need for some degree of secrecy, but the question is how much is necessary. Even though they disagree with the status quo, Orna Ben-Neftali and Roy Peled point out that 'whereas international human rights law (IHRL) explicitly recognizes the public right to know, international humanitarian law (IHL) is essentially silent on the matter, [that secrecy is a priority in war] a silence reflecting a presumption in favour of a State's right to secrecy'.[67]

The question is not so much about whether democracies can conduct secret wars in an accountable fashion, but whether democracies can wage war using means and methods of warfare that are by definition secret, or difficult to observe. There are numerous different proposals for increasing the accountability of the executive branch in America's transnational war. For example, the law professors Amos Guiora and Jeffrey Brand argue for the establishment of 'drone courts' to review executive branch decisions.[68] This proposal, and similar ones, has been attacked by other legal and academic figures who believe that current accountability measures are sufficient.[69] When we consider use of force against ISIS, it is possible to put American accountability mechanisms into perspective, as well as to consider the wider context of transparency and accountability in the present day.

One reason democracies need accountability mechanisms is to prevent governmental overreach. In their examination of the problems associated with drones, John Kaag and Sarah Kreps argued that the asymmetry inherent in these platforms is likely to give rise to a 'moral hazard'—'a situation in which greater risks are taken by individuals who are able to avoid shouldering the cost associated with these risks'.[70] In this framing, the capability of drones increases the likelihood of using them by reducing the costs, and 'it is not at all clear that having more choices leads strategists to make better and more informed ones'. To explain this, they likened the situation to that posed by Plato in the tale of Gyges.[71]

At heart, the ring of Gyges is a myth that explores the interplay of responsibility and justice. In Plato's *Republic*, Glaucon, one of Plato's interlocutors, challenges Socrates to prove that justice is preferable to injustice in and of itself. Glaucon's argument centres on the notion of justice as a compromise, not an inherent good, such that:

> They say that doing injustice is naturally good, and suffering injustice bad, but that the bad in suffering injustice far exceeds the good in doing it; so that, when they do injustice to one another and suffer it and taste of both, it seems profitable—to those who are not able to escape the one and choose the other—to set down a compact among themselves neither to do injustice nor to suffer it. And from there they began to set down their own laws and compacts and to name what the law commands lawful and just. And this, then, is the genesis and being of justice; it is a mean between what is best—doing injustice without paying the penalty—and what is worst—suffering injustice without being able to avenge oneself. The just is in the middle between these two, cared for not because it is good but because it is honored due to a want of vigor in doing injustice.[72]

For Glaucon, 'those who practise it [justice] do so unwillingly, from an incapacity to do injustice', and he raises the issue of the ring of Gyges, so-called because the ring is discovered by a shepherd named Gyges. The ring renders its wearer invisible, and Gyges uses this power to seduce the wife of the king before slaying him. Glaucon explains that this proves that, given freedom from retaliation, 'the actions of the just would be as the actions of the unjust; they would both come at last to the same point'. In secret, the rules that are meant to keep people in line no longer have any hold. Plato's ultimate response to Glaucon is that justice is a form of harmony with one's role in the world, and therefore the just would not behave in the same way as the unjust given the power of Gyges' ring, since they are not slaves to their appetites.

The key question this raises is how to ensure the good conduct of individuals and organisations working in secret to ensure the safety of their peers. How do you ensure that the goal of protecting the country does not lead to behaviour or activities that overstep either political or legal limits? Accountability is a political issue, and one that is usually integral, and particular to, a given society. Democratic societies value accountability, as they draw legitimacy from the support of the population. Although a slippery concept, one way of thinking about accountability is as a measure of official responsiveness to the public. Systems that are entirely unresponsive to the public are unaccountable, yet at the same time political systems that are entirely responsive to public demands are effectively populist in nature, lacking protections for individuals that might fall foul of majoritarian ire. In this way, 'responsiveness is a measure of how much accountability an institutional structure permits'.[73] Another way of thinking about accountability in the United States, which is pertinent to the current context, is offered by Robert D. Behn:

> Our system of accountability has two types of people: Either you are an accountability holder [holding others to account] or you are an accountability holdee [being held to account by others]. It's great to be an accountability holder. It's not so much fun to be an accountability holdee ... Those whom we want to hold accountable have a clear understanding of what accountability means: Accountability means punishment.[74]

Ultimately, this is a question of power: How can the institutions that society assigns the social and political authority to use force be held to account for its use? These are normative issues—implying value judgements as to what is 'normal' and correct—but in democratic societies legitimacy often hinges on perceptions of accountability. A perceived lack of accountability undermines the legitimacy of the system itself, as Garrett Ebbs writes:

> The true danger to the republic right now is an executive establishment that, under the past two presidents, has taken on itself the role of deciding where and whether to make war, has made a mockery of constitutional and statutory restraints on surveillance, and has first conducted and then persistently concealed a shocking campaign of torture. The problem is not

that Obama is better or George W. Bush was worse—what is striking instead is the continuity between administrations on these matters.[75]

The War on Terror has focused attention on this problem. America has had its own issues with enhanced interrogation and rendition, and the UK (and plenty of other states) were complicit in these programmes.[76] Yet important differences exist. The United States might have cancelled Anwar al-Awlaki's passport before he was killed, but he died an American citizen.[77] In contrast, the UK has revoked the citizenship of at least twenty-one dual citizens, two of whom died in American targeted killings.[78] In this, the American example actually demonstrates some of the strengths of the American state. The reporting requirements of the executive branch of government enable limited Congressional oversight, including by politicians from the other party. It also highlights problems. Accountability for the strike that killed Reyaad Khan, for example, is hindered by the fact that the UK's Intelligence and Security Committee has a remit to study intelligence matters, but not military decisions, while the UK's Defence Committee can examine military affairs but lacks the security clearance to examine the intelligence that gave rise to the strike.[79]

The coalition war on ISIS draws attention to the synergies that can be created by states working 'hand in glove' and the problems of holding such behaviour accountable. How do coalitions ensure that the target set does not become the lowest common denominator (or, in legal analysis, the widest possible definitions) of the arrayed states? I do not have an answer to this question, but I think it is an important consideration to bear in mind.

The prospect of accountability matters. Post-hoc judgements found in journalism, criminal investigations, civil claims and international tribunals all render different forms of judgement on the actions of the military. The prospect of such judgements weighs heavily on commanders in contemporary military operations, particularly since the media now broadcasts the results worldwide faster than ever before. In the words of Wesley Clark, who was in charge of NATO's military operations in the 1999 Kosovo War:

American and European leaders were acutely sensitive to the vast change in the flow of information ... The TV reports and press copy that came out of Vietnam were also delayed for hours or days. It took years for the media to build the reporting networks and data flow to bring battlefield events in Vietnam out to the public. In the 1990s all of the information age technologies were available ... The new technologies impacted powerfully at the political levels. The instantaneous flow of news and especially imagery could overwhelm the ability of governments to explain, investigate, coordinate, and confirm.[80]

As a result, Rupert Smith argues that '[w]e are conducting operations now as though we were on a stage, in an amphitheatre or Roman arena'.[81] What is most striking, both about America's transnational war and the coalition war on ISIS, is the role of transnational groups and NGOs in holding governments to account. To return to Behn's differentiation between accountability holders and holdees, the proliferation of groups dedicated to tracking conflicts and identifying the malpractice of states has vastly increased the reach and scope of accountability holders. Therefore, to finish this book on transnational war and warfare, I think we should also pay attention to this range of transnational networks whose actions are shaping the conduct of operations.

If we think of the range of inputs that private citizens and civil society organisations have had in the conduct of America's war, it is sometimes difficult to make sense of it all. America's transnational war also gave rise to civil society networks such as the 'Guantanamo Bay Bar Association'—the lawyers who provided legal representation for prisoners at Guantanamo Bay.[82] The Obama administration had its justification for the use of targeted killings dragged out of it by court cases and journalists. 'Data dumps' of digital archives by whistle-blowers are now a regular occurrence. Nonetheless, the essence of the Obama administration's attitude to law, and the current state of America's war with al Qaeda, is its attentiveness to detail and aim to ensure compliance with the rule of law. The acme of this is the fact that when the law professor Kevin Jon Heller pointed out a flaw in the administration's published legal opinions, the legal bureaucracy running an industrial-scale targeted killing campaign took notice and paused to make sure that this legal issue didn't fatally undermine their lawful authority.[83]

The fear of legal culpability is one form of accountability. Yet the lack of action taken against those responsible for the egregious use of torture during the Bush administration bodes ill for efforts to achieve this form of accountability. The Obama administration's apology for the use of torture was intended to draw a line under the issue. This clearly did not satisfy many critics, both inside the United States as well as around the world, who argued that the matter required criminal convictions of those involved.[84] If we consider the role of accountability to be institutional change, or the mitigation of bad (or illegal) practice, then it is at least arguable that both internal and external accountability measures worked. A government lawyer walked into the Office of Legal Counsel, saw an egregious opinion that legitimised torture and rescinded the memo. The highly partisan reception that the Senate Intelligence Committee's report on CIA interrogations received indicates that this is not a settled political issue,[85] it appears unlikely that another lawyer in John Yoo's position will ever be able to write a memo providing legal permission to use torture again without facing substantial challenge.

Information is essential in order to hold governments accountable. The ICTs that enable targeted killings may greatly increase the internal accountability of militaries,[86] but this is not enough. The Obama administration has sought to shut down and control the leak of information from the executive branch of government by prosecuting whistle-blowers and government employees leaking information to journalists.[87] This is enabled by the same ICTs that I have mentioned before. The digital communications infrastructure that enables the NSA to collect phone call metadata is inherently linked to the increasing capability of governmental bureaucracies to identify people talking to journalists.[88] At the same time, the rise of digital open-source information, or open-source intelligence, gives citizens, journalists and NGOs far greater ability to track the actions of governments.[89] Stephen Grey's investigation of the CIA's rendition programme was enabled by the flight path tracking technology that tracks all commercial flights.[90] If we want to explain the existence of the 'drone debate', then one of the first points of call is the Bureau of Investigative Journalism, the New America Foundation and other organisations that compiled the datasets used to hold the US government to account. The coalition war in Iraq and Syria makes this clear—private individuals now tracking conflicts can use a variety of digital tools and methods to collect and process information that can point towards who is responsible for a given act of violence.[91] This should not be seen as a threat by governments, but it does (and should) create pressure for governments to explain their actions and activities.

* * *

Conclusions

What kind of a democracy can wage a war that apparently has bipartisan support, yet fail to actually authorise that force? The Republican-controlled Congress blames the Democrat president for the impasse, and vice-versa. Ultimately, 'it seems as if Congress is willing—for now—to rest the legal case for war on previous authorizations and ride out the rest of Obama's term'.[92]

Is all of this symptomatic of a 'broken democracy'? From a critical perspective, the conduct of America's war is symbolic of a broken political system. Unaccountable officials take no responsibility for the deaths that they cause worldwide. The democratically elected representatives of the people are too divided to reign in the power of an imperial and unconstitutional executive, and the courts have abdicated responsibility for passing judgement on life and death matters that affect US citizens. Furthermore, the media is complicit in this process due to 'journalism that is incredibly subservient to the American national security state', to quote Glenn Greenwald's criticism of Dean Baquet, the executive editor of the *New York Times*.[93]

An alternate perspective is that this is not a political system 'blinking red', but is instead a normal state of affairs for a country at war. This latter interpretation is more challenging to engage with, because a core assumption of the critical position rests on a change in the status quo as returning America to a more natural state. The problem is that public support for this particular aspect of American foreign policy remains high: roughly two-thirds of Americans support drone strikes on extremists.[94] Moreover, foreign policy is rarely decisive in elections—the American public, like most democracies, tends to vote on political affiliation or economic grounds.[95] The growing political divisions in the United States may be relatively new, but the continuation of transnational warfare represents cross-party agreement on this element of foreign policy.[96] The White House, authorised by Congress, is fulfilling its function, as are the CIA and military that the president orders to protect the

American people. Like it or not, this does not appear to be a democracy in crisis, but a democracy functioning as normal. Given that this book has highlighted four key problems inherent in this normality—the imminence of violence, non-transparent legal categorisations, the reduction of agency from civilian populations and the proliferation of capabilities and norms that enable other states to use these forms of warfare—I hope that this normality leads to examination, not complacency.

AFTERWORD

I was alive during the Cold War, but I was far too young to understand what it meant when the Berlin Wall fell. Growing up in an anti-war household, I attended demonstrations against the first Gulf War, but, again, I was too young to really understand what it meant. When inter-railing around Europe with my mother, we were unable to visit Yugoslavia. Only in my teenage years would it dawn on me that this was because it was the eve of the Yugoslav Wars, and all the horrors that they unleashed.

I write this because I am old enough, just, to remember a time before the War on Terror. In the summer of 2001 I went around the United States on a Greyhound pass. I can remember standing beneath the twin towers of the World Trade Center, framed against the bright blue of a New York summer sky. I cannot accurately recall how I got there, or what I did afterwards, but in that sharp moment they seemed to me the largest buildings ever made. On 11 September I remember sitting in my grandmother's house, watching them collapse into dust on the TV. A couple of weeks later, I started an undergraduate degree in war studies, where our lecturers (some of whom I now count as colleagues) had the unenviable task of attempting to teach us about the concept of war and the principles of the international system while both were being radically altered in theory and practice.

Many of the students that I now teach are too young to remember a time before 9/11, at least in any meaningful sense. America's war, nearly fifteen years and counting, has been the background music to their adult lives. One thing that I have noticed is that it is getting harder and harder to explain what life was like before 9/11. Details matter: there was a time before continuous news tickers on TV, let alone YouTube, social media and the rest of it. Having known a before, and still living the after, I am aware that this perspective on current events is denied to my students just as the experience of having lived through the Cold War was denied to me. I only hope that regardless of what comes next, that none of us will be looking back fondly on a time when states felt it necessary to kill people as standard.

However, I think that the concept of transnational war (and the legal concept of a transnational non-international armed conflict) will both stick. This is not a precise prediction, but given that transnational forms of social organisation are inherent in the globalised world, I think it is likely that we will see a greater number of transnational groups challenging states with violence. As I have outlined in this book, the fact that these kinds of wars are an ill-fit for some of our categories of law will not necessarily matter to terrorist groups, 'criminal insurgencies' and so on. The argument that we should always treat such groups as criminals, through the frame of law enforcement, rests on a condition of certainty that is likely unknown to policy-makers charged with protecting society from violent attacks.

In tandem with this idea, I am also of the opinion that war, and the resort to military means, should be a last resort. The principal challenge I see to this in the contemporary world is not the capability to project force, but the increased visibility of threats, both perceived and actual. Yes, terrorists can kill people, but they do not pose an existential threat to America, nor to the UK. To be clear, I do not think that global governance will provide a solution to this problem, but then I do not think that it is a problem that can be 'solved' to the satisfaction of states. What I hope you can take from this book is that the binary of 'better them than us' needs to give way to a consideration of wider proportionality.

What this book demonstrates is that we need to pay far more attention to the intangible elements of warfare. In particular, 'remote warfare', as a both a term and as a frame of analysis, needs more exploration. I like to think that this book highlights how we need to start placing heavier emphasis on the legal and social construction of violence, and the forms of decision-making involved in war and warfare, rather than physical distance. All wars, once they cross a notional border, are remote from the population that sustains them. The difference is whether they are 'next door' in a physical sense or far away. Distance matters, but the practice of warfare has been remote for some time, is remote in the present day and will likely be remote in the future.

What this book calls attention to is the role of law in violence, and in particular, the tension between various forms of secrecy necessary both in the practice of law and in the functioning of national security structures. What the American experience demonstrates is that legal opinions are integral to public violence, and they shape the wars that democracies wage. From the perspective of a citizen in a democratic society, I think the lack of transparency about these decisions is sometimes unnecessary and undermines the legitimacy of needed government functions. Complete adherence to a standard of 'what we do is secret' is harmful to liberal democracy. There is no single standard of transparency, but publishing policy guidance and the frameworks of legal opinions regarding the right of the executive branch of government to use force is a good thing. It allows lawyers to point out bad law and shaky legal opinions. It provides clarity and security to the people that countries rely upon to ensure their security. It allows democracies to at least debate and object to policy. It allows journalists and activists to hold governments to account. We need the government to work in a legitimate fashion because the contemporary world has no shortage of people and states that are hostile to both democracy and its values. Defending a democratic way of life requires some organisations to work in secret, it requires political leaders to make life-and-death decisions on the basis of fragmentary evidence and it also sometimes requires violence. Where to set the standards for accommodating this within the rule of law is up to us.

NOTES

PREFACE

1. Anderson, Kenneth, 'Targeted Killing and Drone Warfare: How We Came to Debate Whether There Is a "Legal Geography of War"', in Berkowitz, Peter (ed.), *Future Challenges in National Security and Law*, Hoover Institution, Stanford: Stanford University Press, 2011; Carvin, Stephanie. 'The Trouble with Targeted Killing', *Security Studies*, 21, 3 (2012), pp. 529–55.
2. Byman, Daniel, 'Do Targeted Killings Work?', *Foreign Affairs*, 85, 2 (2006), p. 95; Wilner, Alex S., 'Targeted Killings in Afghanistan: Measuring Coercion and Deterrence in Counterterrorism and Counterinsurgency', *Studies in Conflict & Terrorism*, 33, 4 (2010), pp. 307–29; Johnston, Patrick B., and Anoop K. Sarbahi, 'The Impact of US Drone Strikes on Terrorism in Pakistan', *International Studies Quarterly* (2016), pp. 203–219.
3. Zenko, Micah, 'The Long Third War', *Foreign Policy*, October 20, 2012. http://foreignpolicy.com/2012/10/30/the-long-third-war/
4. Boot, Max, 'The New American Way of War', *Foreign Affairs*, 82, 4 (2003), pp. 41–58; Mahnken, Thomas G., *Technology and the American Way of War since 1945*, New York: Columbia University Press, 2010; Carvin, Stephanie, and Michael John Williams, *Law, Science, Liberalism, and the American Way of Warfare*, Cambridge: Cambridge University Press, 2014.

INTRODUCTION: THE BALKAN CRUCIBLE

1. National Security Act of 1947 (P.L. 235).
2. US Congress, 'The Select Committee to Study Governmental Operations with Respect to Intelligence Activities, Foreign and Military Intelligence', Church Committee Report, no. 94–755 (1976).

3. Harder, Tyler J., 'Time to Repeal the Assassination Ban of Executive Order 12,333: A Small Step in Clarifying Current Law', *Military Law Review*, 172 (2002), p. 1.

4. Sullivan, Jeffrey M., 'Revolution or Evolution? The Rise of the UAVs', in *Technology and Society, 2005: Weapons and Wires; Prevention and Safety in a Time of Fear* (ISTAS 2005). Proceedings of International Symposium on pp. 94–101 (IEEE, 2005).

5. Correll, John T., and John T. McNaughton, 'Igloo White', *Air Force Magazine*, 87, 11 (2004), p. 58.

6. Hegghammer, Thomas, 'The Rise of Muslim Foreign Fighters: Islam and the Globalization of Jihad', *International Security*, 35, 3 (2011), pp. 38–48

7. Fulghum, David A., 'Predator to Make Debut over War-Torn Bosnia', *Aviation Week & Space Technology*, 143, 2 (1995), pp. 47–8; Clark, Wesley K., *Waging Modern War: Bosnia, Kosovo, and the Future of Combat*, New York: Public Affairs, 2002, pp. 123–4.

8. Naylor, Sean, *Relentless Strike: The Secret History of Joint Special Operations Command*, New York: St. Martin's Press, 2015, pp. 63–71; Borger, Julian, *The Butcher's Trail: How the Search for Balkan War Criminals Became the World's Most Successful Manhunt*, New York: Other Press, 2016, 77–99.

9. Apple Jr., R.W., 'A War without D-Days Or 4-F's or Riveters', *New York Times*, 30 September 2001.

10. Kaldor, Mary, *New Wars and Old Wars: Organized Violence in a Global Era*, Stanford: Stanford University Press, 1999.

11. Naylor, Sean, *Relentless Strike: The Secret History of Joint Special Operations Command*, New York: St. Martin's Press, 2015, p. 64.

12. Whittle, Richard, *Predator: The Secret Origins of the Drone Revolution*, New York: Henry Holt and Co., 2014, pp. 210–11.

13. Gow, James, *Triumph of the Lack of Will: International Diplomacy and the Yugoslav War*, New York: Columbia University Press, 1997.

14. Isoroku Yamamoto was commander-in-chief of Japan's Combined Fleet during World War II, and was killed when the American navy identified his flight plans and his plane was shot down. Qaed Salim Sinan al-Harithi was a high level al-Qaeda operative killed in Yemen by a Predator drone in 2002.

15. UN Charter, Article 24(1).

16. Werle, Gerhard, and Florian Jessberger, *Principles of International Criminal Law*, Oxford: Oxford University Press, 2014, p. 3.

17. Nollkaemper, André, 'Concurrence between Individual Responsibility and State Responsibility in International Law', *International and Comparative Law Quarterly*, 52, 3 (2003), pp. 615–40.

18. Caplan, Richard, *Europe and the Recognition of New States in Yugoslavia*, Cambridge: Cambridge University Press, 2005.
19. Gow, James, *The Serbian Project and Its Adversaries: A Strategy of War Crimes*, London: Hurst, 2003.
20. Burley, Anne-Marie Slaughter, 'International Law and International Relations Theory: A Dual Agenda', *American Journal of International Law*, 87, 2 (1993), pp. 205–39.
21. Daalder, Ivo H., *Getting to Dayton: The Making of America's Bosnia Policy*, Washington, DC: Brookings Institution Press, 2004, pp. 20–3.
22. Clark, *Waging Modern War*.
23. Roberts, Adam, 'NATO's "Humanitarian War" over Kosovo', *Survival*, 41, 3 (1999), pp. 102–23.
24. Adamsky, Dima, *The Culture of Military Innovation: The Impact of Cultural Factors on the Revolution in Military Affairs in Russia, the US, and Israel*, Stanford: Stanford University Press, 2010, p. 85
25. Carvin and Williams, *Law, Science, Liberalism*, pp. 9–15
26. Mahnken, *Technology and the American Way of War*.
27. Graham, David E., 'Operational Law: A Concept Comes of Age', *Army Lawyer* (1987), p. 9; Warren, Marc L., 'Operational Law: A Concept Matures', *Military Law Review*, 152 (1996), p. 33.
28. Gow, James, *War and War Crimes: The Military, Legitimacy and Success in Armed Conflict*, London: Hurst, 2013.
29. Whittle, *Predator*, p. 141.
30. Ibid., p. 94.
31. Ibid., p. 141.
32. Risen, James, and Ralph Vartabedian, 'Spy Plane Woes Create Bosnia Intelligence Gap', *Los Angeles Times*, 2 December 1995; http://articles.latimes.com/1995–12–02/news/mn-9494_1_military-intelligence
33. Mazzetti, Mark, *The Way of the Knife: The CIA, a Secret Army, and a War at the Ends of the Earth*, New York: Penguin, 2013.
34. Borger, *Butcher's Trail*, pp. 94–7.
35. Ibid.

1. THE CLEANEST WAR

1. Obama, Barack, 'Remarks by the President on a New Strategy for Afghanistan and Pakistan, Speech', White House: Office of the Press Secretary (27 March 2009); https://www.whitehouse.gov/the-press-office/remarks-president-a-new-strategy-afghanistan-and-pakistan
2. Department of Justice, 'Lawfulness of a Lethal Operation Directed against a U.S. Citizen Who Is a Senior Operational Leader of Al-Qa'ida or an Associated Force', Washington, DC: DoJ (2011).

3. Bureau of Investigative Journalism, 'Get the Data: Drone Wars' https://www.thebureauinvestigates.com/category/projects/drones/drones-graphs/. Figure is calculated from data for Pakistan, Yemen and Somalia, excluding 'possible' drone strikes (accessed 12 June 2016).

4. Coker, Christopher, *War in an Age of Risk*, Cambridge: Polity, 2009, Chapter 1, Loc 393/5396.

5. Strachan, Hew, and Sibyl Schiepers (eds), *The Changing Character of War*, Oxford: Oxford University Press, 2011.

6. Kaag, John, and Sarah Kreps, *Drone Warfare*, Cambridge: Polity, 2014, p. 108.

7. For an in-depth explanation of the novel technical aspects of Predators vs earlier UAVs, see Whittle, *Predator*.

8. For an overview of Israeli targeted killings, see Byman, Daniel, *A High Price: The Triumphs and Failures of Israeli Counterterrorism*, Oxford: Oxford University Press, 2011.

9. For data, see the Bureau of Investigative Journalism, a London-based journalism group that has produced one of the best datasets on covert US actions: https://www.thebureauinvestigates.com/category/projects/drones/drones-graphs/

10. Yoo, John, 'Assassination or Targeted Killings after 9/11', *New York Law School Review* (2011), p. 64.

11. Potter, *Nimitz*, p. 233. See also Kahn, David, *The Codebreakers; the Story of Secret Writing*, New York: Macmillan, 1967, pp. 598–9.

12. Costello, John, *The Pacific War*, New York: Quill, 1982, p. 401.

13. Kahn, *Codebreakers*, pp. 598–9; Potter, E.B., *Nimitz*, Annapolis, MD: Naval Institute Press, 1976, p. 233.

14. Potter, *Nimitz*, p. 233.

15. Woods, Chris, *Sudden Justice: America's Secret Drone Wars*, London: Hurst, 2015, pp. 23–6.

16. Ibid., p. 56

17. Kahn, *Codebreakers*, p. 598.

18. Johnsen, Gregory D., *The Last Refuge: Yemen, Al-Qaeda, and the Battle for Arabia*, London: Oneworld, 2013, pp. 121–3.

19. Woods, *Sudden Justice*, p. 57.

20. Hedges, Stephen J., 'U.S. Kills 6 Al Qaeda Suspects', *Chicago Tribune*, 5 November 2002; http://articles.chicagotribune.com/2002–11–05/news/0211050289_1_al-qaeda-yemeni-government-officials-al-harthi

21. Coker, Christopher, *Ethics and War in the 21st Century*, London: Routledge, 2008, pp. 9, 201, loc. 468.

22. DoD News, 'Obama, Hagel Mark End of Operation Enduring Freedom', DoD News, 28 December 2014; http://www.defense.gov/news/newsarticle.aspx?id=123887

23. See Heuser, Beatrice, *Reading Clausewitz*, New York: Random House, 2011; also note that Marie von Clausewitz played a significant role in the work. See Bellinger, Vanya Eftimova, *Marie von Clausewitz: The Woman Behind the Making of 'On War'*, Oxford: Oxford University Press, 2015.

24. Paret, Peter, 'Clausewitz', in Paret, Peter (ed.), *Makers of Modern Strategy from Machiavelli to the Nuclear Age*, Princeton: Princeton University Press, 1986, p. 199.

25. Gow, *War and War Crimes*, p. 1.

26. Coker, *War in an Age of Risk*, loc. 1410/5356.

27. Dickinson, Laura A., 'Military Lawyers on the Battlefield: An Empirical Account of International Law Compliance', *American Journal of International Law*, 104, 1 (January 2010), pp. 1–28.

28. Clausewitz, *On War*, Book 1.2

29. Oppenheim, L., *International Law Vol. II.—War and Neutrality*, London: Longmans, Green and Co, 1912, p. 60.

30. Goldsmith, Jack, *The Terror Presidency: Law and Judgement inside the Bush Administration*, New York: W.W. Norton, 2009, pp. 104–5.

31. Greenwood, Christopher, 'The Concept of War in Modern International Law', *International and Comparative Law Quarterly*, 36, 2 (April 1987), p. 295.

32. Solis, Gary D., *The Law of Armed Conflict: International Humanitarian Law in War*, Cambridge: Cambridge University Press, 2010, p. 153.

33. Goldsmith, Jack L., and Posner, Eric A., *The Limits of International Law*, Oxford: Oxford University Press, 2005.

34. Clausewitz, Carl von, *On War*, trans. Howard, Michael, and Peter Paret, Princeton: Princeton University Press, 1989, Book 1.2.

35. Oxford English Dictionary definition.

36. Nye, Joseph S., and Robert Keohane, 'Transnational Relations and World Politics: An Introduction', *International Organisation*, 25, 3 (1971), p. 331.

37. Gerges, Fawaz A., *The Far Enemy: Why Jihad Went Global*, Cambridge: Cambridge University Press, 2005.

38. Smith, Jackie, 'Transnational Social Movements', in Snow, David (ed.), *The Wiley-Blackwell Encyclopedia of Social and Political Movements*, Malden, MA: Wiley-Blackwell, 2013.

39. See Sandler, Todd, 'Collective Action and Transnational Terrorism', *World Economy*, 26, 6 (2003), pp. 779–802.

40. Smith, Rupert, *The Utility of Force: The Art of War in the Modern World*, New York: Penguin, 2006, p. 1.

41. Ibid.

42. Clausewitz, *On War*, Book 1.2.

43. Goldsmith and Posner, *Limits of International Law*, p. 169.

44. Ibid., p. 180.
45. Ohlin, Jens D., *The Assault on International Law*, Oxford: Oxford University Press, 2015, p. 49.
46. Ibid., 145.
47. See Wendt, Alexander, 'Anarchy Is What States Make of It: The Social Construction of Power Politics', *International Organization*, 46, 2 (1992), pp. 391–425; Wendt, *Social Theory of International Politics*, Cambridge: Cambridge University Press, 1999.
48. Lebow, Ned, *A Cultural Theory of International Relations*, Cambridge: Cambridge University Press, 2008.
49. Ohlin, *Assault on International Law*, p. 11.
50. Gow, *War and War Crimes*, p. 140.
51. Dill, Janina, *Legitimate Targets? Social Construction, International Law and US Bombing*, Cambridge: Cambridge University Press, 2015, p. 63.
52. Coker, *Ethics and War*, p. 114.
53. Bobbitt, Philip, *The Shield of Achilles: War, Peace and the Course of History*, London: Allen Lane, 2002.
54. Grey, Stephen, *Ghost Plane: The Inside Story of the CIA's Secret Rendition Programme*, London: Hurst, 2006, pp. 245–58.
55. Mayer, Jane, 'The Black Sites: A Rare Look inside the C.I.A.'s Secret Interrogation Program', *New Yorker*, 13 August 2007; http://www.newyorker.com/magazine/2007/08/13/the-black-sites?currentPage=1; also ee United States Senate Select Committee on Intelligence, 'Committee Study of the Central Intelligence Agency's Detention and Interrogation Program', SSCI, 2014.
56. Risen, James, 'American Psychological Association Bolstered C.I.A. Torture Program, Report Says', *New York Times*, 30 April 2015; http://www.nytimes.com/2015/05/01/us/report-says-american-psychological-association-collaborated-on-torture-justification.html
57. Goldsmith, *Terror Presidency*, pp. 152–5.
58. Obama, Barack, 'Remarks by the President on National Security', National Archives, Washington, DC, 21 May 2009; https://www.whitehouse.gov/the-press-office/remarks-president-national-security-5-21-09
59. Scahill, Jeremy, *Dirty Wars: The World Is a Battlefield*, London: Serpent's Tail, 2013, p. 515.
60. Obama, 'Remarks by the President on National Security'.
61. For example, see Hasan, Medhi, 'On Wiretaps and Drone Strikes, It's Time for Liberals to Accept That Obama Is Worse Than Bush', *New Statesman*, 13 June 2013; http://www.newstatesman.com/politics/2013/06/wiretaps-and-drone-strikes-its-time-liberals-accept-obama-worse-bush

62. Rohde, David, 'Obama's Many Contradictions on Foreign Policy', The Atlantic, 9 September 2013; http://www.theatlantic.com/international/archive/2013/09/obamas-many-contradictions-on-foreign-policy/279479/

63. Goldsmith, Jack, *Power and Constraint: The Accountable Presidency after 9/11*, New York: W.W. Norton, 2012.

64. Holmes, Stephen, *Passions & Constraint: On the Theory of Liberal Democracy*, Chicago: University of Chicago Press, 1995.

65. Savage, Charlie, *Power Wars*, Boston: Little, Brown, 2015, pp. 47–67.

66. Cheney, Dick, 'Speech to the Veterans of Foreign Wars (VFW) National Convention in Nashville, Tennessee', August 2002; http://www.theguardian.com/world/2002/aug/27/usa.iraq

67. Bridgstock, Martin, *Science, Technology, and Society: An Introduction*, Cambridge: Cambridge University Press, 1998, p. 6.

68. Creveld, Martin Van, *Technology and War: From 2000 BC to the Present*, New York: Touchstone, 1991, p. 311.

69. McNeal, Gregory S., 'Are Targeted Killings Unlawful? A Case Study in Empirical Claims without Empirical Evidence', in Finkelstein, Claire, Jens David Ohlin and Andrew Altman (eds), *Targeted Killings: Law and Morality in an Asymmetrical World*, Oxford: Oxford University Press, 2012, pp. 326–46.

70. Ellis, John, *The Social History of the Machine Gun*, Baltimore: Johns Hopkins University Press, 1986.

71. Lynn, John A., 'Discourse, Reality, and the Culture of Combat', *International History Review*, 27, 3 (2005).

72. Ellis, *Social History of the Machine Gun*, p. 17.

2. THE LENS OF LAW

1. Elton, Ben, Lloyd, John, Curtis, Richard, Atkinson, Rowan, *Blackadder: The Whole Damn Dynasty*, London: Penguin, 1999, p. 442.

2. Melzer, Nils, *Targeted Killing in International Law*, Oxford: Oxford University Press, 2008, pp. 138–9.

3. McChrystal, Stanley, *My Share of The Task: A Memoir*, New York: Penguin, 2014, p. 230, loc 4962.

4. Riedel, Bruce, 'Al Qaeda Strikes Back', *Foreign Affairs*, 86, 3 (2007), pp. 27–8.

5. See, e.g., Lubell, Noam, *Extraterritorial Use of Force against Non-state Actors*, Oxford: Oxford University Press, 2010, pp. 112–21.

6. Office of the Assistant Attorney General, 'Memorandum for the Attorney General Re: Applicability of Federal Criminal Laws and the Constitution to Contemplated Lethal Operations against Shaykh Anwar al-Aulaqi',

US Department of Justice, Office of Legal Counsel, 16 July 2010, p. 24.

7. Most notably, the transitions between international armed conflict and non-international armed conflict, as well as the cessation of hostilities with foreign forces remaining in place. For example, see Roberts, Adam, 'The End of Occupation: Iraq 2004', *International and Comparative Law Quarterly*, 54, 1 (2005)

8. Bush, George W., 'Address to the Joint Session of the 107th Congress', Washington, DC, 20 September 2001; http://georgewbush-white-house.archives.gov/infocus/bushrecord/documents/Selected_Speeches_George_W_Bush.pdf

9. Cassese, Antonio, "Terrorism Is Also Disrupting Some Crucial Legal Categories of International Law', *European Journal of International Law*, 12, 5 (2001), pp. 993–1001.

10. Article 51 of the Charter of the United Nations states that 'Nothing in the present Charter shall impair the inherent right of individual or collective self-defence if an armed attack occurs against a Member of the United Nations, until the Security Council has taken measures necessary to maintain international peace and security.'

11. Murphy, Sean D., 'Terrorism and the Concept of "Armed Attack" in Article 51 of the U.N. Charter', *Harvard International Law Journal*, 53, 1 (2002), p. 51.

12. Stahn, Carsten, 'Terrorist Acts as Armed Attack: The Right to Sef-Defense, Article 51(1/2) of the UN Charter, and International Terrorism', *Fletcher Forum of World Affairs*, 27, 2 (2003), p. 36.

13. Byers, Michael, 'Terrorism, the Use of Force and International Law after 11 September', *International and Comparative Law Quarterly*, 51 (April 2002), p. 409.

14. Van den hole, Leo, 'Anticipatory Self-Defence under International Law', *American University International Law Review*, 19 (2003), p. 69.

15. Mary Ellen O'Connell is a leading example, see O'Connell, Mary Ellen, 'Respect the Battlefield', CBS News, 8 April 2010; http://www.cbsnews.com/news/respect-the-battlefield/

16. Howard, Michael, 'What's in a Name? How to Fight Terrorism', *Foreign Affairs*, 81, 1 (2002), p. 8.

17. Ibid., p. 10.

18. Bobbitt, Philip, *Terror and Consent: The Wars for the Twenty-First Century*, New York: Penguin, 2009, p. 133.

19. Ibid., p. 181.

20. Cassese, 'Terrorism Is Also Disrupting Crucial Legal Categories of International Law', p. 993.

21. Greenwood, Christopher, 'War, Terrorism, and International Law', *Current Legal Problems*, 56, 1 (2003), p. 512.

22. Solis, *Law of Armed Conflict*, pp. 20–1.

23. Notably the 1949 Geneva Conventions, as well as the general prohibition on war as a tool of states in the UN Charter.

24. Dinstein, Yoram, *War, Aggression and Self-Defence*, 3rd edn, Cambridge: Cambridge University Press, 2004, p. 136.

25. Most notably in the speeches of the Obama administration, see McDonald, Jack, 'The Ethics and Legality of the American Targeted Killing Programme', PhD thesis, King's College London, 2013; Anderson, Kenneth, and Benjamin Wittes, *Speaking the Law: The Obama Administration's Addresses on National Security Law*, Stanford: Hoover Institution Press, 2015.

26. Brennan, John, 'The Ethics and Efficacy of the President's Counterterrorism Strategy', Washington, DC: Wilson Center, 30 April 2012.

27. Greenwood, 'War, Terrorism, and International Law', p. 513.

28. See Solis, *Law of Armed Conflict*, pp. 205–6.

29. Use of Force Committee, 'Final Report on the Meaning of Armed Conflict in International Law', International Law Association, The Hague Conference, 2010, p. 1.

30. McDougall, Carrie, *The Crime of Aggression Under the Rome Statute of the International Criminal Court*, Cambridge: Cambridge University Press, 2013.

31. Use of Force Committee, 'Final Report on the Meaning of Armed Conflict', pp. 3–4.

32. Schabas, William A., 'Lex Specialis—Belt and Suspenders—The Parallel Operation of Human Rights Law and the Law of Armed Conflict, and the Conundrum of Jus Ad Bellum', *Israel Law Review*, 40 (2007), p. 592.

33. O'Connell, 'Defining Armed Conflict', p. 397.

34. Datasets: Roggio, Bill, 'Charting the Data for US Airstrikes in Pakistan, 2004–2015', Long War Journal; http://www.longwarjournal.org/pakistan-strikes; Roggio, Bill, and Bob Barry, 'Charting the Data for US Airstrikes in Yemen, 2002–2015', Long War Journal; http://www.longwarjournal.org/yemen-strikes/; New America Foundation, 'Drone Wars Pakistan: Analysis', New America Foundation; http://securitydata.newamerica.net/drones/pakistan-analysis.html; New America Foundation, 'Drone Wars Yemen: Analysis', New America Foundation; http://securitydata.newamerica.net/drones/yemen-analysis.html; Bureau of Investigative Journalism, 'Get the Data: Drone Wars', Bureau of Investigative Journalism; https://www.thebureauinvestigates.com/category/projects/drones/drones-graphs/; Pakistan Body Count, 'Pakistan Body Count', Pakistan Body Count; http://pakistanbodycount.org/

35. Blank, Laurie R., and Benjamin R. Farley, 'Characterizing US Operations in Pakistan: Is the United States Engaged in an Armed Conflict?', *Fordham International Law Journal*, 34, 2 (2011) p. 154.

36. Warrick, Joey, 'CIA Places Blame for Bhutto Assassination', *Washington Post*, 18 January 2008; http://www.washingtonpost.com/wp-dyn/content/article/2008/01/17/AR2008011703252.html

37. Duguid, Gordon, 'Press Statement: Rewards for Justice; Baitullah Mehsud', Bureau of Public Affairs: Office of the Spokesman, 25 March 2009; http://www.state.gov/r/pa/prs/ps/2009/03/120863.htm

38. Bureau of Investigative Journalism, 'Obama 2009 Pakistan Strikes', 2009, Data entry OB29; http://www.thebureauinvestigates.com/2011/08/10/obama-2009-strikes/

39. O'Connell, Mary Ellen, 'Unlawful Killing with Combat Drones: A Case Study of Pakistan, 2004–2009', Notre Dame Legal Studies Paper no. 09–43 (2009), p. 10; http://papers.ssrn.com/sol3/papers.cfm?abstract_id=1501144

40. Reprieve, 'You Never Die Twice: Multiple Kills in the US Drone Program', Reprieve, 2014, p. 2; http://www.reprieve.org/uploads/2/6/3/3/26338131/2014_11_24_pub_you_never_die_twice_-_multiple_kills_in_the_us_drone_program.pdf

41. Bellal, Annyssa, Gilles Giacca and Stuart Casey-Maslen, 'International Law and Armed Non-state Actors in Afghanistan', *International Review of the Red Cross*, 93, 881 (March 2011); https://www.icrc.org/eng/assets/files/review/2011/irrc-881-maslen.pdf

42. Woods, *Sudden Justice*, p. 223.

43. See Shapiro, Jacob N., and C. Christine Fair, 'Understanding Support for Islamist Militancy in Pakistan', *International Security*, 34, 3 (Winter 2009/10).

44. Mazzetti, Mark, and David Sanger, 'Obama Expands Missile Strikes inside Pakistan', *New York Times*, 21 February 2009, p. A1; http://www.nytimes.com/2009/02/21/washington/21policy.html

45. Bureau of Investigative Journalism, 'Naming the Dead: Baitullah Mehsud'; https://www.thebureauinvestigates.com/namingthedead/people/nd223/?lang=en

46. McDonald, 'Ethics and Legality of the American Targeted Killing Programme', p. 11.

47. Alston, Philip, 'The CIA and Targeted Killings beyond Borders', *Harvard National Security Journal*, 2 (2011); http://harvardnsj.org/wp-content/uploads/2011/02/Vol.-2_Alston1.pdf

48. Bull, Hedley, *The Anarchical Society: A Study of Order in World Politics*, Basingstoke: Palgrave Macmillan, 2012.

49. Solis, *Law of Armed Conflict*, p. 20.

50. Gathii, James Thuo, 'International Law and Eurocentricity', *European Journal of International Law*, 9 (1998), pp. 184–211.

51. Henkin, Louis, *How Nations Behave*, 2nd edn, New York: Columbia University Press, 1979, p. 47.

52. Solis, *Law of Armed Conflict*, p. 20.

53. Also referred to as 'Common article 2'.

54. UN Charter, Article 2(4).

55. UN Charter, Article 51.

56. For interested readers, I would suggest Dinstein, *War, Aggression and Self-Defence*, 2004.

57. Dinstein, Yoram, 'The Initiation, Suspension, and Termination of War', *International Law Studies* US Naval War College 75 (2000), p. 133.

58. Aldrich, George H., 'Prospects for United States Ratification of Additional Protocol I to the 1949 Geneva Conventions', *American Journal of International Law*, 85, 1 (1991), pp. 1–4.

59. This task often falls on the ICRC, see Mack, Michelle, and Jelena Pejic, 'Increasing Respect for International Humanitarian Law in Non-international Armed Conflicts', ICRC, February 2008; https://www.icrc.org/eng/assets/files/other/icrc_002_0923.pdf

60. Also sometimes referred to as 'state terror', see Sluka, Jeffrey A., 'Introduction', in Sluka, Jeffrey A. (ed.), *State Terror and Anthropology*, Philadelphia: University of Pennsylvania Press, 2000.

61. UN Charter Article 23(1)

62. Weiss, Thomas G., 'The Illusion of UN Security Council Reform', *Washington Quarterly*, 26, 4 (2003), pp. 147–61.

63. Shelton, Dinah, *Commitment and Compliance: The Role of Non-binding Norms in the International Legal System*, Oxford: Oxford University Press, 2003.

64. Glennon, Michael J., "Nicaragua v. United States: Constitutionality of US Modification of ICJ Jurisdiction', *American Journal of International Law* (1985), pp. 682–9.

65. International Court of Justice, 'Case Concerning the Military and Paramilitary Activities in and against Nicaragua (Nicaragua v. United States of America)', Judgment of 27 June 1986, p. 6.

66. United Nations Security Council, Resolution 827, 25 May 1993.

67. Finnemore, Martha, and Kathryn Sikkink, 'International Norm Dynamics and Political Change', *International Organization*, 52, 4 (1998), pp. 887–917.

68. Koh, Harold Hongju, 'How Is International Human Rights Law Enforced', *Indiana Law Journal*, 74 (1998), p. 1409.

69. Moyn, Samuel, *The Last Utopia*, Cambridge, MA: Harvard University Press, 2010, Chapter 5.

70. Wexler, Lesley, 'The International Deployment of Shame, Second-Best Responses, and Norm Entrepreneurship: The Campaign to Ban Landmines and the Landmine Ban Treaty', *Arizona Journal of International and Comparative Law*, 20 (2003), p. 561.

71. Koh, Harold Hongju et al., 'Why Do Nations Obey International Law?', *Yale Law Journal* (1997), p. 2650.

72. Akande, Dapo, 'Classification of Armed Conflicts: Relevant Legal Concepts', in Wilmshurst, Elizabeth (ed.), *International Law and the Classification of Armed Conflicts*, Oxford: Oxford University Press, 2012, p. 32.

73. Wilmshurst, Elizabeth, 'Introduction', in Wilmshurst, *International Law*, p. 2.

74. Alston, Philip, 'Report of the UN Special Rapporteur on Extrajudicial, Summary or Arbitrary Executions: Study on Targeted Killings', UN Doc. A/HRC/14/24/Add.6 2010, p. 15; http://www2.ohchr.org/english/bodies/hrcouncil/docs/14session/A.HRC.14.24.Add6.pdf

75. Corn, Geoffrey S., 'Hamdan, Lebanon, and the Regulation of Armed Hostilities: The Need to Recognize a Hybrid Category of Armed Conflict', *Vanderbilt Journal of Transnational Law*, 40 (2006).

76. Akande, 'Classification of Armed Conflicts', p. 41.

77. Ibid.

78. Solis, *Law of Armed Conflict*, p. 152.

79. Schmitt, Michael N., 'Responding to Transnational Terrorism under the Jus ad bellum: A Normative Framework', in Schmitt, *Essays on Law and War at the Fault Lines*, The Hague: TMC Asser Press, 2011, pp. 49–86.

80. Anderson, Kenneth, 'Targeted Killing and Drone Warfare: How We Came to Debate Whether There Is a "Legal Geography of War"', Washington College of Law Research Paper no. 2011–16 (2011), p. 3; https://www.law.upenn.edu/live/files/3484-anderson-k-targeted-killing-and-drone-warfare

81. For legal analysis of this particular question, see Murphy, Sean D., 'The International Legality of US Military Cross-Border Operations from Afghanistan into Pakistan', in Schmitt, Michael N. (ed.), 'The War in Afghanistan: A Legal Analysis', *International Law Studies*, 85 (2008).

82. Harbom, Lotta, and Peter Wallensteen, 'Armed Conflict and Its International Dimensions, 1946–2004', *Journal of Peace Research*, 42, 5 (2005), p. 629.

83. Tadic, 'Opinion and Judgment', ICTY, 7 May 1997; http://www.haguejusticeportal.net/Docs/Court%20Documents/ICTY/Tadic_judgement.pdf

84. Tadić, 'Decision on Motion for Interlocutory Appeal on Jurisdiction', ICTY, paragraph 70, note 174.

85. Ibid.

86. Protocol Additional to the Geneva Conventions of 12 August 1949, and relating to the Protection of Victims of Non-international Armed Conflicts (Protocol II), 8 June 1977. Article 1(2) states that: 'This Protocol shall not apply to situations of internal disturbances and tensions, such as riots, isolated and sporadic acts of violence and other acts of a similar nature, as not being armed conflicts.'

87. Lubell, Noam, 'The War(?) against Al Qaeda,' in Wilmshurst, *International Law*, p. 2050.

88. See Keegan, John, *A History of Warfare*, New York: Random House, 2011; Huntington, Samuel P., *The Soldier and the State: The Theory and Politics of Civil–Military Relations*, Cambridge, MA: Harvard University Press, 1981.

89. Clunan, Anne L., and Harold A. Trinkunas (eds), *Ungoverned Spaces Alternatives to State Authority in an Era of Softened Sovereignty*, Stanford: Stanford University Press, 2010.

90. Jackson, Robert H., *Quasi-States Sovereignty, International Relations and the Third World*, Cambridge: Cambridge University Press, 1993.

91. Alston, Philip, 'Report of the UN Special Rapporteur on Extrajudicial, Summary or Arbitrary Executions: Study on Targeted Killings', UN Doc. A/HRC/14/24/Add.6 2010, p. 16; http://www2.ohchr.org/english/bodies/hrcouncil/docs/14session/A.HRC.14.24.Add6.pdf

92. Shaw, Malcolm N., *International Law*, 5th edn, Cambridge: Cambridge University Press, 2003, p. 69.

93. Ibid.

94. Keen, David, *Useful Enemies: When Waging Wars Is More Important Than Winning Them*, New Haven: Yale University Press, 2012.

95. Ohlin, Jens David, *The Assault on International Law*, Oxford: Oxford University Press, 2015, p. 174.

96. Goldsmith and Posner, *Limits of International Law*, Chapter 1.

3. IN WASHINGTON'S SHADOW

1. Klaidman, Daniel, *Kill or Capture: The War on Terror and the Soul of the Obama Presidency*, Boston: Houghton Mifflin Harcourt, 2012, p. 50.

2. Joint Resolution, 8 December 1941, Public Law 77–328, 55 STAT 795.

3. Elsea, Jennifer K., and Grimmett, Richard F., 'Declarations of War (DOW) and Authorizations for the Use of Military Force: Historical Background and Legal Implications', Washington, DC: Congressional Research Service, 17 March 2011.

4. Greenwood, 'Concept of War', p. 285.

5. 'Authorization for Use of Military Force against Iraq', Resolution of 2002, Public Law 107–243, 116 Stat. 1498.

6. 'Authorization for Use of Military Force (AUMF)', Public Law 107–40 (2001).

7. Zenko, Micah, 'The Long Third War', *Foreign Policy* (30 October 2012); http://www.cfr.org/drones/long-third-war/p29368

8. McElroy, Damien, Adrian Blomfield and Nasser Arrabyee, 'Anwar al-Awlaki: Drone Kills US-Born Preacher Who Inspired Lone Wolf Terrorists', *Daily Telegraph*, 30 September 2011; http://www.telegraph.co.uk/news/worldnews/al-qaeda/8800346/Anwar-al-Awlaki-Drone-kills-US-born-preacher-who-inspired-lone-wolf-terrorists.html

9. Douthat, Ross, 'The Making of an Imperial President', *New York Times*, 22 November 2014; http://www.nytimes.com/2014/11/23/opinion/sunday/ross-douthat-the-making-of-an-imperial-president.html

10. Paul, Rand, 'Show Us the Drone Memos', *New York Times*, 11 May 2014; http://www.nytimes.com/2014/05/12/opinion/show-us-the-drone-memos.html?hp&rref=opinion&_r=0

11. Mazzetti, *Way of the Knife*, p. 87.

12. Miller, Greg, 'Muslim Cleric Aulaqi Is 1st U.S. Citizen on List of Those CIA Is Allowed to Kill', *Washington Post*, 7 April 2010; http://www.washingtonpost.com/wp-dyn/content/article/2010/04/06/AR2010040604121.html

13. Berger, J.M., 'Anwar Al-Awlaki's Links to the September 11 Hijackers', The Atlantic, 9 September 2011; http://www.theatlantic.com/international/archive/2011/09/anwar-al-awlakis-links-to-the-september-11-hijackers/244796/

14. Shane, Scott, and Mekhennet, Souad, 'Imam's Path from Condemning Terror to Preaching Jihad', *New York Times*, 8 May 2010; http://www.nytimes.com/2010/05/09/world/09awlaki.html

15. Savage, *Power Wars*, p. 232.

16. Important examples are: O'Connell, "Unlawful Killing with Combat Drones'; Alston, 'CIA and Targeted Killings'; Benjamin, Medea, *Drone Warfare: Killing by Remote Control*, London: Verso, 2013.

17. Waxman, Matthew C., 'Guantánamo, Habeas Corpus, and Standards of Proof: Viewing the Law through Multiple Lenses', *Case Western Reserve Journal of International Law* 42 (2009), p. 245.

18. 'Authorization for Use of Military Force (AUMF)', Public Law 107–40, 115 Stat. 224

19. Department of Justice, 'Lawfulness of a Lethal Operation', 2011, p. 1; Office of the Assistant Attorney General, 'Memorandum for the Attorney General Re: Applicability of Federal Criminal Laws and the Constitution

to Contemplated Lethal Operations against Shaykh Anwar al-Aulaqi', US Department of Justice, Office of Legal Counsel, 16 July 2010.

20. Becker, Jo, and Scott Shane, 'Secret "Kill List" Proves a Test of Obama's Principles and Will', *New York Times*, 29 May 2012, p. A1; http://www.nytimes.com/2012/05/29/world/obamas-leadership-in-war-on-al-qaeda.html; Currier, Cora, 'The Kill Chain', The Intercept, 15 October 2015; https://theintercept.com/drone-papers/the-kill-chain/

21. Cole, David, 'Killing Citizens in Secret', *New York Review of Books*: NYR Daily, 9 October 2011; http://www.nybooks.com/blogs/nyrblog/2011/oct/09/killing-citizens-secret/

22. Not to be confused with *Al-Aulaqi v Panetta*, launched after Anwar's death to challenge the government's right to kill US citizens. See ACLU/CCR, 'Al-Aulaqi V. Panetta: Constitutional Challenge to Killing of Three U.S. Citizens', ACLU, 4 June 2014; https://www.aclu.org/cases/al-aulaqi-v-panetta-constitutional-challenge-killing-three-us-citizens

23. *Al-Aulaqi v Obama*, Complaint, 30 August 2010, p. 2.

24. *Al-Aulaqi v. Panetta*.

25. Miller, Greg, 'Legal Memo Backing Drone Strike That Killed American Anwar al-Awlaki Is Released', *Washington Post*, 23 June 2014.

26. ACLU, 'Frequently Asked Questions about Targeted Killing'; https://www.aclu.org/frequently-asked-questions-about-targeting-killing

27. Obama, Barack, 'Remarks by the President at the "Change of Office" Chairman of the Joint Chiefs of Staff Ceremony', Fort Myer, Virginia, 30 September 2011; https://www.whitehouse.gov/the-press-office/2011/09/30/remarks-president-change-office-chairman-joint-chiefs-staff-ceremony

28. Klaidman, *Kill or Capture*, p. 216.

29. US Supreme Court, Ex Parte Quirin, 317 US 1 (1942)

30. There are specific protections in Article 3 of the constitution, not to be confused with the military crime of 'war treason' of aiding enemy forces with information, etc. See Lieber Code, Article 90.

31. See *In re territo* (1946)

32. Cronin, Audrey Kurth, 'ISIS Is Not a Terrorist Group: Why Counterterrorism Won't Stop the Latest Jihadist Threat', *Foreign Affairs*, 94, 2 (March/April 2015).

33. Bobbitt, *Terror and Consent*, p. 539.

34. Yoo, John, *War by Other Means: An Insider's Account of the War on Terror*, New York: Atlantic Monthly Press, 2006, p. 130.

35. Ibid., p. 16.

36. Ibid., p. 17.

37. Byman, Daniel, 'Comparing Al Qaeda and ISIS: Different Goals,

Different Targets', Brookings: Prepared testimony before the Sub-committee on Counterterrorism and Intelligence of the House Committee on Homeland Security, 29 April 2015; http://www.brookings.edu/research/testimony/2015/04/29-terrorism-in-africa-byman

38. Berger, J.M., 'The Islamic State vs. al Qaeda: Who's Winning the War to Become the Jihadi Superpower?', *Foreign Policy* (2 September 2014); http://foreignpolicy.com/2014/09/02/the-islamic-state-vs-al-qaeda/

39. Hoffman, Bruce, 'A First Draft of the History of America's Ongoing Wars on Terrorism', *Studies in Conflict & Terrorism*, 38, 1 (2015), p. 76.

40. Jackson, Brian A., 'Groups, Networks, or Movements: A Command-and-Control-Driven Approach to Classifying Terrorist Organizations and Its Application to Al Qaeda', *Studies in Conflict & Terrorism*, 29, 3 (2006) p. 242.

41. Mattis, James N., 'Commanding General's Message to All Hands', 1st Marine Division (REIN), March 2003.

42. Market states, according to Philip Bobbitt, are states that predicate their legitimacy on their ability to maximise opportunities for their citizens. Bobbitt argues that these market-centric entities represent the future, and a turn away from the nation states that defined the nineteenth and twentieth centuries. Bobbitt, Philip, *The Shield of Achilles: War, Peace, and the Course of History*, New York: Anchor Books, 2002, p. 230.

43. Singer, P.W., 'Can't Win with'—Can't Go to War without'—: Private Military Contractors and Counterinsurgency', Brookings Policy Paper, no 4 (September 2007).

44. O'Connell, Mary Ellen, 'To Kill or Capture Suspects in the Global War on Terror', *Case Western Reserve Journal of International Law*, 35, 2 (2003); http://scholarship.law.nd.edu/cgi/viewcontent.cgi?article=1682&context=law_faculty_scholarship

45. Radsan, Afsheen John, and Richard W. Murphy, 'The Evolution of Law and Policy for CIA Targeted Killing', *Journal of National Security Law and Policy*, 5 (2012), p. 462.

46. Brennan, John O., 'The Efficacy and Ethics of U.S. Counterterrorism Strategy', Speech, Wilson Center, 30 April 2012; http://www.wilsoncenter.org/event/the-efficacy-and-ethics-us-counterterrorism-strategy

47. Elias, Barbara (ed.), 'Bush Administration's First Memo on al-Qaeda Declassified', National Security Archive Electronic Briefing Book no. 147 (2006); http://nsarchive.gwu.edu/NSAEBB/NSAEBB147/

48. 'Authorization for Use of Military Force (AUMF)', Public Law 107–40 (2001) 2(a).

49. See Savage, *Power Wars*; Mazzetti, *Way of the Knife*; Klaidman, *Kill or Capture*; Goldsmith, *Power and Constraint*.

50. Armed conflict from the Hamdan decision, contained in Department of Justice, 'Lawfulness of a Lethal Operation', 2011, p. 1; Office of the Assistant Attorney General, 'Memorandum for the Attorney General Re: Applicability of Federal Criminal Laws and the Constitution to Contemplated Lethal Operations against Shaykh Anwar al-Aulaqi', US Department of Justice, Office of Legal Counsel, 16 July 2010.
51. Use of Force Committee, 'Final Report on the Meaning of Armed Conflict in International Law', International Law Association, The Hague Conference, 2010, p. 4.
52. Ibid.
53. Powell, Emilia Justyna, and Sara McLaughlin Mitchell, 'The International Court of Justice and the World's Three Legal Systems', *Journal of Politics*, 69, 2 (May 2007), p. 397.
54. Paust, Jordan J., 'The US and the ICC: No More Excuses', *Washington University Global Studies Law Review*, 12 (2013), pp. 569–70.
55. *Hamdan v. Rumsfeld*, 548 US 557 (2006)
56. See, for example, Brennan, 'Efficacy and Ethics of U.S. Counterterrorism Strategy'; Office of the Assistant Attorney General, 'Memorandum for the Attorney General Re: Applicability of Federal Criminal Laws and the Constitution to Contemplated Lethal Operations against Shaykh Anwar al-Aulaqi', US Department of Justice, Office of Legal Counsel, 16 July 2010.
57. 'Authorization for Use of Military Force (AUMF)', Public Law 107–40 (2001).
58. See United States Senate Select Committee on Intelligence, 'Committee Study of the Central Intelligence Agency's Detention and Interrogation Program', SSCI (2014).
59. See Office of General Counsel Department of Defense, 'Department of Defense Law of War Manual', Department of Defense, June 2015.
60. Cook, Martin L., *The Moral Warrior: Ethics and Service in the US Military*, New York: SUNY Press, 2004, p. 41.
61. Joint resolution concerning the war powers of Congress and the president, PL 93–148, 87 State, 555 (1973).
62. The Uniform Code of Military Justice, 64 Stat. 109, 10 U.S.C. §§801–946.
63. See Relyea, Harold C., 'Presidential Directives: Background and Overview', Congressional Research Service, 98–611 GOV, 26 November 2008.
64. Greenwald, Glenn, 'Chilling Legal Memo from Obama DOJ Justifies Assassination of US Citizens', *Guardian*, 5 February 2013; http://www.theguardian.com/commentisfree/2013/feb/05/obama-kill-list-doj-memo

65. Friedersdorf, Conor, 'Waging War in Secret vs. American Democracy', The Atlantic, 7 February 2012; http://www.theatlantic.com/politics/archive/2012/02/waging-war-in-secret-vs-american-democracy/252677/

66. Woods, Chris, 'Drones: Barack Obama's Secret War', *New Statesman*, 13 June 2012; http://www.newstatesman.com/politics/politics/2012/06/drones-barack-obamas-secret-war

67. Taylor, Marisa, and Jonathan S. Landay, 'Obama's Crackdown Views Leaks as Aiding Enemies of U.S.', McClatchy DC, 20 June 2013; http://www.mcclatchydc.com/news/special-reports/insider-threats/article24750244.html#.UkSv9dKsgyo

68. O'Connell, Mary Ellen, 'The Choice of Law Against Terrorism', *Journal of National Security Law and Policy*, 4 (2010), p. 368.

69. Menkhaus, Ken, 'Governance without Government in Somalia: Spoilers, State Building, and the Politics of Coping', *International Security*, 31, 3 (Winter 2006/7), pp. 74–106.

70. Fukuyama, Francis, *State-Building: Governance and World Order in the 21st Century*, Ithaca: Cornell University Press, 2004.

71. For example, the problems caused by using militias to extend state authority in Afghanistan. See Goodhand, Jonathan, and Aziz Hakimi, 'Counterinsurgency, Local Militias and Statebuilding in Afghanistan', United States Institute of Peace, Peaceworks no. 90 (2014) p. 44; http://www.usip.org/sites/default/files/PW90-Counterinsurgency-Local-Militias-and-Statebuilding-in-Afghanistan.pdf

72. Jones, Seth G., and C. Christine Fair, 'Counterinsurgency in Pakistan', RAND Corporation, 2010, p. 75; http://www.rand.org/content/dam/rand/pubs/monographs/2010/RAND_MG982.pdf

73. Huntington, Samuel P., 'The Lonely Superpower', *Foreign Affairs*, 78, 2 (1999).

74. WikiLeaks, 'Secret US Embassy Cables', Wikileaks.org, 28 November 2010; https://wikileaks.org/cablegate.html

75. 'US Embassy Cables: Yemen Trumpets Strikes on al-Qaida That Were Americans' Work', *Guardian*, 4 December 2010; http://www.the-guardian.com/world/us-embassy-cables-documents/240955; 'US Embassy Cables: Pakistan Backs US Drone Attacks on Tribal Areas', *Guardian*, 30 November 2010; http://www.theguardian.com/world/us-embassy-cables-documents/167125

76. Mazzetti, *Way of the Knife*, p. 109.

77. Entous, Adam, Julian E. Barnes and Margaret Coker, 'U.S. Doubts Intelligence That Led to Yemen Strike', *Wall Street Journal*, 29 December 2011; http://www.wsj.com/articles/SB10001424052970203899504577126883574284126

78. Mazzetti, Mark, 'A Secret Deal on Drones, Sealed in Blood', *New York Times*, 6 April 2013; http://www.nytimes.com/2013/04/07/world/asia/origins-of-cias-not-so-secret-drone-war-in-pakistan.html?_r=0

79. White House, 'U.S. Policy Standards and Procedures for the Use of Force in Counterterrorism Operations outside the United States and Areas of Active Hostilities', fact sheet, 23 May 2015; https://www.whitehouse.gov/sites/default/files/uploads/2013.05.23_fact_sheet_on_ppg.pdf

80. Ibid.

81. Anderson, Kenneth, 'Targeted Killing in U.S. Counterterrorism Strategy and Law', Working Paper, Brookings Institution, 11 May 2009, p. 4; http://www.brookings.edu/~/media/research/files/papers/2009/5/11-counterterrorism-anderson/0511_counterterrorism_anderson.pdf

82. Savage, *Power Wars*, p. 264.

83. Zenko, Micah, 'Policy Innovation Memorandum No. 31: Transferring CIA Drone Strikes to the Pentagon', Council on Foreign Relations, 16 April 2013.

84. Woods, *Sudden Justice*, pp. 226–35.

85. Mackinlay, John, *The Insurgent Archipelago*, London: Hurst, 2009.

86. Galula, David, *Counterinsurgency Warfare: Theory and Practice*, New York: Praeger Security International, 2006, p. 4.

87. Jaffe, Greg, Adam Goldman and Greg Miller, 'Officials Fear CIA Missed Opportunity to Identify Western Hostage', *Washington Post*, 10 September 2015; https://www.washingtonpost.com/world/national-security/officials-fear-cia-missed-opportunity-to-identify-western-hostage/2015/09/10/6a159bf6–571e-11e5-b8c9–944725fcd3b9_story.html

88. Watkins, Ali, 'Obama Administration on Plan to Take Away CIA's Drones: Never Mind, Keep 'Em', Huffington Post, 24 June 2015; http://www.huffingtonpost.com/2015/06/24/obama-cia-drones_n_7649702.html

89. Miller, Greg, 'U.S. Launches Secret Drone Campaign to Hunt Islamic State Leaders in Syria', *Washington Post*, 1 September 2015; https://www.washingtonpost.com/world/national-security/us-launches-secret-drone-campaign-to-hunt-islamic-state-leaders-in-syria/2015/09/01/723b3e04–5033–11e5–933e-7d06c647a395_story.html

90. Ibid.

91. Mazzetti, *Way of the Knife*, pp. 286–7

92. Miller, Greg, 'Lawmakers Seek to Stymie Plan to Shift Control of Drone Campaign from CIA to Pentagon', Washington Post, 15 January 2014; https://www.washingtonpost.com/world/national-security/law-

makers-seek-to-stymie-plan-to-shift-control-of-drone-campaign-from-cia-to-pentagon/2014/01/15/c0096b18–7e0e-11e3–9556–4a4bf7b-cbd84_story.html

93. Libicki, Martin C., 'The Specter of Non-obvious Warfare', *Strategic Studies Quarterly*, 6, 3 (Fall 2012), p. 88.
94. Ibid., 89.
95. McChrystal, *My Share of the Task*, p. 162, loc 3506.
96. Robinson, Linda, 'The Future of Special Operations', *Foreign Affairs*, 91, 6 (2012), p. 111.
97. This is a general definition, though some academics dispute this, most notably Mary Calder's concept of 'new wars,' which blurs war and crime. See Kaldor, Mary, *New & Old Wars: Organised Violence in a Global Era*, Cambridge: Polity Press, 2002.
98. Elsea, Jennifer K., and Richard F. Grimmett, 'Declarations of War and Authorizations for the Use of Military Force: Historical Background and Legal Implications', Congressional Research Service, RL31133, 2011, p. 1.

4. LAWFUL ANNIHILATION?

1. Dill, Janina, *Legitimate Targets? Social Construction, International Law and US Bombing*, Cambridge: Cambridge University Press, 2015, p. 79.
2. The United States has now given consent to be bound by the Protocol on Blinding Laser Weapons. See Carnahan, Burrus M., and Marjorie Robertson, 'The Protocol on "Blinding Laser Weapons": A New Direction for International Humanitarian Law', *American Journal of International Law*, 90, 3 (1996), pp. 484–90.
3. US War Department General Orders no. 100, 24 April 1863: article 14.
4. Office of General Counsel, Department of Defense, 'The Department of Defense Law of War Manual', Department of Defense, 2015, p. 52.
5. Ibid., 53.
6. Smith, *Utility of Force*, p. 6.
7. Clausewitz, *On War*, Book 1, Section 3.
8. Ibid, Chapter 1, sections 23–6; Book 8, Chapter 6.
9. Freedman, Lawrence, *Strategy: A History*, Oxford: Oxford University Press, 2013, p. 3.
10. Heuser, Beatrice, *The Evolution of Strategy: Thinking War from Antiquity to the Present*, Cambridge: Cambridge University Press, 2010.
11. Sidebottom, Harry, *Ancient Warfare: A Very Short Introduction*, Oxford: Oxford University Press, 2004, p. 35, quoted in Heuser, *Evolution of Strategy*.

12. Goldsmith, *Power and Constraint*, p. 128.

13. Johnson, Jeh, 'Speech at the Oxford Union', 30 November 2012; http://www.lawfareblog.com/jeh-johnson-speech-oxford-union

14. Clausewitz, *On War*, Book 1(2) definition.

15. Strachan, Hew, *The Direction of War: Contemporary Strategy in Historical Perspective*, Cambridge: Cambridge University Press, 2013, p. 16.

16. Woodward, Bob, *Bush at War*, New York: Simon & Schuster, 2002, p. 45.

17. Lewis, Paul H., *Guerrillas and Generals: The 'Dirty War' in Argentina*, Westport: Greenwood, 2002, pp. 139–41.

18. See, for example, Honig, Jan Willem, 'Strategy and Genocide: Srebrenica as an Analytical Challenge', *Southeast European and Black Sea Studies*, 7, 3 (2007).

19. See Chapter 11, 'Bombing', in Glover, Jonathan, *Humanity: A Moral History of the Twentieth Century*, London: Pimlico, 2001.

20. 'Direct participation in hostilities' will be explained in Chapter 6. Solis, *Law of Armed Conflict*, pp. 205–6.

21. Smith, M.L.R., and Sophie Roberts, 'War in the Gray: Exploring the Concept of Dirty War', *Studies in Conflict & Terrorism*, 31, no. 5 (2008), p. 382.

22. Although both frameworks legitimate violence, the use of torture is prohibited and constitutes a war crime. See ICRC, 'Customary IHL: Rule 90; Torture and Cruel, Inhuman or Degrading Treatment', ICRC (2005); https://www.icrc.org/customary-ihl/eng/docs/v1_rul_rule90

23. Scahill, *Dirty Wars*.

24. Schmitt, Carl, *The Theory of the Partisan: A Commentary/Remark on the Concept of the Political*, Ann Arbor: Michigan State University Press, 2004.

25. Ibid., p. 64.

26. Ibid.

27. Ibid., p. 7.

28. Paret, Peter, 'Clausewitz', in Paret, Peter (ed.), *Makers of Modern Strategy from Machiavelli to the Nuclear Age*, Princeton: Princeton University Press, 1986, p. 199.

29. Schmitt, Carl, *Political Theology: Four Chapters on the Concept of Sovereignty*, trans. Gerge Schwab, Chicago: University of Chicago Press, 2005, p. 6.

30. Butler, Judith, 'Guantanamo Limbo', *The Nation*, 1 April 2002; http://www.thenation.com/article/guantanamo-limbo/

31. Mehring, Reinhard, *Carl Schmitt: A Biography*, Cambridge: Polity, 2014, pp. 188–93.

32. Smith and Roberts, 'War in the Gray', p. 378.

33. Ibid., p. 382.

34. Ibid., p. 393.

35. Robben, Antonius, 'The Fear of Indifference: Combatants' Anxieties about the Political Identity of Civilians during Argentina's Dirty War', in Koonings, Kees, and Dirk Krujit (eds), *Societies of Fear: The Legacy of Civil War, Violence and Terror in Latin America*, New York: Zed Books, 1999, p. 129.

36. Weigley, Russell F., *The American Way of War: A History of United States Military Strategy and Policy*, New York: Macmillan, 1973.

37. Ibid., xxii.

38. Echevarria, Antulio II, *Reconsidering the American Way of War: US Military Practice from the Revolution to Afghanistan*, Washington, DC: Georgetown University Press, 2014, loc. 196/4791.

39. Ibid., Chapter 2

40. Linn, Brian M., 'The American Way of War Revisited', *Journal of Military History*, 66, 2 (April 2002), p. 502.

41. Ibid., p. 503.

42. Echevarria II, *Reconsidering the American Way of War*, loc. 223.

43. Ibid., loc. 696.

44. Ibid., loc. 3566.

45. Carvin, Stephanie, and Michael John Williams, *Law, Science, Liberalism, and the American Way of Warfare*, Cambridge: Cambridge University Press, 2014, p. 204.

46. Rosenberg, Carol, 'Pentagon Envisions up to 7 More Guantánamo Trials', *Miami Herald*, 26 March 2015; http://www.miamiherald.com/news/nation-world/world/americas/guantanamo/article16415225.html

47. The four landmark cases are: Rasul v. Bush (2004); Hamdi v. Rumsfeld (2004); Hamdan v. Rumsfeld (2006); and Boumediene v. Bush (2008). Significant laws include the Detainee Treatment Act (2005), Military Commissions Act (2006), Military Commissions Act (2009).

48. Bush, George W., 'Detention, Treatment, and Trial of Certain Non-citizens in the War Against Terrorism', White House: Presidential Military Order, 13 November 2001; http://georgewbush-whitehouse.archives.gov/news/releases/2001/11/20011113–27.html

49. Supreme Court of the United States, Salim Ahmed Hamdan, Petitioner v. Donald H. Rumsfeld, Secretary of Defense, et al., Opinion of the Court, 29 June 2006; https://www.law.cornell.edu/supct/html/05–184.ZO.html

50. Notable detention cases include: Hamdi v. Rumsfeld; Rasul v. Bush; Rumsfeld v. Padilla; Hamdan v. Rumsfeld; Boumediene v. Bush.

51. Office of Public Affairs, 'Department of Justice Withdraws "Enemy Combatant" Definition for Guantanamo Detainees', US Department of Justice, 13 March 2009; http://www.justice.gov/opa/pr/department-justice-withdraws-enemy-combatant-definition-guantanamo-detainees

52. Chesney, Robert M., 'Who May Be Killed? Anwar al-Awlaki as a Case Study in the International Legal Regulation of Lethal Force', *Yearbook of International Humanitarian Law*, 13 (December 2010), pp. 3–60.

53. Chesney, Robert M., 'Who May Be Held? Military Detention through the Habeas Lens', *Boston College Law Review*, 52 (2011).

54. Rasmussen, Mikkel Vedby, *The Risk Society at War: Terror, Technology and Strategy in the Twenty-First Century*, Cambridge: Cambridge University Press, 2006, p. 164.

55. Abrahms, Max, 'Why Terrorism Does Not Work', *International Security*, 31, 2 (2006), pp. 42–78.

56. Sheffer, Gabriel, 'Diasporas and Terrorism', in Richardson, Louise (ed.), *The Roots of Terrorism*, London: Routledge (2013).

57. Cronin, Audrey Kurth, *How Terrorism Ends: Understanding the Decline and Demise of Terrorist Campaigns*, Princeton: Princeton University Press, 2009, pp. 142–3.

58. Kilcullen, David, and Andrew Exum, 'Death from Above, Outrage Down Below', *New York Times*, 17 May 2009; http://www.nytimes.com/2009/05/17/opinion/17exum.html?pagewanted=all&_r=0

59. Byman, 'Do Targeted Killings Work?', p. 97.

60. Rid, Thomas, 'Deterrence beyond the State: The Israeli Experience', *Contemporary Security Policy*, 33 (2012).

61. Kilcullen, David, 'Countering Global Insurgency', *Journal of Strategic Studies*, 28, 4 (2005), p. 610.

62. White House, 'National Security Strategy for Counterterrorism', US Government, June 2011, p. 6.

63. Jenkins, Brian Michael, 'Al Qaeda after Bin Laden: Implications for American Strategy', Testimony presented before the House Armed Services Committee, Subcommittee on Emerging Threats and Capabilities, 22 June 2011, p. 6; http://www.dtic.mil/dtic/tr/fulltext/u2/a545812.pdf

64. Obama, Barack, 'Remarks by the President on a New Strategy for Afghanistan and Pakistan', White House, 27 March 2009; https://www.whitehouse.gov/the-press-office/remarks-president-a-new-strategy-afghanistan-and-pakistan

65. Cronin, How Terrorism Ends, pp. 31–2.

66. Cronin, Audrey Kurth, 'Why Drones Fail: When Tactics Drive Strategy', *Foreign Affairs*, 92 (2013).

67. Smith, *Utility of Force*, p. 6.

68. Cronin, *How Terrorism Ends*, pp. 207–8.

69. Ibid., p. 91.

70. Ibid., p. 94.

71. Ibid., pp. 146–8.

72. Ibid., p. 115.

73. Ibid., p. 142.

74. Ibid., 179.

75. Ibid., p. 179.

76. Jordan, Javier, 'The Effectiveness of the Drone Campaign against Al Qaeda Central: A Case Study', *Journal of Strategic Studies*, 37, 1 (2014), pp. 4–29.

77. Jordan, Jenna, 'Attacking the Leader, Missing the Mark: Why Terrorist Groups Survive Decapitation Strikes', *International Security*, 38, 4 (2014), pp. 7–38.

78. Cronin, *How Terrorism Ends*, p. 191.

79. Cronin, 'Why Drones Fail', p. 45.

80. Ibid., p. 47.

81. Cronin, *How Terrorism Ends*, pp. 122–7

82. Byman, Daniel, *A High Price: The Triumphs & Failures of Israeli Counterterrorism*, Oxford: Oxford University Press, 2011, p. 365.

83. McChrystal, *My Share of the Task*, p. 149.

84. Cronin, *How Terrorism Ends*, p. 129.

85. Dror Moreh (dir.), *The Gatekeepers*, Sony, 2012.

86. Freedman, Lawrence, 'Terrorism as a Strategy', *Government and Opposition*, 42, 3 (2007), p. 331.

5. UNTO OTHERS

1. Bush, George W., '9/11 Address to the Nation', 11 September 2001.

2. BBC News, 'Infinite Justice, Out: Enduring Freedom, In', BBC News, 25 September 2001; http://news.bbc.co.uk/1/hi/world/americas/1563722.stm

3. Obama, Barack, 'Remarks by the President on Osama Bin Laden', White House, 1 May 2011; http://www.whitehouse.gov/blog/2011/05/02/osama-bin-laden-dead

4. Bureau of Investigative Journalism, 'US strikes in Yemen, 2002 to Present', TBIJ: Dataset, accessed 1 July 2015, Strike ID YEM 144; https://docs.google.com/spreadsheets/d/1lb1hEYJ_omI8lSe33iz-wS2a2lbiygs0hTp2Al_Kz5KQ/edit#gid=492674230

5. Dozier, Kimberley, 'US Officials: Drone Targeted Embassy Plot Leader', AP, 20 December 2013; http://bigstory.ap.org/article/us-officials-drone-targeted-embassy-plot-leader

6. Al Jazeera, 'Yemen Drone Strike "Targeted al-Qaeda leader"', www. aljazeera.com, 20 December 2013; http://www.aljazeera.com/news/ middleeast/2013/12/yemen-drone-strike-targeted-al-qaeda-leader-20131220192937914455.html

7. Emmerson, Ben, 'Report of the Special Rapporteur on the Promotion and Protection of Human Rights and Fundamental Freedoms while Countering Terrorism', UN Human Rights Council, A/HRC/25/59, 28 February 2014, p. 16; http://justsecurity.org/wp-content/uploads/ 2014/02/Special-Rapporteur-Rapporteur-Emmerson-Drones-2014.pdf

8. Ibid., p. 10.

9. Data taken from https://www.thebureauinvestigates.com/category/ projects/drones/drones-graphs/ (accessed 9 June 2016).

10. See, for example, Benjamin, *Drone Warfare*, loc. 1549.

11. Office of General Counsel, Department of Defense, 'The Department of Defense Law of War Manual', Department of Defense, 2015, p. 22.

12. Ohlin, Jens David, *The Assault on International Law*, Oxford: Oxford University Press, 2015, p. 180.

13. O'Driscoll, Cian, 'Talking about Just War: Obama in Oslo, Bush at War', *Politics*, 31, 2 (2011).

14. Carty, Anthony, *Philosophy of International Law*, Edinburgh: Edinburgh University Press, 2007; Besson, Samantha, and John Tasioulas (eds), *The Philosophy of International Law*, Oxford: Oxford University Press, 2010.

15. Guthrie, Charles, and Michael Quinlan, *Just War: The Just War Tradition: Ethics in Modern Warfare*, London: Bloomsbury, 2007, p. 11.

16. Biggar, Nigel, *In Defence of War*, Oxford: Oxford University Press, 2013, p. 169.

17. Guthrie and Quinlan, *Just War*, p. 11.

18. For an outstanding survey of the differing approaches that constitute the just war tradition, see Reichberg, Gregory M., Henrik Syse and Endre Begby (eds), *The Ethics of War: Classic and Contemporary Readings*, Malden, MA: Blackwell, 2006.

19. Walzer, Michael, *Just and Unjust Wars: A Moral Argument with Historical Illustrations*, 3rd edn, New York: Basic Books, 2000, p. 16.

20. Guthrie and Quinlan, *Just War*, pp. 12–14.

21. Lippman, Walter, *U.S Foreign Policy: Shield of the Republic*, Boston: Little, Brown, 1943, p. 5.

22. Walzer, *Just and Unjust Wars*, p. 3.

23. Machiavelli, Niccolò, *The Prince*, 2nd edn, trans. Harvey C. Mansfield, Chicago: University of Chicago Press, 1998, p. 65.

24. Ibid., p. 67.

25. Williams, Bernard, *Morality: An Introduction to Ethics*, Cambridge: Cambridge University Press, 2012, p. 5.

26. Ibid., p. 11.

27. Walzer, *Just and Unjust Wars*, p. 4.

28. Guthrie and Quinlan, *Just War*, p. 1.

29. Strawser, Bradley J., 'Revisionist Just War Theory and the Real World: A Cautiously Optimistic Proposal', in *Routledge Handbook of Ethics and War: Just War Theory in the 21st Century*, New York: Routledge, 2013, p. 76.

30. McMahan, Jeff, *Killing in War*, Oxford: Oxford University Press, 2009.

31. Wolfers, Arnold, 'National Security as an Ambiguous Symbol', *Political Science Quarterly*, 67, 4 (1952), pp. 498–9.

32. Macintyre, Alasdair, *Whose Justice? Which Rationality?* London: Duckworth, 1988, p. 343.

33. Kelsey, John, 'The Triumph of Just War Theory and Imperial Overstretch', in Lang Jr, Anthony F., Cian O'Driscoll and John Williams (eds), *Just War: Authority, Tradition, and Practice*, Washington, DC: Georgetown University Press, 2013, pp. 269–70.

34. See Walzer, *Just and Unjust Wars*, Chapter 7.

35. Also included are virtue ethicists; for a discussion of all three, see Fisher, David, *Morality and War: Can War Be Just in the Twenty-first Century?* Oxford: Oxford University Press, 2011.

36. O'Driscoll, 'Talking about Just War', p. 88.

37. Banks, Cyndi, *Criminal Justice Ethics: Theory and Practice*, 3rd edn, Thousand Oaks: Sage, 2013, Chapter 8.

38. Dershowitz, Alan, 'Want to Torture? Get a Warrant', *San Francisco Chronicle*, 22 January 2002, p. A19; http://www.sfgate.com/opinion/openforum/article/Want-to-torture-Get-a-warrant-2880547.php

39. Frost, Mervyn, *Global Ethics: Anarchy, Freedom and International Relations*, London: Routledge, 2008.

40. Obama, Barack, 'Remarks by the President on National Security', National Archives, Washington, DC, 21 May 2009; https://www.whitehouse.gov/the-press-office/remarks-president-national-security-5-21-09

41. Morgenthau, Hans J., *Politics among Nations: The Struggle for Power and Peace*, New York: Alfred A. Knopf, 1948, Chapters 13 and 14.

42. Niebuhr, Reinhold, *The Irony of American History*, Chicago: University of Chicago Press, 2008, p. 1.

43. Morgenthau, *Politics among Nations*, pp. 174–5.

44. Bobbitt, Philip, *The Shield of Achilles: War, Peace and the Course of History*, London: Allen Lane, 2002, p. 779.

45. See, for example, Dillon, Michael, and Julian Reid, *The Liberal Way of War: Killing to Make Life Live*, London: Routledge, 2009.

46. Brown, Chris, 'From Humanised War to Humanitarian Intervention:

Carl Schmitt's Critique of the "Just War Tradition"', in Odysseos, L., and F. Petito (eds), *The International Political Thought of Carl Schmitt: Terror, Liberal War and the Crisis of Global Order*, London: Routledge, 2007, p. 59.

47. Slomp, Gabriella, 'Carl Schmitt's Five Arguments against the Idea of Just War', *Cambridge Review of International Affairs*, 19, 3 (2006).

48. Coates, A.J. *The Ethics of War*, Manchester: Manchester University Press, 1997, p. 97.

49. McDonald, 'Ethics and Legality of the American Targeted Killing Programme'.

50. Slomp, 'Carl Schmitt's Five Arguments', p. 437.

51. Schmitt, Carl, *The Theory of the Partisan: A Commentary/Remark on the Concept of the Political*, trans. A.C. Goodson, Michigan: Michigan State University Press, 2004.

52. Walzer, *Just and Unjust Wars*, p. 41.

53. Biggar, *In Defence of War*, p. 172.

54. See Elbe, Joachim von, 'The Evolution of the Concept of the Just War in International Law', *American Journal of International Law*, 33, 4 (1939), pp. 665–88.

55. Grotius, Hugo, *The Rights of War and Peace*, Indianapolis: Liberty Fund, 2005, Book II, I.IX.I, p. 403.

56. It should be mentioned that this Requerimiento was criticised by a leading figure in the history of the just war tradition, Francisco de Vitoria. See Hernández, Ramón, O.P., 'The Internationalization of Francisco de Vitoria and Domingo de Soto', *Fordham International Law Journal*, 15, 4 (1991), pp. 1046–47.

57. 'Convention (II) with Respect to the Laws and Customs of War on Land and Its Annex: Regulations concerning the Laws and Customs of War on Land', The Hague, 29 July 1899; https://www.icrc.org/applic/ihl/ihl.nsf/Article.xsp?action=openDocument&documentId=9 FE084CDAC63D10FC12563CD00515C4D

58. 'Protocol Additional to the Geneva Conventions of 12 August 1949, and relating to the Protection of Victims of International Armed Conflicts (Protocol I)', 8 June 1977. Article 1.2.

59. Meron, Theodor, 'The Martens Clause, Principles of Humanity, and Dictates of Public Conscience', *American Journal of International Law* (2000), p. 88.

60. United States Declaration of Independence, 1776.

61. UN General Assembly, 'Universal Declaration of Human Rights', UN General Assembly, 1948.

62. ICCPR Art 6(1)

63. King, Hugh, 'The Extraterritorial Human Rights Obligations of States', *Human Rights Law Review*, 9, 4 (2009), pp. 521–56.

64. Moyn, Samuel, *The Last Utopia: Human Rights in History*, Cambridge, MA: Belknap Press of Harvard University Press, 2012, p. 215.
65. Meron, Theodor, 'The Humanization of Humanitarian Law', *American Journal of International Law*, 94, 2 (2000), pp. 239, 251–2.
66. Corn, Geoffrey, 'Mixing Apples and Hand Grenades: The Logical Limit of Applying Human Rights Norms to Armed Conflict', *Journal of International Humanitarian Legal Studies*, 1, 1 (2010), pp. 52–94.
67. Schabas, "Lex Specialis', p. 592.
68. Bennett, Wells C., 'The Extraterritorial Effect of Human Rights: The ECHR's Al-Skeini Decision', Lawfare, 12 July 2011; https://www.lawfareblog.com/extraterritorial-effect-human-rights-echrs-al-skeini-decision
69. Milanovic, Marko, 'Al-Skeini and Al-Jedda in Strasbourg', *European Journal of International Law*, 23, 1 (2012), pp. 121–39.
70. Dennis, Michael J., 'Application of Human Rights Treaties Extra-territorially in Times of Armed Conflict and Military Occupation', *American Journal of International Law*, 99, 1 (January 2005), p. 141
71. Office of General Counsel, Department of Defense, 'Department of Defense Law of War Manual', pp. 21–2.
72. See Melzer, Nils, 'Targeted Killing or Less Harmful Means? Israel's High Court Judgment on Targeted Killing and the Restrictive Function of Military Necessity', *Yearbook of International Humanitarian Law*, 9 (2006).
73. Gaita, Raymond, *A Common Humanity: Thinking about Love and Truth and Justice*, London: Routledge, 2002.
74. Fabre, Cécile, *Cosmopolitan War*, Oxford: Oxford University Press, 2012.
75. Ibid., p. 49.
76. Ibid., p. 36.
77. Brennan, 'Ethics and Efficacy of the President's Counterterrorism Strategy'.
78. See Tom J. Farer's contribution in Farer, Tom J., with Daniele Archibugi, Chris Brown, Neta C. Crawford, Thomas G. Weiss and Nicholas J. Wheeler, 'Roundtable: Humanitarian Intervention After 9/11', *International Relations*, 19, 2 (2005)
79. See Kant, Immanuel, *Groundwork for the Metaphysics of Morals*, trans. Allen W. Wood, New Haven: Yale University Press (2002)
80. See Berlin, Isaiah, 'Two Concepts of Liberty', in Berlin, Isaiah, *Liberty*, Oxford: Oxford University Press, 2002.
81. Taylor, Charles, 'Atomism', in Taylor, Charles, *Philosophical Papers: Volume 2, Philosophy and the Human Sciences*, Cambridge: Cambridge University Press, 1985, pp. 190–1.

82. Rawls, *Theory of Justice*, pp. 136–41.
83. Fabre, *Cosmopolitan War*, p. 25.
84. Buchanan, Allen E., 'Assessing the Communitarian Critique of Liberalism', *Ethics*, 99, 4 (July 1989), pp. 852–3.
85. Rawls, John, *Political Liberalism*, New York: Columbia University Press, 1993, pp. 5–6.
86. Rawls, John, *The Law of the Peoples; With, 'The Idea of Public Reason Revisited'*, Cambridge, MA: Harvard University Press, 1999, p. 89.
87. Fabre, Cecile, 'Cosmopolitanism, Just War Theory and Legitimate Authority', *International Affairs*, 84, 5 (2008), p. 965.
88. Rawls, *Law of Peoples*, p. 82.
89. Ibid., p. 83.
90. Ibid., p. 91.
91. Kuper, Andrew, 'Rawlsian Global Justice: Beyond the Law of Peoples to a Cosmopolitan Law of Persons', *Political Theory*, 28, 5 (2000), p. 666.
92. Rawls, *Law of Peoples*, p. 119.
93. Rawls, *Law of the Peoples; With, 'The Idea of Public Reason Revisited'*, p. 96.
94. See, for example, Calhoun, Laurie L., *War and Delusion: A Critical Examination*, Basingstoke: Palgrave Macmillan, 2013.
95. Nye Jr, Joseph S., *Soft Power: The Means to Success in World Politics*, New York: Public Affairs, 2005, chapter 1
96. Ibid., chapter 5
97. Obama, Barack, 'Renewing American Leadership', *Foreign Affairs*, 86, 4 (2007).

6. INDIVIDUATED WARFARE

1. Pontecorvo, Gillo (dir.), *The Battle of Algiers (La Battaglia Di Algeri)*, Italy: 1966.
2. Reprieve, 'You Never Die Twice: Multiple Kills in the US Drone Program', Reprieve, 24 November 2014, p. 2.
3. Grissom, Adam, 'The Future of Military Innovation Studies', *Journal of Strategic Studies*, 29, 5 (2006), p. 926.
4. Nagl, John A., *Learning to Eat Soup with a Knife: Counterinsurgency Lessons from Malaya and Vietnam*, Chicago: University of Chicago Press, 2009, pp. 213–23.
5. Rabinovich, Abraham, *The Yom Kippur War: The Epic Encounter That Transformed the Middle East*, New York: Knopf Doubleday, 2005, pp. 107–11.
6. Issacharoff, Samuel, and Richard H. Pildes, 'Targeted Warfare: Individuating Enemy Responsibility', *New York University Law Review*, 88 (2013),

pp. 12–40; There is also a European University Institute project entitled 'The Individualisation of War: Reconfiguring the Ethics, Law, and Politics of Armed Conflict', led by Professor Jennifer Welsh. https://iow.eui.eu/

7. Garcia, Rosanna, and Roger Calantone, 'A Critical Look at Technological Innovation Typology and Innovativeness Terminology: A Literature Review', *Journal of product Innovation Management*, 19, no. 2 (2002), pp. 110–32.

8. Helpman, Elhanan, *General Purpose Technologies and Economic Growth*, Cambridge, MA: MIT press, 1998.

9. International law (and other rules and regulations) is translated into operational law, see Warren, Marc L., 'Operational Law: A Concept Matures', *Military Law Review*, 152 (1996). Day-to-day practice is guided by rules of engagement that ensure compliance with operational law (and thereby ensure compliance with international law), see Grunawalt, Richard J., 'The JCS Standing Rules of Engagement: A Judge Advocate's Primer', *Air Force Law Review*, 42 (1997).

10. Franklin, Ursula M., *The Real World of Technology*, Berkeley: House of Anansi Press, 1999, p. 1.

11. O'Connell, Mary Ellen, 'Combatants and the Combat Zone', *University of Richmond Law Review*, 43 (2008–9), p. 858.

12. Alston, Philip, 'Report of the UN Special Rapporteur on Extrajudicial, Summary or Arbitrary Executions: Study on Targeted Killings', UN Doc. A/HRC/14/24/Add.6 2010, pp. 18–19; http://www2.ohchr.org/english/bodies/hrcouncil/docs/14session/A.HRC.14.24.Add6.pdf

13. Chamayou, Grégoire, *Manhunts: A Philosophical History*, trans. Steven Rendall, Princeton: Princeton University Press, 2012; Chamayou, *A Theory of the Drone*, New York: New Press, 2015

14. Chamayou, Theory of the Drone, p. 91.

15. Foust, Joshua, 'Do Drones Work?', The American Prospect, 15 May 2013; http://prospect.org/article/do-drones-work

16. Alston, 'Report of the UN Special Rapporteur on Extrajudicial, Summary or Arbitrary Executions', p. 18.

17. Keegan, John, *A History of Warfare*, London: Hutchinson, 1993, p. 271.

18. Luttwak, Edward N., 'A Post-heroic Military Policy', *Foreign Affairs*, 75, 4 (1996), pp. 36–7.

19. For example, Britain in Afghanistan. See Mark Clegg, 'Protecting British Soldiers in Afghanistan', *RUSI Journal*, 157, 3 (2012), p. 25.

20. Gavin, James M., 'Two Fighting Generals: Patton and MacArthur', *Atlantic* (February 1965), p. 55.

21. Bailey, Jonathan B.A., *Field Artillery and Firepower*, Annapolis: Naval Institute Press, 2004, pp. 212–14.

22. Perfidy covers actions where a combatant pretends to be someone deserving protection under the law of armed conflict, so as to take advantage of this protection in order to attack their opponent: for example, pretending to be incapacitated, or pretending to surrender, in order to attack someone. ICRC, 'Customary IHL: Rule 65. Perfidy', ICRC; https://www.icrc.org/customary-ihl/eng/docs/v1_rul_rule 65

23. Whittle, *Predator*, p. 152.

24. McChrystal, *My Share of the Task*, p. 148.

25. Wasserman, Stanley, and Katherine Faust, *Social Network Analysis: Methods and Applications*, Cambridge: Cambridge University Press, 1994, p. 5.

26. Joint Chiefs of Staff, 'Joint Publication 3–60 Joint Targeting', JCS, 2013, pp. vii–ix; http://cfr.org/content/publications/attachments/ Joint_Chiefs_of_Staff-Joint_Targeting_31_January_2013.pdf

27. Ibid.

28. Kenny, Michael, *From Pablo to Osama*, University Park: Pennsylvania State University Press, 2007, Chapter 6.

29. Pfanner, Toni, 'Military Uniforms and the Law of War', *International Review of the Red Cross*, 86, 853 (2004); https://www.icrc.org/eng/ assets/files/other/irrc_853_pfanner.pdf

30. Keegan, *History of Warfare*, pp. 109–11.

31. Flynn, Michael T., Rich Juergens and Thomas L. Cantrell, 'Employing ISR SOF Best Practices', *Joint Force Quarterly*, 50 (2008), p. 57.

32. Uniforms in part define armed forces in law. See International Committee of the Red Cross, 'Practice Relating to Rule 4. Definition of Armed Forces', ICRC; https://www.icrc.org/customary-ihl/eng/ docs/v2_rul_rule4. Improper use of uniforms, for example, is prohibited in the law of armed conflict. See International Committee of the Red Cross, 'Practice Relating to Rule 62. Improper Use of Flags or Military Emblems, Insignia or Uniforms of the Adversary', ICRC; https://www.icrc.org/customary-ihl/eng/docs/v2_rul_rule62

33. Gow, *Serbian Project and Its Adversaries*.

34. Horne, Alistair, *A Savage War of Peace: Algeria 1954–1962*, New York: New York Review Books Classics, 2006, p. 196.

35. Lewis, *Guerrillas and Generals*, p. 147.

36. Klaidman, *Kill or Capture*, p. 203.

37. Cronin, *How Terrorism Ends*, pp. 115–17.

38. Flynn, Juergens and Cantrell, 'Employing ISR SOF Best Practices', p. 57.

39. McChrystal, *My Share of The Task*, pp. 153–6.

40. Flynn, Juergens and Cantrell, 'Employing ISR SOF Best Practices', p. 57.

41. Woods, *Sudden Justice*, p. 81.
42. Flynn, Juergens, and Cantrell, 'Employing ISR SOF Best Practices', p. 57.
43. Woods, *Sudden Justice*, pp. 251–4.
44. White House, 'U.S. Policy Standards and Procedures for the Use of Force in Counterterrorism Operations outside the United States and Areas of Active Hostilities', fact sheet, 23 May 2015; https://www.whitehouse.gov/sites/default/files/uploads/2013.05.23_fact_sheet_on_ppg.pdf
45. Currier, Cora, 'The Kill Chain: the Lethal Bureaucracy behind Obama's Drone War', The Intercept, 15 October 2015; https://theintercept.com/drone-papers/the-kill-chain/
46. White House, 'U.S. Policy Standards and Procedures for the Use of Force'.
47. Woods, *Sudden Justice*, pp. 240–2.
48. Chamayou, *Theory of the Drone*, pp. 37–41.
49. Brennan, Scott, and Daniel Kreiss, 'Digitalization and Digitization', Culture Digitally, 8 September 2014; http://culturedigitally.org/2014/09/digitalization-and-digitization/
50. Rosenau, William, and Austin Long, *The Phoenix Program and Contemporary Counterinsurgency*, Santa Monica: RAND Corporation, 2009, p. 4.
51. Weiner, Tim, *Legacy of Ashes: The History of the CIA*, New York: Anchor, 2008, pp. 267–9.
52. Rosenau and Long, *Phoenix Program and Contemporary Counterinsurgency*, p. 9.
53. Urban, Mark, *Task Force Black*, Boston: Little, Brown, 2010, loc. 1856.
54. Codd, E.F., 'A Relational Model of Data for Large Shared Data Banks', *Communications of the ACM*, 13, 6 (1970), pp. 377–8.
55. Ibid.
56. Singer, Natasha, 'Mapping, and Sharing, the Consumer Genome', *New York Times*, 16 June 2012; http://www.nytimes.com/2012/06/17/technology/acxiom-the-quiet-giant-of-consumer-database-marketing.html?pagewanted=all
57. Omand, David, 'Understanding Digital Intelligence and the Norms That Might Govern It', Global Commission on Internet Governance, Paper Series, no. 8, March 2015; https://www.cigionline.org/sites/default/files/gcig_paper_no8.pdf
58. Mayer-Schonberger, Viktor, and Kenneth Cukier, *Big Data: A Revolution That Will Transform How We Live, Work, and Think*, Boston: Houghton Mifflin Harcourt, 2013, p. 29.
59. Shubber, Kadhim, 'A Simple Guide to GCHQ's Internet Surveillance Programme Tempora', Wired, 24 June 2013; http://www.wired.co.uk/news/archive/2013-06/24/gchq-tempora-101

60. Urban, *Task Force Black*, loc. 1856.
61. Graham, Stephen, and David Wood, 'Digitizing Surveillance: Categorization, Space, inequality', *Critical Social Policy*, 23, 2 (2003), p. 228.
62. 'President of Yemen Flees by Sea; Saudis Begin Airstrikes', *New York Times*, 25 March 2015; http://www.nytimes.com/aponline/2015/03/25/world/middleeast/ap-ml-yemen.html?_r=0
63. Byman, Daniel, 'The Intelligence War on Terrorism', *Intelligence and National Security*, 29, 6 (2014), p. 847.
64. Atwood, Chandler P., 'Activity-Based Intelligence: Revolutionizing Military Intelligence Analysis', Joint Force Quarterly, 77 (2015), p. 26.
65. Becker, Jo, and Scott Shane, 'Secret "Kill List" Proves a Test of Obama's Principles and Will', *New York Times*, 29 May 2012, p. A1; http://www.nytimes.com/2012/05/29/world/obamas-leadership-in-war-on-al-qaeda.html?_r=0
66. Woods, *Sudden Justice*, drone pilot testimony on p. 175.
67. McNeal, Greg, 'The U.S. Practice of Collateral Damage Estimation and Mitigation', Pepperdine University School of Law Working Paper, 2011; http://papers.ssrn.com/sol3/papers.cfm?abstract_id=1819583
68. Woods, Chris, *Sudden Justice*, pp. 14–15.
69. Brennan, 'Efficacy and Ethics of U.S. Counterterrorism Strategy'.
70. Galula, *Counterinsurgency Warfare*, pp. 39–40.
71. Petraeus, David H., and James F. Amos, *Counterinsurgency: FM 3–24*, Boulder: Paladin Press, 2007, pp. 1–149, 1–27
72. A feature of war the world over. See Scott, James C., *The Art of Not Being Governed: An Anarchist History of Upland Southeast Asia*, New Haven: Yale University Press, 2014, pp. 149–59
73. Gertler, Jeremiah, 'U.S. Unmanned Aerial Systems', Congressional Research Service R42136, 3 January 2012, p. 35; http://www.fas.org/sgp/crs/natsec/R42136.pdf
74. Solis, *Law of Armed Conflict*, p. 188.
75. International Human Rights and Conflict Resolution Clinic (Stanford Law School), Global Justice Clinic (NYU School of Law), 'Living Under Drones: Death, Injury, and Trauma to Civilians From US Drone Practices in Pakistan', Stanford Law School/NYU School of Law, 2012.
76. Murthy, R. Srinivasa, and Rashmi Lakshminarayana, 'Mental Health Consequences of War: A Brief Review of Research Findings', *World Psychiatry*, 5, 1 (2006), p. 28.
77. Emery, John R., and Daniel R. Brunstetter, 'Drones as Aerial Occupation', *Peace Review* 27, 4 (2015), p. 424.
78. Lewis, *Guerrillas and Generals*, p. 155.
79. Lieblich, Eliav, 'Beyond Life and Limb: Exploring Incidental Mental

Harm under International Law', in Jinks, Derek, Jackson Nyamuya Maogoto and Solon Solomon (eds), *Applying International Humanitarian Law in Judicial and Quasi-Judicial Bodies: International and Domestic Aspects*, The Hague: T.M.C. Asser Press, 2014, p. 187.

80. Ibid., p. 202.
81. Sherman, William T., 'Letter of William T. Sherman to James M. Calhoun, E.E. Rawson, and S.C. Wells, September 12, 1864', in Berlin, Jean V., and Brooks D. Simpson (eds), *Sherman's Civil War: Selected Correspondence of William T. Sherman, 1860–1865*, Chapel Hill: University of North Carolina Press, 1999, pp. 707–9.
82. An archive of these documents is available from the Canadian Journalists for Free Expression, see https://cjfe.org/snowden
83. Perlroth, Nicole, Jeff Larson and Scott Shane, 'N.S.A. Able to Foil Basic Safeguards of Privacy on Web', *New York Times*, 5 September 2013; http://www.nytimes.com/2013/09/06/us/nsa-foils-much-internet-encryption.html
84. Schneier, Bruce, 'The US Government Has Betrayed the Internet: We Need to Take It Back', *Guardian*, 5 September 2013; http://www.the-guardian.com/commentisfree/2013/sep/05/government-betrayed-internet-nsa-spying
85. Intelligence and Security Committee of Parliament, 'Privacy and Security: A Modern and Transparent Legal Framework', House of Commons, 12 March 2015, p. 67; http://isc.independent.gov.uk/files/20150312_ISC_P+S+Rpt(web).pdf
86. Tufekci, Zeynep, 'Engineering the Public: Big Data, Surveillance and Computational Politics', *First Monday*, 19, 7 (2014).
87. 'Foreign Intelligence Surveillance Act of 1978' ('FISA' Public Law 95–511, 92 Stat. 1783, 50 U.S.C. Chapter 36)
88. 50 US Code Chapter 36, Subchapter I: §1802 and §1804
89. Gellman, Barton, and Laura Poitras, 'U.S., British Intelligence Mining Data from Nine U.S. Internet Companies in Broad Secret Program', *Washington Post*, 7 June 2013; http://www.washingtonpost.com/investigations/us-intelligence-mining-data-from-nine-us-internet-companies-in-broad-secret-program/2013/06/06/3a0c0da8-cebf-11e2–8845-d970ccb04497_story.html

7. KILLING THROUGH A MONITOR, DARKLY

1. Dick, Philip K., *A Scanner Darkly*, London: Gollancz, 1999, p. 146.
2. Obama, Barack, 'Remarks by the President on Osama Bin Laden', White House, Office of the Press Secretary, 2 May 2011; https://www.whitehouse.gov/the-press-office/2011/05/02/remarks-president-osama-bin-laden

3. Melzer, Nils, 'Interpretive Guidance on the Notion of Direct Participation in Hostilities under International Humanitarian Law', ICRC, 2009, p. 4.

4. See Chapter 4 ('Strategy and Justice') in Gow, *War and War Crimes*.

5. For details of the changing status of republican prisoners, see Moore, Jonathan, 'Paramilitary Prisoners and the Peace Process in Northern Ireland', in O'Day, Alan (ed.), *Political Violence in Northern Ireland: Conflict and Conflict Resolution*, Westport: Praeger 1997.

6. Department of Justice, 'Lawfulness of a Lethal Operation', 2011, p. 1.

7. Miller, Greg, 'Plan for Hunting Terrorists Signals U.S. Intends to Keep Adding Names to Kill Lists', *Washington Post*, 23 October 2012; https://www.washingtonpost.com/world/national-security/plan-for-hunting-terrorists-signals-us-intends-to-keep-adding-names-to-kill-lists/2012/10/23/4789b2ae-18b3–11e2-a55c-39408fbe6a4b_story.html

8. 'Small Footprint Operations 2/13', The Intercept, 15 October 2015; https://theintercept.com/document/2015/10/14/small-footprint-operations-2–13/. Figure taken from slide 41.

9. American Civil Liberties Union, 'ACLU Comment on Targeted Killing "Disposition Matrix"', ACLU, 24 October 2012; https://www.aclu.org/news/aclu-comment-targeted-killing-disposition-matrix

10. See, for example, Human Rights Watch, '"Between a Drone and al-Qaeda": The Civilian Cost of US Targeted Killings in Yemen', Human Rights Watch, 22 October 2013; https://www.hrw.org/sites/default/files/reports/yemen1013_ForUpload_1.pdf

11. According to the Bureau of Investigative Journalism, between 168 and 204 in Pakistan as of 31 January 2015. See Serle, Jack, 'Almost 2,500 Now Killed by Covert US Drone Strikes since Obama Inauguration Six Years Ago: The Bureau's Report for January 2015', Bureau of Investigative Journalism, 2 February 2015; https://www.thebureauinvestigates.com/2015/02/02/almost-2500-killed-covert-us-drone-strikes-obama-inauguration/

12. Wheeler, Marcy, 'SCOTUS Reviews the "Military Age Male" Standard on Thursday', Emptywheel.net, 6 June 2012; https://www.emptywheel.net/2012/06/06/scotus-reviews-the-military-age-male-standard-on-thursday/

14. Heller, Kevin Jon '"One Hell of a Killing Machine": Signature Strikes and International Law', *Journal of International Criminal Justice*, 11 (2013), pp. 97–100.

15. Engel, Richard, and Robert Windrem, 'CIA Didn't Always Know Who It Was Killing in Drone Strikes, Classified Documents Show', NBC News, 5 June 2013; http://investigations.nbcnews.com/_news/2013/06/05/18781930-cia-didnt-always-know-who-it-was-killing-in-drone-strikes-classified-documents-show

16. Becker, Job, and Scott Shane, 'Secret "Kill List" Proves a Test of Obama's Principles and Will', *New York Times*, 29 May 2012; http://www.nytimes.com/2012/05/29/world/obamas-leadership-in-war-on-al-qaeda.html?pagewanted=all

17. Greenwald, Glenn, 'Three Key Lessons from the Obama Administration's Drone Lies', *Guardian*, 11 April 2013; http://www.theguardian.com/commentisfree/2013/apr/11/three-lessons-obama-drone-lies

18. Issacharoff, Samuel, and Richard H. Pildes, 'Targeted Warfare: Individuating Enemy Responsibility', *New York University Law Review*, 88 (2013), p. 1570.

19. Ibid., p. 1523.

20. Ibid., p. 1523.

21. Klaidman, *Kill or Capture*, pp. 199–204.

22. Smith, *Utility of Force*, p. 16.

23. Parrott, David, 'Cultures of Combat in the Ancien Régime: Linear Warfare, Noble Values, and Entrepreneurship', *International History Review*, 27, 3 (2005), pp. 526–7.

24. Groebner, Valentin, *Who Are You? Identification, Deception, and Surveillance in Early Modern Europe*, trans. Mark Kyburz and John Peck, New York: Zone Books, 2007, p. 26.

25. See, for example, the leveé en masse, a feature of international armed conflicts without parallel in non-international armed conflict.

26. See Pfanner, 'Military Uniforms and the Law of War'.

27. Scahill, *Dirty Wars*, p. 76.

28. Wendt, 'Anarchy Is What States Make of It', pp. 412–13.

29. Treaty text 1977 protocols

30. General Counsel of the Department of Defense, 'Department of Defense Law of War Manual'.

31. Melzer, Nils, 'Interpretive Guidance on the Notion of Direct Participation in Hostilities under International Humanitarian Law', ICRC, 2009.

32. Bellinger, John B. III, and William J. Haynes II, 'A US Government Response to the International Committee of the Red Cross Study Customary International Humanitarian Law', *International Review of the Red Cross*, 89, 866 (June 2007); https://www.icrc.org/eng/assets/files/other/irrc_866_bellinger.pdf

33. General Counsel of the Department of Defense, 'Department of Defense Law of War Manual', p. 197.

34. Article 50(1), API 1977

35. Melzer, 'Interpretive Guidance', p. 27.

36. Ibid.

37. Ibid., p. 332
38. Ibid., p. 33
39. Ibid.
40. Ibid., p. 56.
41. Ibid., p. 51.
42. Ibid., p. 46.
43. Ibid., p. 70.
44. Ibid., p. 70
45. General Counsel of the Department of Defense, 'Department of Defense Law of War Manual', pp. 218–20.
46. Ibid., p. 218.
47. Ibid., pp. 218–19.
48. Ibid., p. 220.
49. Watkin, Kenneth, 'Opportunity Lost: Organized Armed Groups and the ICRC Direct Participation in Hostilities Interpretive Guidance', *NYU Journal of International Law & Policy*, 42 (2009), p. 655.
50. Ibid., p. 656.
51. Melzer, Nils, 'Keeping the Balance between Military Necessity and Humanity: A Response to Four Critiques of the ICRC's Interpretive Guidance on the Notion of Direct Participation in Hostilities', *NYU Journal of International Law & Policy*, 42 (2009).
52. Ibid., p. 850.
53. Schmitt, Michael N., 'The Interpretive Guidance on the Notion of Direct Participation in Hostilities: A Critical Analysis', *Harvard National Security Journal*, 1 (2010), p. 37.
54. Ibid., p. 38.
55. McNeal, Gregory S., 'Targeted Killing and Accountability', *Georgetown Law Journal*, 102 (2014), p. 759.
56. Carvin, Stephanie, and Michael John Williams, *Law, Science, Liberalism, and the American Way of Warfare*, Cambridge: Cambridge University Press, 2014, p. 126.
57. See, Joint Chiefs of Staff, 'Joint Publication 3–60: Joint Targeting', Joint Chiefs of Staff, 13 April 2007.
58. Spiegel Staff, 'Obama's Lists: A Dubious History of Targeted Killings in Afghanistan', Spiegel Online, 28 December 2014; http://www.spiegel.de/international/world/secret-docs-reveal-dubious-details-of-targeted-killings-in-afghanistan-a-1010358.html
59. Standing US rules governing the use of force are classified secret; however, an unclassified version is available. Enclosure A to the Chairman of the Joint Chiefs of Staff Instruction 3121.01B details 'standing rules of engagement for US forces'. See, Chairman of the Joint Chiefs of Staff, 'Instruction 3121.01B', Joint Chiefs of Staff, 13 June 2005;

http://navybmr.com/study%20material/CJCSI%203121.01B%20 ENCLOSURE%20(L),%20STANDING%20RULES%20OF%20 ENGAGEMENT%20STANDING%20RULES%20OF%20THE%20 USE%20OF%20FORCE%20FOR%20U.%20S.%20FORCES.pdf

60. Gregory, Derek, 'From a View to a Kill: Drones and Late Modern War', *Theory, Culture & Society*, 28, 7–8 (2011), pp. 188–215.

61. Bowden, Mark, 'The Killing Machines: How to Think about Drones', The Atlantic, September 2013; http://www.theatlantic.com/magazine/archive/2013/09/the-killing-machines-how-to-think-about-drones/309434/

62. Joint Chiefs of Staff, 'Joint Publication 3–09: Joint Fire Support', Joint Chiefs of Staff, 12 December 2014, p. A-9; http://fas.org/irp/doddir/dod/jp3_09.pdf

63. Ibid.

64. Alston, 'CIA and Targeted Killings', p. 405.

65. Zenko, Micah, 'Policy Innovation Memorandum No. 31: Transferring CIA Drone Strikes to the Pentagon', Council on Foreign Relations, 16 April 2013, p. 1. http://www.cfr.org/drones/transferring-cia-drone-strikes-pentagon/p30434

66. Becker, Jo, and Scott Shane, 'Secret "Kill List" Proves a Test of Obama's Principles and Will', *New York Times*, 29 May 2012; http://www.nytimes.com/2012/05/29/world/obamas-leadership-in-war-on-al-qaeda.html

67. Gregory, Derek, 'Targeted Killings and Signature Strikes', Geographical Imaginations, 6 November 2012; http://geographicalimaginations.com/2012/11/06/targeted-killings-and-signature-strikes/

68. Flynn, Juergens and Cantrell, 'Employing ISR SOF Best Practices', p. 57.

69. Klaidman, *Kill or Capture*.

70. Currier, 'Kill Chain'.

71. Klaidman, *Kill or Capture*, pp. 212–13.

72. Butler, Judith, *Frames of War: When Is a Life Grievable?* London: Verso, 2009, p. 38.

73. Hayden, Michael, 'Threat, Responses, Law and Liberty', Speech, American Bar Association, 8 September 2015.

74. Al-Aulaqi v. Obama (2010)

75. Coll, Steve, 'Kill of Capture', *New Yorker*, 2 August 2012; http://www.newyorker.com/news/daily-comment/kill-or-capture

76. American Civil Liberties Union, 'Al-Aulaqi v. Obama: Constitutional Challenge to Proposed Killing Of U.S. Citizen', ACLU, 19 October 2011; https://www.aclu.org/cases/al-aulaqi-v-obama-constitutional-challenge-proposed-killing-us-citizen

77. Boothby, William H., *The Law of Targeting*, Oxford: Oxford University Press, 2012, p. 4.

78. Schmitt, Carl, *Political Theology: Four Chapters on the Concept of Sovereignty*, trans. George Schwab, Chicago: University of Chicago Press, 2005, p. 5.

79. Schmitt, Carl, *Dictatorship: From the Origin of the Modern Concept of Sovereignty to Proletarian Class Struggle*, trans. Michael Hoelzl and Graham Ward, Cambridge: Polity Press, 2014, p. 150.

80. Agamben, Giorgio, *Homo Sacer: Sovereign Power and Bare Life*, trans. Daniel Heller-Roazen, Stanford: Stanford University Press, 1995, Chapter 1.

81. McDonald, 'Ethics and Legality of the American Targeted Killing Programme', Chapter 6.

82. Agamben, *Homo Sacer*, p. 28.

83. Ibid., pp. 28–9.

84. Agamben, Giorgio, *State of Exception*, trans. Kevin Attell, Chicago: Chicago University Press, 2005, p. 3.

85. Goldsmith, *Power and Constraint*, pp. 139–40.

86. Cole, David, 'An Executive Power to Kill?', New York Review of Books Blog, 6 March 2012; http://www.nybooks.com/blogs/nyrblog/2012/mar/06/targeted-killings-holder-speech/

87. Scahill, *Dirty Wars*, Chapter 36, p. 352.

88. Greenwald, Glenn, 'America's Drone Sickness', Salon, 19 April 2012; http://www.salon.com/2012/04/19/americas_drone_sickness/

89. Shane, Scott, 'Drone Strikes Reveal Uncomfortable Truth: U.S. Is Often Unsure about Who Will Die', *New York Times*, 23 April 2015; http://www.nytimes.com/2015/04/24/world/asia/drone-strikes-reveal-uncomfortable-truth-us-is-often-unsure-about-who-will-die.html?_r=0

90. Corn, Geoffrey, and Chris Jenks, 'Two Sides of the Combatant Coin: Untangling Direct Participation in Hostilities from Belligerent Status in Non-international Armed Conflicts', *University of Pennsylvania Journal of International Law*, 33 (2011), p. 314.

91. Phillips, Mark, 'A Brief Overview of Activity Based Intelligence and Human Domain Analytics', *Trajectory Magazine*, 28 September 2012; http://trajectorymagazine.com/civil/item/1369-human-domain-analytics.html

92. Steadman, Ian, 'IBM's Watson Is Better at Diagnosing Cancer than Human Doctors', Wired, 11 February 2013; http://www.wired.co.uk/news/archive/2013–02/11/ibm-watson-medical-doctor

8. THE BODY AS THE BATTLEFIELD

1. Chaucer, Geoffrey, *The Canterbury Tales*, London: Penguin Classics, 2005.
2. For examples, see Mazzetti, *Way of the Knife*, pp. 226–8, 242–7.
3. Salehyan, Idean, 'No Shelter Here: Rebel Sanctuaries and International Conflict', *Journal of Politics*, 70, 1 (2008), pp. 54–66.
4. Lubell, Noam, and Nathan Derejko, 'A Global Battlefield? Drones and the Geographical Scope of Armed Conflict', *Journal of International Criminal Justice*, 11, 1 (2013), p. 79.
5. O'Connell, Mary Ellen, 'The Choice of Law against Terrorism', *Journal of National Security Law & Policy*, 4 (2010), p. 361.
6. See, for example, Birch, Marion, Gay Lee and Tomasz Pierscionek, Drones: The Physical and Psychological Implications of a Global Theatre of War', Medact, 2012, p. 6; http://www.medact.org/wp-content/uploads/2012/10/report-drones-2012.pdf
7. Libicki, Martin C., 'The Specter of Non-obvious Warfare', *Strategic Studies*, 89 (2012), p. 88.
8. Brennan, 'Efficacy and Ethics of U.S. Counterterrorism Strategy'.
9. Alston, 'CIA and Targeted Killings', p. 321.
10. For example, the role of resource exploitation in prolonging political conflicts in Africa. See Ballentine, Karen, and Heiko Nitzschke, 'Beyond Greed and Grievance: Policy Lessons from Studies in the Political Economy of Armed Conflict', in Picciotto, Robert, and Rachel Weaving (eds), *Security and Development: Investing in Peace and Prosperity*, London: Routledge, 2006, p. 161.
11. Walzer, *Just and Unjust Wars*, pp. 138–42.
12. Ibid., p. 38.
13. King, Anthony, *The Combat Soldier: Infantry Tactics and Cohesion in the Twentieth and Twenty-First Centuries*, Oxford: Oxford University Press, 2013, Chapter 9.
14. Jones, Edgar, 'The Psychology of Killing: The Combat Experience of British Soldiers during the First World War', *Journal of Contemporary History*, 41, 2 (2006), p. 245.
15. See, for example, Sharkey, Noel, 'Automating Warfare: Lessons Learned from the Drones', *Journal of Law, Information & Science*, 21 (2011), p. 145.
16. Royakkers, Lamber, and Rinie Van Est, 'The Cubicle Warrior: The Marionette of Digitalized Warfare', *Ethics and Information Technology*, 12, 3 (2010).
17. Woods, *Sudden Justice*, pp. 174–5.
18. Lambeth, Benjamin S., *NATO's Air War for Kosovo: A Strategic and Operational Assessment*, Santa Monica: RAND, 2001, p. 39.

19. Arkin, William M., *Divining Victory: Airpower in the 2006 Israel–Hezbollah War*, Maxwell Airforce Base, AL: Air University Press, 2007, p. 78.

20. Ignatieff, Michael, *Virtual War: Kosovo and Beyond*, London: Vintage, 2001, p. 92.

21. McNeal, Gregory S., 'Are Targeted Killings Unlawful? A Case Study in Empirical Claims Without Empirical Evidence', in Finkelstein, Claire, Jens David Ohlin and Andrew Altman (eds), *Targeted Killings: Law and Morality in an Asymmetrical World*, Oxford: Oxford University Press, 2012, pp. 326–46.

22. Strawser, Bradley Jay, 'Moral Predators: The Duty to Employ Uninhabited Aerial Vehicles', *Journal of Military Ethics*, 9, 4 (2010), pp. 342–68.

23. Holder, Eric, 'Attorney General Eric Holder Speaks at Northwestern University School of Law'; http://www.justice.gov/opa/speech/attorney-general-eric-holder-speaks-northwestern-university-school-law

24. 'Declaration Renouncing the Use, in Time of War, of Certain Explosive Projectiles', St. Petersburg, 29 November/11 December 1868; https://www.icrc.org/applic/ihl/ihl.nsf/Article.xsp?action=openDocument&documentId=568842C2B90F4A29C12563CD0051547C

25. 'Convention (IV) Relative to the Protection of Civilian Persons in Time of War', Geneva, 12 August 1949, Article 3.1.a.; https://www.icrc.org/applic/ihl/ihl.nsf/ART/380-600006?OpenDocument

26. Pictet, Jean, 'Humanitarian Law and the Protection of War Victims', Henry Dunant Institute, Geneva, 1975, p. 32.

27. Ibid.

28. Parks, W. Hays, 'Part IX of the ICRC Direct Participation in Hostilities Study: No Mandate, No Expertise, and Legally Incorrect', *NYU Journal of International Law & Policy*, 42 (2009), pp. 785–7.

29. Swiss, Shana, and Joan E. Giller, 'Rape as a Crime of War: A Medical Perspective', *Journal of the American Medical Association*, 270, 5 (1993), p. 614.

30. Brennan, 'Efficacy and Ethics of U.S. Counterterrorism Strategy'.

31. Schmitt, Michael N., 'Precision Attack and International Humanitarian Law', *International Review of the Red Cross*, 87, 859 (2005), p. 454.

32. Woods, Chris, 'US Claims of "No Civilian Deaths" Are Untrue', Bureau of Investigative Journalism, 18 July 2011; https://www.thebureauinvestigates.com/2011/07/18/washingtons-untrue-claims-no-civilian-deaths-in-pakistan-drone-strikes/

33. Manes, Jonathan, 'Civilian Deaths from CIA Drone Strikes: Zero or Dozens?' ACLU 19 July 2011; https://www.aclu.org/blog/civilian-deaths-cia-drone-strikes-zero-or-dozens

34. Even if humanitarian concerns do alter the calculus that military com-

manders use to assess proportionality, they will not eliminate or outlaw this form of calculation. Meron, Theodor, 'The Humanization of
Humanitarian Law', *American Journal of International Law*, 94, 2 (2000),
p. 241.

35. United States v. Wilhelm List et al. ('The Hostage Case'), 1948, XI
    TWC 1253–54. Quoted in Solis, *Law of Armed Conflict*, p. 259.
36. Notably arising from article 57 of Additional Protocol I, see Quéguiner,
    Jean-François, 'Precautions under the Law Governing the Conduct of
    Hostilities', *International Review of the Red Cross*, 88, 864 (December
    2006), pp. 796–8.
37. Corn, Geoffrey S., 'Precautions to Minimize Civilian Harm Are a
    Fundamental Principle of the Law of War', Just Security, 8 July 2015;
    https://www.justsecurity.org/24493/obligation-precautions-fundamental-
    principle-law-war/
38. Brennan, 'Efficacy and Ethics of U.S. Counterterrorism Strategy'.
39. Reprieve, 'Yemen "Set up a Counselling Centre" for Children Because
    of Drone Strikes', Reprieve.org.uk, 17 January 2014; http://www.
    reprieve.org.uk/press/counselling_centre_yemeni_children_drone_
    strikes/
40. International Human Rights and Conflict Resolution Clinic (Stanford
    Law School) and Global Justice Clinic (NYU School Of Law), 'Living
    Under Drones: Death, Injury, and Trauma to Civilians from US Drone
    Practices in Pakistan', Stanford/NYU, 2012, pp. 55–102.
41. See Cigar, Norman, *Genocide in Bosnia: The Policy of Ethnic Cleansing*,
    College Station: Texas A&M University Press, 1995. Forced displace-
    ment of a population (without violent attack) is permissible in inter-
    national law under certain circumstances during armed conflicts. See
    International Committee of the Red Cross, 'Customary IHL: Rule 129;
    The Act of Displacement', ICRC, 2015; https://www.icrc.org/cus-
    tomary-ihl/eng/docs/v1_cha_chapter38_rule129#refFn_61_3
42. Blank, Laurie R., 'Where Is the Battlefield in the "War on Terror"?
    The Need for a Workable Framework', JURIST: Forum, 1 December
    2010; http://jurist.org/forum/2010/12/where-is-the-battlefield-in-
    the-war-on-terror-the-need-for-a-workable-framework.php
43. Blum, Gabriella, and Philip B. Heymann, 'Law of Policy of Targeted
    Killing', *Harvard National Security Journal*, 1 (2010), p. 169.
44. Lubell, Noam, and Nathan Derejko, 'A Global Battlefield? Drones and
    the Geographical Scope of Armed Conflict', *Journal of International
    Criminal Justice*, 11, 1 (2013), pp. 65–88.
45. O'Connell, 'Unlawful Killing with Combat Drones', p. 19.
46. Lubell, Noam, *The Extraterritorial Use of Force against Non-state Actors*,
    Oxford: Oxford University Press, 2010, p. 255.

47. Scahill, *Dirty Wars*.
48. Bailey, *Field Artillery and Firepower*, p. 118.
49. Howard, Michael, *The Franco-Prussian War: The German Invasion of France 1870–1871*, London: Routledge, 2005, p. 5.
50. Smith, *Utility of Force*, p. 1.
51. Ibid.
52. Development, Concepts and Doctrine Centre, 'Joint Doctrine Publication 3–70, Battlespace Management', Ministry of Defence, 2008, pp. 1–2.
53. Lubell and Derejko, 'Global Battlefield?' p. 74.
54. International Human Rights and Conflict Resolution Clinic at Stanford Law School and Global Justice Clinic at NYU School of Law, 'Living under Drones', p. 80.
55. Clausewitz, *On War*, Book 1.25.
56. Rasmussen, *Risk Society at War*, p. 60.
57. See Bond, Brian, *The Pursuit of Victory: From Napoleon to Saddam Hussein*, Oxford: Oxford University Press, 1998.
58. Blank, Laurie R., 'Defining the Battlefield in Contemporary Conflict and Counterterrorism: Understanding the Parameters of the Zone of Combat', *Georgia Journal of International and Comparative Law*, 39, 1 (2010), p. 37.
59. Solis, *Law of Armed Conflict*, pp. 205–6.
60. Miller, Greg, 'Plan for Hunting Terrorists Signals U.S. Intends to Keep Adding Names to Kill Lists', *Washington Post*, 23 October 2012.
61. Lewis, Michael W., 'Drones and the Boundaries of the Battlefield', *Texas International Law Journal*, 47 (2011), p. 300.
62. Lubell and Derejko, 'Global Battlefield?' p. 82
63. Solis, *Law of Armed Conflict*, p. 188.
64. See generally 'Convention (III) Relative to the Treatment of Prisoners of War', Geneva, 12 August 1949, Article 3(1).
65. See Boothby, Bill, 'And for Such Time As: The Time Dimension to Direct Participation in Hostilities', *NYU Journal of international law & Policy*, 42 (2009).
66. ICRC, 'Customary IHL: Rule 20; Advance Warning, ICRC (2015)'; https://www.icrc.org/customary-ihl/eng/docs/v1_cha_chapter5_rule20
67. Mazzetti, *Way of the Knife*, p. 311.
68. Scahill, *Dirty Wars*, p. 509.
69. Ibid., p. 507.
70. Cook, Jonathan, 'Gaza: Life and Death under Israel's Drones', Aljazeera, 28 November 2013; http://www.aljazeera.com/indepth/features/2013/11/gaza-life-death-under-israel-drones-20131125124214350423.html

71. Israeli Defense Forces, 'How Is the IDF Minimizing Harm to Civilians in Gaza?' IDF Blog, 16 July 2014; https://www.idfblog.com/blog/2014/07/16/idf-done-minimize-harm-civilians-gaza/

72. Libman, Liron A., 'Legal Advice in the Conduct of Operations in the Israel Defense Forces', *Military Law and Law of War Review*, 67 (2011), p. 78.

73. Dill, Janina, 'Guest Post: Israel's Use of Law and Warnings in Gaza', Opinio Juris, 30 July 2014; http://opiniojuris.org/2014/07/30/guest-post-israels-use-law-warnings-gaza/

74. United Nations Independent Commission of Inquiry on the 2014 Gaza Conflict, 'Report of the Detailed Findings of the Commission of Inquiry on the 2014 Gaza Conflict', A/HRC/29/CRP.4, UNHRC 2014, paragraph 236.

75. Joronen, Mikko, '"Death Comes Knocking on the Roof": Thanatopolitics of Ethical Killing during Operation Protective Edge in Gaza', *Antipode*, 8, 2 (2015), p. 9.

76. See Benvenisti, Eval, *The International Law of Occupation*, Oxford: Oxford University Press, 2012.

77. Ackerman, Spencer, 'U.S. Holds on to Biometrics Database of 3 Million Iraqis', Wired, 21 December 2011; https://www.wired.com/2011/12/iraq-biometrics-database/

9. GYGES' KNIFE

1. Ignatieff, Michael, *Virtual War*, London: Vintage, 2001, p. 215.

2. BBC News, 'Cardiff Jihadist Reyaad Khan, 21, Killed by RAF Drone', BBC News, 7 September 2015.

3. Stern, Jessica, and Berger, J.M., *ISIS: The State of Terror*, New York: William Collins, 2015, pp. 44–51.

4. Cameron, David, 'Syria: Refugees and Counter-Terrorism: Prime Minister's Statement', gov.uk, 7 September 2015; https://www.gov.uk/government/speeches/syria-refugees-and-counter-terrorism-prime-ministers-statement

5. Anderson, Kenneth, 'Targeted Killing in U.S. Counterterrorism Strategy and Law', Working Paper, 11 May 2009; http://ssrn.com/abstract=1415070 or http://dx.doi.org/10.2139/ssrn.1415070

6. Obama, Barack, 'Letter from the President: War Powers Resolution regarding Syria', White House, 23 September 2014; https://www.whitehouse.gov/the-press-office/2014/09/23/letter-president-war-powers-resolution-regarding-syria

7. Chesney, Robert et al., 'A Statutory Framework for Next-Generation Terrorist Threats', Jean Perkins Task Force on National Security and

Law, Stanford: Hoover Institution, 25 February 2013; Brooks, Rosa, 'Mission Creep in the War on Terror', *Foreign Policy*, 14 March 2013; Waxman, Matthew, 'AUMF Reform: A Response to Brook and Others', Lawfare, 15 March 2013; Chivvis, Christopher S., and Andrew M. Liepman, 'Authorities for Military Operations against Terrorist Groups: The State of the Debate and Options for Congress', Santa Monica: RAND, 2015, p. 41; http://www.rand.org/content/dam/rand/pubs/research_reports/RR1100/RR1145/RAND_RR1145.pdf

8. White House, 'U.S. Policy Standards and Procedures for the Use of Force in Counterterrorism Operations outside the United States'.

9. Stern and Berger, *ISIS*, 2015, p. 8.

10. Wood, Graeme, 'What ISIS Really Wants', The Atlantic, March 2015.

11. Mcinnes, Kathleen J., 'CRS Report R44135: Coalition Contributions to Countering the Islamic State', Congressional Research Service, 13 April 2016.

12. McCants, Will, *The ISIS Apocalypse: The History, Strategy, and Doomsday Vision of the Islamic State*, New York: St. Martin's Press, 2015.

13. Stern and Berger, *ISIS*, Chapter 2.

14. Ibid., pp. 33–8.

15. Ibid., pp. 42–3.

16. Smith, Alexander, 'Iraqi PM Haider Al-Abadi Says Forces Lost 2,300 Humvees to ISIS', NBC News, 1 June 2015; http://www.nbcnews.com/storyline/isis-terror/iraqi-prime-minister-haider-al-abadi-says-his-forces-lost-n367596

17. Council on Foreign Relations, 'James Clapper on Global Intelligence Challenges: A Conversation with James R. Clapper Jr.', Council on Foreign Relations, 2 March 2015; http://www.cfr.org/homeland-security/james-clapper-global-intelligence-challenges/p36195

18. United Nations Security Council, 'Letter Dated 19 May 2015 from the Chair of the Security Council Committee Pursuant to resolutions 1267 (1999) and 1989 (2011) concerning Al-Qaida and Associated Individuals and Entities Addressed to the President of the Security Council', UNSC, 19 May 2015, p. 8; http://www.un.org/en/ga/search/view_doc.asp?symbol=S/2015/358

19. McCants, *ISIS Apocalypse*, pp. 116–123.

20. Anderson, Jon Lee, 'ISIS Rises in Libya', *New Yorker*, 4 August 2015; http://www.newyorker.com/news/news-desk/isis-rises-in-libya

21. Windrem, Robert, and William M. Arkin, "Why Hasn't the U.S. Killed Bin Laden's Wingman Ayman al-Zawahiri?' NBC News, 17 May 2016; http://www.nbcnews.com/news/us-news/why-hasn-t-u-s-kill-bin-laden-s-wingman-n574986

22. Hegghammer, Thomas, and Petter Nesser, 'Assessing the Islamic State's

Commitment to Attacking the West', *Perspectives on Terrorism*, 9, 4 (2015); http://www.terrorismanalysts.com/pt/index.php/pot/article/view/440/html

23. Miller, Greg, and Souad Mekhennet, 'Inside the Surreal World of the Islamic State's Propaganda Machine', *Washington Post*, 20 November 2015, https://www.washingtonpost.com/world/national-security/inside-the-islamic-states-propoganda-machine/2015/11/20/05/e997a-8ce6-11e5-acff-673ae92ddd2b_story.html; Koerner, Brendan I., 'Why ISIS Is Winning the Social Media War', Wired, March 2016; https://www.wired.com/2016/03/isis-winning-social-media-war-heres-beat/

24. Borger, Julian, 'Paris Gunman Amedy Coulibaly Declared Allegiance to Isis', *Guardian*, 12 January 2015; https://www.theguardian.com/world/2015/jan/11/paris-gunman-amedy-coulibaly-allegiance-isis

25. Kalfood, Mohammed Ali, Kareem Fahim and Eric Schmitt, 'Suicide Attacks at Mosques in Yemen Kill More than 130', *New York Times*, 20 March 2015; http://www.nytimes.com/2015/03/21/world/middleeast/suicide-attacks-at-shiite-mosques-in-yemen.html

26. Samti, Farah and Carlotta Gall, 'Tunisia Attack Kills at Least 38 at Beach Resort Hotel', *New York Times*, 26 June 2015; http://www.nytimes.com/2015/06/27/world/africa/gunmen-attack-hotel-in-sousse-tunisia.html

27. Faiola, Anthony, and Souad Mekhennet, 'Paris Attacks Were Carried Out by Three Groups Tied to Islamic State, Official Says', *Washington Post*, 15 November 2015; https://www.washingtonpost.com/world/string-of-paris-terrorist-attacks-leaves-over-120-dead/2015/11/14/066df55c-8a73–11e5-bd91-d385b244482f_story.html

28. Holland, Steve, and Roberta Rampton, 'Obama Orders U.S. Airstrikes in Syria against Islamic State', Reuters, 11 September 2014; http://www.reuters.com/article/2014/09/11/us-iraq-crisis-obama-idUSKBN0H527Z20140911

29. Obama, Barack, 'Statement by the President on ISIL', White House, 10 September 2014; https://www.whitehouse.gov/the-press-office/2014/09/10/statement-president-isil-1

30. https://airwars.org/data/. Data taken on 8 June 2016

31. BBC News, 'Syria Crisis: Cameron Loses Commons Vote on Syria Action', BBC News, 30 August 2013; http://www.bbc.co.uk/news/uk-politics-23892783

32. 'MPs Approve Motion on ISIL in Syria', parliament.uk, 2 December 2015; http://www.parliament.uk/business/news/2015/december/mps-debate-motion-on-isil-in-syria/

33. Cameron, 'Syria: Refugees and Counter-Terrorism'.

34. Andnan, Ghassan, 'Iraqi Counterterrorism Forces Enter Fallujah',

Wall Street Journal, 8 June 2016; http://www.wsj.com/articles/iraqi-counterterrorism-forces-enter-fallujah-1465389277

35. Archive: https://airwars.org/daily-reports/
36. Soufan Group, 'Foreign Fighters: An Updated Assessment of the Flow of Foreign Fighters into Syria and Iraq', Soufan Group, December 2015; http://soufangroup.com/wp-content/uploads/2015/12/TSG_ForeignFightersUpdate3.pdf
37. Malet, David, *Foreign Fighters: Transnational Identity in Civil Conflicts*, Oxford: Oxford University Press, 2013, p. 10.
38. Johnson, Jeh, 'Speech at the Oxford Union', 30 November 2012; http://www.lawfareblog.com/jeh-johnson-speech-oxford-union
39. 'A New Prescription', *Economist*, 10 August 2013; http://www.economist.com/news/leaders/21583270-new-zealands-plan-regulate-designer-drugs-better-trying-ban-them-and-failing-new
40. See, for example: Bąkowski, Piotr, and Laura Puccio, 'Briefing: Foreign Fighters' Member States' Responses and EU Action in an International Context', European Parliamentary Research Service, February 2015; http://www.europarl.europa.eu/EPRS/EPRS-Briefing-548980-Foreign-fighters-FINAL.pdf
41. Hegghammer, Thomas, *Jihad in Saudi Arabia: Violence and Pan-Islamism since 1979*, Cambridge: Cambridge University Press, 2010, Chapter 2.
42. Birmingham Policy Commission, 'The Security Impact of Drones: Challenges and Opportunities for the UK', University of Birmingham, 2014, p. 43.
43. Obama, Barack, 'Letter from the President: War Powers Resolution Regarding Iraq", White House, 8 August 2014; https://www.whitehouse.gov/the-press-office/2014/08/08/letter-president-war-powers-resolution-regarding-iraq
44. Obama, Barack, 'Letter from the President: War Powers Resolution Regarding Iraq', The White House, 23 September 2014; https://www.whitehouse.gov/the-press-office/2014/09/23/letter-president-war-powers-resolution-regarding-iraq; Obama, Barack, 'Letter from the President: War Powers Resolution Regarding Syria', White House, 23 September 2014; https://www.whitehouse.gov/the-press-office/2014/09/23/letter-president-war-powers-resolution-regarding-syria
45. Chivvis and Liepman, 'Authorities for Military Operations against Terrorist Groups'.
46. House of Lords Constitution Committee, '2nd Report of Session 2013–14: Constitutional Arrangements for the Use of Armed Force', HMSO, 24 July 2013; http://www.publications.parliament.uk/pa/ld201314/ldselect/ldconst/46/46.pdf
47. Cameron, "Syria: Refugees and Counter-Terrorism'.

48. Ibid.

49. Customary law regarding self-defence is usually described and debated in the formula of the Caroline test, from an incident involving a ship called the Caroline in the nineteenth century. Customary self-defence must be both necessary and proportionate to the threat, and states need to demonstrate that the threat was 'instant, overwhelming, leaving no choice of means, and no moment for deliberation.'

50. United Kingdom Mission to the United Nations, 'Letter to the UN Security Council (S/2015/688)', 7 September 2015; https://www.justsecurity.org/wp-content/uploads/2015/09/UK_UNSC_Letter_on_Drone_Strike_7Sept2015.pdf

51. BBC News, 'Ambassador Gives "Iraq Defence" for UK's Syria Drone Strike', BBC News, 11 September 2015; http://www.bbc.com/news/uk-34215799

52. Fallon, Michael, 'Letter to the Joint Committee on Human Rights', Ministry of Defence, 14 December 2015; http://www.parliament.uk/documents/joint-committees/human-rights/Letter_from_SoS_for_Defence_111215.pdf

53. Joint Committee on Human Rights, 'Oral Evidence: The UK Government's Policy on the Use of Drones for Targeted Killing, HC 574', Joint Committee on Human Rights, 16 December 2015, Question 24; http://data.parliament.uk/writtenevidence/committeeevidence.svc/evidencedocument/human-rights-committee/the-uk-governments-policy-on-the-use-of-drones-for-targeted-killing/oral/27633.html

54. Kreps, Sarah, and Micah Zenko, 'The Next Drone Wars: Preparing for Proliferation', *Foreign Affairs*, 93, 2 (March/April 2014), pp. 68–79.

55. The 'Five Eyes' group originates in the post-war UK–US intelligence agreement.

56. BBC News, '"Jihadi John": US "Reasonably Certain" Strike Killed IS Militant', BBC News, 13 November 2015; http://www.bbc.co.uk/news/uk-34805924

57. Wintour, Patrick, 'Cameron Says Airstrike on Mohammed Emwazi Was Act of Self-Defence', *Guardian*, 13 November 2015; https://www.theguardian.com/world/2015/nov/13/cameron-says-airstrike-on-mohammed-emwazi-was-act-of-self-defence

58. Alston, Philip, 'Report of the UN Special Rapporteur on Extrajudicial, Summary or Arbitrary Executions: Study on Targeted Killings', UN Doc. A/HRC/14/24/Add.6 2010; http://www2.ohchr.org/english/bodies/hrcouncil/docs/14session/A.HRC.14.24.Add6.pdf

59. The case was dismissed on appeal, see Reprieve, 'UK Must Not Hide Drone War Involvement behind "Special Relationship", Court Hears', Reprieve, 3 December 2013; http://reprieve.webfactional.com/press/uk_must_not_hide_drone_war_involvement/

60. Townsend, Mark, 'GCHQ Civilian Staff Face War Crimes Charge over Drone Strikes in Pakistan', *Guardian*, 11 March 2012; http://www.theguardian.com/world/2012/mar/11/gchq-staff-war-crimes-drones

61. Ross, Alice, and James Ball, 'GCHQ Documents Raise Fresh Questions over UK Complicity in US Drone Strikes', *Guardian*, 24 June 2015; http://www.theguardian.com/uk-news/2015/jun/24/gchq-documents-raise-fresh-questions-over-uk-complicity-in-us-drone-strikes

62. Eckhardt, Andy, 'Drone War: German Court Throws Out Case by Family of Slain Yeminis', NBC News, 27 May 2015; http://www.nbcnews.com/news/world/drone-war-germany-aiding-americas-targeted-killings-n365116

63. Airwars, 'Summary Findings on Coalition Airstrikes: August 8th 2014 to June 6th 2016', Airwars, 6 June 2016; https://airwars.org/civilian-casualty-claims/

64. Priest, Dana, 'Covert Action in Colombia', *Washington Post*, 21 December 2013; http://www.washingtonpost.com/sf/investigative/2013/12/21/covert-action-in-colombia/

65. Secretary of State for Defence (Michael Fallon), 'House of Commons: Written Statement (HCWS149): UK Embedded Forces', Ministry of Defence, 20 July 2015.

66. Akande, Dapo, 'Embedded Troops and the Use of Force in Syria: International and Domestic Law Questions', EJIL: Talk, 11 September 2015; http://www.ejiltalk.org/embedded-troops-and-the-use-of-force-in-syria-international-and-domestic-law-questions/

67. Ben-Neftali, Orna, and Roy Peled, 'How Much Secrecy Does Warfare Need?' in Bianchi, Andrea, and Anne Peters (eds), *Transparency in International Law*, Cambridge: Cambridge University Press, 2013, p. 321.

68. Guiora, Amos N., and Jeffrey S. Brand, 'Establishment of a Drone Court: A Necessary Restraint on Executive Power', in Barela, Steven J. (ed.), *Legitimacy and Drones: Investigating the Legality, Morality and Efficacy of UCAVs*, Burlington: Ashgate, 2015.

69. Vladeck, Steve, 'Drone Courts: The Wrong Solution to the Wrong Problem', Just Security, 2 December 2014; https://www.justsecurity.org/17914/drone-courts-wrong-solution-wrong-problem/

70. Kaag, John, and Sarah Kreps, 'The Moral Hazard of Drones', *New York Times*, 22 July 2012; http://opinionator.blogs.nytimes.com/2012/07/22/the-moral-hazard-of-drones/?_r=0

71. Ibid.

72. Bloom, Allan, *The Republic of Plato 2nd Ed.*, New York: Basic Books, 1991, pp. 36–37.

73. Ferejohn, John, 'Accountability and Authority: Toward a Theory of Political Accountability', in Przeworski, Adam, and Susan C. Stokes

(eds), *Democracy, Accountability, and Representation*, Cambridge: Cambridge University Press, 1999, p. 131.

74. Behn, Robert D., *Rethinking Democratic Accountability*, Washington, DC: Brookings Institution Press, 2001, pp. 3–4.

75. Epps, Garrett, 'The Real Constitutional Crisis is Hidden', The Atlantic, 30 December 2014; http://www.theatlantic.com/politics/archive/2014/12/there-is-a-constitutional-crisis-but-not-the-one-many-people-think-nsa-war-torture/384120/

76. Cobain, Ian, *Cruel Britannia: A Secret History of Torture*, London: Portobello Books, 2013; Grey, Stephen, *Ghost Plane: The Inside Story of the CIA's Secret Rendition Programme*, London: Hurst, 2006.

77. Gerstein, Josh, 'U.S. Revoked Anwar Al-Awlaki's Passport Six Months before Death', Politico, 28 November 2012; http://www.politico.com/blogs/under-the-radar/2012/11/us-revoked-anwar-al-awlakis-passport-six-months-before-death-150521

78. Woods, Chris, and Alice Ross, '"Medieval Exile": The 42 Britons Stripped of Their Citizenship', Bureau of Investigative Journalism, 26 February 2013; https://www.thebureauinvestigates.com/2013/02/26/medieval-exile-the-21-britons-stripped-of-their-citizenship/

79. Grieve, Dominic, 'Open Letter to the Chair of the Joint Committee on Human Rights', 14 January 2016; http://isc.independent.gov.uk/files/20160114-ISC-6.5–114-to-Chair-JCHR.pdf

80. Clark, *Waging Modern War*, p. 8.

81. Smith, *Utility of Force*, p. 284.

82. Sullivan, Stacy, 'The Minutes of the Guantánamo Bay Bar Association', *New York Magazine*, 2006.

83. Savage, *Power Wars*, pp. 249–51.

84. Laughland, Oliver, 'CIA Report: "Torture Is a Crime and Those Responsible Must Be Brought to Justice"', *Guardian*, 10 December 2014; http://www.theguardian.com/us-news/2014/dec/09/torture-cia-amnesty-international-human-rights-watch

85. Bruck, Connie, 'The Inside War', *New Yorker*, 22 June 2015.

86. Whetham, David, 'Killer Drones: The Moral Ups and Downs', *RUSI Journal*, 158, 3 (2013), pp. 26–7.

87. Ackerman, Spencer, and Ed Pilkington, 'Obama's War on Whistle-blowers Leaves Administration Insiders Unscathed', *Guardian*, 16 March 2015; http://www.theguardian.com/us-news/2015/mar/16/whistleblowers-double-standard-obama-david-petraeus-chelsea-manning

88. Maass, Peter, 'Destroyed by the Espionage Act', The Intercept, 18 February 2015; https://theintercept.com/2015/02/18/destroyed-by-the-espionage-act/

89. Hobbs, Christopher, Matthew Moran and Daniel Salisbury, *Open Source*

Intelligence in the Twenty-First Century: New Approaches and Opportunities, Basingstoke: Palgrave Macmillan, 2014.

90. Grey, *Ghost Plane*.
91. Notably OSINT organisations such as Bellingcat; see www.bellingcat.com
92. French, David, 'Reminder: Congress Rejected the AUMF against ISIS Because It Didn't Want a Third Obama Term', National Review, December 15, 2015; http://www.nationalreview.com/corner/428532/congress-rejected-aumf-against-isis-because-it-didnt-want-third-obama-term
93. HuffPost Live, 'Glenn Greenwald on Dean Baquet: A "Disturbing History" of Journalism "Subservient" to National Security State', Huffington Post, 16 May 2014; http://www.huffingtonpost.com/2014/05/16/glenn-greenwald-new-york-times_n_5337486.html
94. Pew Research Centre, 'Public Continues to Back U.S. Drone Attacks', Pew Research Centre, 28 May 2015; http://www.people-press.org/2015/05/28/public-continues-to-back-u-s-drone-attacks/
95. See Lewis-Beck, Michael S., and Mary Stegmaier, 'Economic Determinants of Electoral Outcomes', *Annual Review of Political Science*, 3 (2000).
96. Curry, Tom, 'Drone Issue Creating Unusual Bipartisan Alliances', NBC News, 24 April 2013; http:// nbcpolitics.nbcnews.com/_news/2013/04/24/17895849-drone-issue-creating-unusual-bipartisan-alliances?lite

INDEX

INDEX

asymmetry, 139–46, 163, 170, 241
attrition, 10, 92, 98–9, 103–4,
　106–9, 111, 209
al-Aulaqi v. Obama, 67, 186
Australia, 236
Authorization for Use of Military
　Force (AUMF), 64, 66, 74, 76,
　81, 167, 183, 222, 228, 233
al-Awlaki, Abdulrahman, 215–19
al-Awlaki, Anwar, 64–9, 166–7,
　184–8, 215, 234, 243
Aztecs, 147

B-2 bombers, 8, 213
Baathism, 124, 224
al-Badani, Shawqi Ali Ahmad, 112
al-Baghdadi, Abu Bakr, 224
Balkan Wars, *see* Yugoslav Wars
al-Banna, Ibrahim, 215
Basra, Iraq, 126
Battle of Algiers (1956–57), 148
Battle of Cannae (216 BC), 144
Battle of Midway (1942), 18
Battle of Solferino (1859), 50
Battle of Verdun (1916), 209
battlefields, 206–19
Berlin Wall, 249
Bhutto, Benazir, 44
big data, 155, 191, 244
Bill of Rights, 65
Bin Laden, Osama, viii, 2, 8, 20,
　83, 111, 139, 165
biometric data, 218
black letter law, 47, 173; *see also*
　treaty law
black sites, 30
Black, Cofer, 93
blinks, 149–50
body as battlefield, 211–19
Bosnian War (1992–95), 2, 5, 6–7,
　10, 55, 75
Brennan, John, 73, 129, 159, 197

Bureau of Investigative Journalism,
　14, 43, 112, 245
Bush administration (2001–2009)
　and accountability, 244
　and al-Awlaki, 66
　and dirty war, 94, 96–7
　and enmity, 96–7
　and Guantanamo Bay, vii, 96,
　　100–101
　al-Harithi, killing of (2002), 3,
　　17–20, 22–3, 36, 65, 172
　and illegal enemy combatants,
　　100
　and just war, 113, 117–19
　Mehsud, killing of (2007), 43–5
　and national security, 117, 132
　Nek Muhammad, killing of
　　(2004), 81
　and torture, 30–31, 70, 77,
　　100–101, 244–5
　and War on Terror, vii, 24, 37–8,
　　70, 93, 100, 111, 113
　al-Zarqawi, killing of (2006), 36,
　　85–6, 107, 138, 146, 150, 156

Cameron, David, 16, 221, 230–32,
　236
Canada, 236, 239
cancer, 191
Carthage, 74, 144
Cartwright, James 'Hoss', 63
Caucasus, 224, 227
CENTCOM, US, 18
Center for Constitutional Reform
　(CCR), 67, 185
Central Intelligence Agency (CIA),
　1, 22, 31, 34, 81–4, 196
　Church Committee, 1, 83
　in Colombia, 238
　Counterterrorism Center
　　(CTC), 93
　extraordinary rendition, 30, 245

INDEX